FROM WEALTH TO POWER

For Helen —

PRINCETON STUDIES IN

INTERNATIONAL HISTORY AND POLITICS

Series Editors
Jack L. Snyder, Marc Trachtenberg, and Fareed Zakaria

Recent titles:

*The Moral Purpose of the State: Culture, Social Identity, and
Institutional Rationality in International Relations* by
Christian Reus-Smit

Entangling Relations: American Foreign Policy in Its Century
by David Lake

*A Constructed Peace: The Making of the European
Settlement, 1945–1963* by Marc Trachtenberg

*Regional Orders at Century's Dawn: Global and Domestic
Influences on Grand Strategy* by Etel Solingen

*From Wealth to Power: The Unusual Origins
of America's World Role* by Fareed Zakaria

*Changing Course: Ideas, Politics, and the Soviet Withdrawal
from Afghanistan* by Sarah E. Mendelson

Disarming Strangers: Nuclear Diplomacy with North Korea
by Leon V. Sigal

*Imagining War: French and British Military Doctrine
between the Wars* by Elizabeth Kier

*Roosevelt and the Munich Crisis: A Study of Political
Decision-Making* by Barbara Rearden Farnham

*Useful Adversaries: Grand Strategy, Domestic Mobilization,
and Sino-American Conflict, 1947–1958*
by Thomas J. Christensen

*Satellites and Commissars: Strategy and Conflict in the
Politics of Soviet-Bloc Trade* by Randall W. Stone

*Does Conquest Pay? The Exploitation of Occupied
Industrial Societies* by Peter Liberman

*Cultural Realism: Strategic Culture and Grand Strategy in
Chinese History* by Alastair Iain Johnston

The Korean War: An International History
by William Stueck

Fareed Zakaria

FROM WEALTH TO POWER

THE UNUSUAL ORIGINS OF AMERICA'S
WORLD ROLE

PRINCETON UNIVERSITY PRESS   PRINCETON, NEW JERSEY

Fourth printing, and first paperback printing, 1999

Paperback ISBN 0-691-01035-8

The Library of Congress has cataloged the cloth edition
of this book as follows

Zakaria, Fareed.
From wealth to power : the unusual origins of America's world role /
Fareed Zakaria.
p.   cm.
Includes bibliographical references and index.
ISBN 0-691-04496-1 (cl : alk. paper)
1. United States—Foreign relations—1865–1921. 2.   International
relations.   I. Title.
E661.7.Z35   1998
327.73—dc21   97-34245

This book has been composed in Sabon

The paper used in this publication meets the minimum
requirements of ANSI/NISO Z39.48-1992
(R1997) (*Permanence of Paper*)

http://pup.princeton.edu

Printed in the United States of America

10   9   8   7   6   5   4

————————— To my parents —————————

RAFIQ AND FATMA ZAKARIA

Contents

Preface

THIS BOOK is a product of interest and frustration; interest in history and political science, and frustration with the study of international relations. International relations is studied nowadays with a serious involvement in either history or social science theory, but rarely both. (This is partly a reflection of the ever-increasing professionalization of disciplines in the academy.) I have tried to make a small contribution to what I think is a necessary joint enterprise, examining the historical record for insights and evidence that shed light on broad theoretical topics in world politics, such as the rise of new great powers.

I was fortunate to have been in two ideal environments for scholarship, first as an undergraduate and then as a Ph.D. student. My interest in history was nurtured at Yale's dazzling history department, where Paul Kennedy, Robin Winks, and Vasily Rudich were particularly generous with their time and attention. At Harvard I learned to think like a social scientist. The Department of Government at Harvard was an extraordinary place, crammed with wide-ranging intelligence, erudition, and, above all, argument. For their advice, encouragement, and friendship I am deeply grateful to Samuel P. Huntington, Stanley Hoffmann, Robert Keohane, Joseph Nye, and the late Judith Shklar. I was awarded fellowships by the Center for Science and International Affairs, the Center for International Affairs, and the Olin Institute for Strategic Studies, which were indispensible to completing this project. At *Foreign Affairs,* James Hoge has generously allowed me the time and flexibility to write, which made it possible to turn a dissertation into a book. Princeton University Press has been enthusiastic and helpful from the start, for which I owe thanks to its director, Walter Lippincott; Malcolm Debevoise; and Malcolm Litchfield. Ronald Krebs helped greatly with the final revisions. Ib Ohlsson drew an elegant map to help me make my point.

Over the years, many friends have listened to parts of this project as it progressed from an outline to a book. I want to thank them all, but especially those who read some part of it: Gideon Rose, Andrew Moravscik, Sean Lynn-Jones, Robert Lieberman, Timothy Naftali, Thomas Christensen, and Nicholas Rizopoulos. The final product has lost many of its early scars because of their constructive criticism.

Finally, some personal thanks. As I was growing up in India, my interest in the world was kindled by two extraordinary people: Khushwant Singh, who taught me how to write, and the late Girilal Jain, who taught me how to think. Gideon, Dan, and Joanna Rose and Sheri Berman have been a wondrous combination of friends and family. My brother, Arshad, has been a pillar of support since we both left home for college fourteen years ago. I did not know my wife, Paula, when most of this book was written. Had I, she would have lifted my spirits then as she does each day now. Finally and most importantly, thanks to my parents, Fatma and Rafiq Zakaria, to whom this book is dedicated and who gave me more than I can ever explain, let alone repay.

FROM WEALTH TO POWER

CHAPTER ONE

Introduction

WHAT MAKES A GREAT POWER?

WHAT TURNS rich nations into "great powers"? Why, as states grow increasingly wealthy, do they build large armies, entangle themselves in politics beyond their borders, and seek international influence? What factors speed or retard the translation of material resources into political interests? These questions, central to the theory and history of international relations as well as the world we live in today, guide this study of the rise of the United States. Throughout history, few events in international life have been as regular or as disruptive as the arrival of a new great power on the world scene. From the Peloponnesian War over two thousand years ago—caused, in Thucydides' famous words, by "the growth of Athenian power and the fear which this caused in Sparta"[1]—to the rise of Germany in this century, almost every new addition to the ranks of the great powers has resulted in global instability and war. E. H. Carr correctly identified the "problem of peaceful change" as the central dilemma of international relations.[2]

The strong are all the same, Michael Mandelbaum writes: "They expand. They send their soldiers, ships, and public and private agents abroad. They fight wars, guard borders, and administer territories and people of different languages, customs, and beliefs far from their own capitals. They exert influence on foreigners in a variety of ways. . . . The strong do to others what others cannot do to them."[3] Over the course of history, states that have experienced significant growth in their material resources have relatively soon redefined and expanded their political interests abroad, measured by their increases in military spending, initiation of wars, acquisition of territory, posting of soldiers and diplomats, and participation in great-power decision-making. Paul Kennedy concludes that "there is a very clear connection between an indi-

[1] Thucydides, *History of the Peloponnesian War*, trans. Rex Warner, rev. ed. (New York: Penguin Books, 1972), 49.

[2] Edward Hallett Carr, *The Twenty Years Crisis, 1919–1939: An Introduction to the Study of International Relations*, 2d ed. (New York: Harper and Row, 1964), 208–23.

[3] Michael Mandelbaum, *The Fate of Nations: The Search for National Security in the Nineteenth and Twentieth Centuries* (Cambridge: Cambridge University Press, 1988), 134–35.

vidual Great Power's economic rise and fall and its growth and decline as an important military power (or world empire)."[4] Consider the brief rise and fall of Sweden. At the start of the seventeenth century, Sweden was hardly a bright prospect for great powerdom. With a largely peasant population, little industry, few towns, and a barter economy, its economic foundation was extremely weak. But after significant foreign investment and internal reforms, Sweden's fortunes changed, and in a short time it became one of Europe's richest countries and the leading producer of iron and copper. This new wealth paved the way for a more powerful military and a more assertive diplomacy. By 1630, Gustavus Adolphus had eagerly joined the European political fray on behalf of the Protestant cause, and Sweden's tremendous military force was critical in checking Habsburg ambitions over the next twenty years. In subsequent decades, it acquired several trans-Baltic territories, intervened repeatedly in Poland, and dreamed of uniting Scandinavia under its throne. Then, over the next sixty years, Sweden's economic might declined, compared to that of the industrializing economies of western Europe, and correspondingly its role as a great European power dwindled.[5]

Sweden is a clear example of a trend one can see among nearly all rising powers, from the Netherlands in the late sixteenth century to Britain in the late eighteenth century to Japan in the late nineteenth century. Prussia, for example, remained a second-rank power until its economic takeoff in the 1850s. Between 1830 and 1880, the German state's share of world manufacturing output climbed nearly 150 percent, while its two great continental rivals, France and the Habsburg Empire, saw rises of just 50 percent and 40 percent respectively. Germany's GNP doubled between 1840 and 1870, growing more than that of any other European state. Joined with the Prussian military revolution of the 1860s, this growth underlay the successful wars of German unification and the new Germany's triumph over France. After 1870 Germany, backed by its unparalleled industrial power and led by the adroit Bismarck, would dominate the European great-power system. Diplomats at the time noted that now all roads led to Berlin.[6]

So common was this pattern that European statesmen viewed the state that did not turn its wealth into political influence as an anomaly. In the eighteenth century, they spoke in astonishment and scorn of "the Dutch disease, a malady that prevented a nation enjoying unequalled

---

[4] Paul M. Kennedy, *The Rise and Fall of the Great Powers: Economic Change and Military Conflict from 1500 to the Present* (New York: Random House, 1987), xxii.

[5] Ibid., 64–66.

[6] Ibid., 149, 160–62, 171, 185–88.

individual prosperity and commercial prowess from remaining a state of great influence and power."[7] With greater wealth, a country could build a military and diplomatic apparatus capable of fulfilling its aims abroad; but its very aims, its perception of its needs and goals, all tended to expand with rising resources. As European statesmen raised under the great-power system understood so clearly, capabilities shape intentions.

In the second half of the nineteenth century, the United States was afflicted with the Dutch disease. While America emerged from the Civil War as a powerful industrial state, unquestionably one of the three or four richest nations in the world, its foreign policy was marked by a persistent reluctance to involve itself abroad. Many historians of the period have asked why America expanded in the 1890s. But for the political scientist, viewing the country's power and expansion in comparative perspective, the more puzzling question is why America did not expand more and sooner. The period 1865–1908, particularly before 1890, presents us with many instances in which the country's central decision-makers noticed and considered clear opportunities to expand American influence abroad and rejected them. Certainly, between the time when they get rich and when they acquire expansive political interests abroad, countries often experience a time lag, frequently because policymakers fail to perceive the shift in their country's relative economic position. But America's central decision-makers were well aware of its economic strength and proudly proclaimed it. Nevertheless, the country hewed to a relatively isolationist line, with few exceptions, until the 1890s—a highly unusual gap between power and interests, for it lasted some thirty years. The United States would thus seem to represent an exception to the historical record and a challenge to the great-power rule. (Before proceeding any further, I should note that historians of American foreign policy sometimes restrict the meaning of the term *expansion* to the acquisition of colonial territories. This study employs a broader, more commonsensical definition of the term; expansion can certainly involve imperialism, but it more generally refers to an activist foreign policy that ranges from attention to international events to increases in diplomatic legations to participation in great-power diplomacy. The Soviet Union, by this definition, could be called expansionist in the 1970s even though it was not formally annexing parts of Africa and Central Asia. Using territorial annexation as *one* measure of expansionism, the thirty years from 1865 to 1896 still stand out as an anomaly in American history.)

---

[7] John Brewer, *The Sinews of Power: War, Money, and the English State, 1688–1783* (London: Unwin Hyman, 1989), xv.

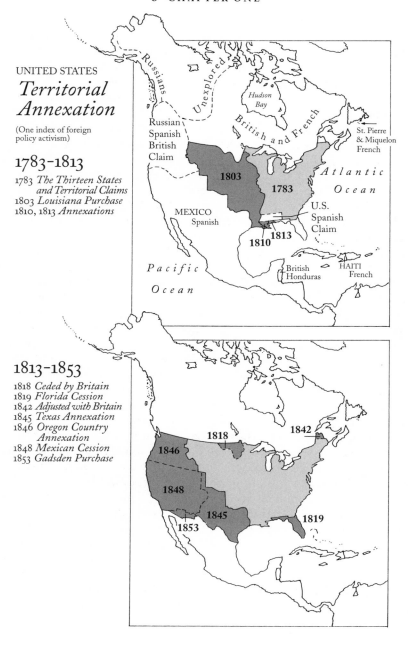

UNITED STATES

Territorial Annexation

(One index of foreign policy activism)

1783–1813

1783 *The Thirteen States and Territorial Claims*
1803 *Louisiana Purchase*
1810, 1813 *Annexations*

1813–1853

1818 *Ceded by Britain*
1819 *Florida Cession*
1842 *Adjusted with Britain*
1845 *Texas Annexation*
1846 *Oregon Country Annexation*
1848 *Mexican Cession*
1853 *Gadsden Purchase*

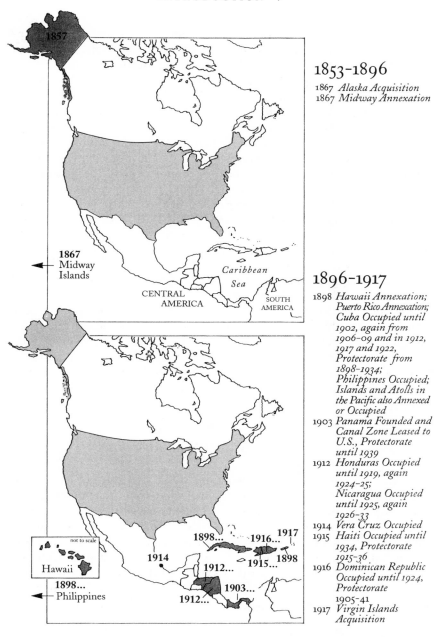

1853–1896

1867 *Alaska Acquisition*
1867 *Midway Annexation*

1867
Midway
Islands

1896–1917

1898 *Hawaii Annexation;*
       Puerto Rico Annexation;
       Cuba Occupied until
       1902, again from
       1906–09 and in 1912,
       1917 and 1922,
       Protectorate from
       1898–1934;
       Philippines Occupied;
       Islands and Atolls in
       the Pacific also Annexed
       or Occupied
1903 *Panama Founded and*
       Canal Zone Leased to
       U.S., Protectorate
       until 1939
1912 *Honduras Occupied*
       until 1919, again
       1924–25;
       Nicaragua Occupied
       until 1925, again
       1926–33
1914 *Vera Cruz Occupied*
1915 *Haiti Occupied until*
       1934, Protectorate
       1915–36
1916 *Dominican Republic*
       Occupied until 1924,
       Protectorate
       1905–41
1917 *Virgin Islands*
       Acquisition

1857

Caribbean
Sea
CENTRAL
AMERICA
SOUTH
AMERICA

not to scale
Hawaii
1898...
Philippines

1914
1912...
1898...
1912...
1903...
1916...
1915...
1917
1898

This study offers an explanation for this apparent aberration that is rooted in a more general theory of foreign policy. The search for a dominant cause that explains the course of late-nineteenth-century American foreign policy may seem misguided. Historians' accounts of the cases of expansion and nonexpansion stress different factors in each case, ranging from the balance of power to the influence of various interest groups to ideology—racism or social Darwinism or manifest destiny—to the idiosyncrasies of America's leaders. Such a complete account would, no doubt, be more accurate than either of this study's two contending theories of foreign policy, which rely on just one or two of these factors. But a list of facts and factors cannot explain the general dynamic motivating foreign policy that would result in nonexpansion in the 1870s and 1880s and yet expansion in the 1890s. William Henry Seward, secretary of state between 1861 and 1869, possessed as expansionist an ideology as did William McKinley and Theodore Roosevelt, and all three were equally aware of the relationship between power and interests. Why did the latter two succeed where the former failed? Some historians maintain that the expansion of the 1890s was prompted in large part by the depression of 1893 and the widespread sense that the country needed to expand to gain access to larger export markets, yet those same historians point to the economic troubles of the 1870s as preventing expansion in that era; if hard times can explain both expansion and isolation, how central can that factor be? The aim here is to tease out a plausible explanation for both expansion and nonexpansion, and for that we need a first-cut theory, not a full historical account.

TWO FIRST-CUT THEORIES

The literature on international relations offers two first-cut answers to the central question of this study: under what conditions do states expand their political interests abroad? These two theories of foreign policy, which explain national behavior—the *attempt* at expansion, not its success—are classical realism and defensive realism.[8] Both start with the logic that the international system presents states with powerful constraints and opportunities that they cannot easily ignore, but they make radically different fundamental assumptions. Classical realism supposes that a nation's interests are determined by its power (meaning its mate-

[8] A theory of foreign policy explains why and when a nation would pursue expansion. Whether that attempt succeeds or fails depends on the international environment. To understand the outcome of that effort, one must consult a theory of international politics, such as Kenneth Waltz's balance-of-power theory.

rial resources) relative to other nations: nations thus expand when they can. They do not expand in a mad frenzy—anywhere, anytime—but in a rational manner, in places and at times that minimize costs and risks, in areas that are weaker than they, and when their power is on the rise. As Robert Gilpin argues, all states seek control over at least territory, the behavior of other states, and the world economy; the difference is that only rich states can act on these preferences.[9] Scholars as diverse as Gilpin, Kennedy, Glenn Snyder, Bruce Bueno de Mesquita, and Aaron Friedberg—as well as traditional realists like Hans Morgenthau and E. H. Carr—all adopt some version of this theory in their work.

But classical realism's emphasis on national power as the most important factor affecting a nation's foreign policy overlooks an important distinction. Foreign policy is made not by the nation as a whole but by its government; consequently, what matters is state power, not national power. State power is that portion of national power the government can extract for its purposes and reflects the ease with which central decision-makers can achieve their ends. This variation on classical realism, which I call state-centered realism, maintains the logic that capabilities shape intentions, but it recognizes that state structure limits the availability of national power. Thus the structure, scope, and capacity of the state are crucial factors in explaining the process by which nations become increasingly active on the world stage. While models of how state structures can affect national policy have long been advanced by scholars of comparative politics—from Alexis de Tocqueville and James Bryce to Samuel Huntington and Theda Skocpol—the connection between the structure of the state and foreign policy has not been explored sufficiently. Domestic causes have often been regarded as competing with international pressures as explanations of foreign policy. This study demonstrates that a domestic variable, state power, can be introduced into a systemic theory without undermining the theory's basic premises. In fact, the logic of realism fits nicely with an appreciation of state structure. States may be billiard balls, but each is made of a different material, affecting its speed, spin, and bounce on the international plane.

The second theory of foreign policy, defensive realism, presents a more benign view of the pressures of the international system. It posits that states seek security rather than influence and so predicts that nations expand their interests abroad when threatened. They expand in times of insecurity, against powerful nations with aggressive intentions. Absent a threatening environment, states have no systemic incentive to

[9] Robert Gilpin, *War and Change in World Politics* (Cambridge: Cambridge University Press, 1981), 23–25.

expand: they expand not when they can but when they must. Stephen Walt, Stephen Van Evera, and Jack Snyder—and before them, John Herz—are the most prominent exponents of this variant of realism.

However, this study shows why defensive realism's emphasis on threats is theoretically unhelpful. The concept of threat is highly malleable, and statesmen, rather than acknowledge their desires for influence and even hegemony, understandably often manufacture, consciously or unconsciously, "threats" and "dangers to security" to justify expansion. When statesmen cry "national security" to defend obviously aggressive behavior, this explanation for expansion becomes meaningless. More important still, defensive realism explains very little actual foreign policy. The international system, according to defensive realism, pushes states toward minimalist foreign policies. But since most great powers have been expansionist, they all must be considered exceptions to the rule. Great-power behavior is seen largely as abnormal and thus pathological, the result of domestic deformities. Defensive realists believe that states know from history that expansion is pointless: states balance against you rather than jump on your bandwagon, defense is often stronger than offense, and so on. Maybe, but the lessons of history are not scientific truths. Perhaps the defensive realists are right that states *should* glean certain lessons, but do they? Good theory explains how the world works, not how it should work.

This study tests these two theories of foreign policy by examining American attempts to expand its influence abroad in the late nineteenth century. Did the United States expand to counter threats, as defensive realism would predict, or to promote its influence, narrowing the gap between state power and foreign political interests, as state-centered realism would contend? Did the United States expand to balance against strong nations, which posed significant threats to its security, or did it expand in the direction of least resistance? And, equally important, when the United States did not expand, was it because of a benign international environment, the perception that security was "plentiful," or rather because America's weak state structure left its statesmen without access to its national potential?

THE HISTORICAL RECORD

The pattern of American foreign policy from the end of the Civil War to the close of Theodore Roosevelt's term as president largely confirms the predictions of state-centered realism: central decision-makers, which in the American case means the president and his closest advisers, expanded American influence abroad when they perceived increases in state power. The decades after the Civil War saw the beginning of a long period of growth in America's material resources. But this national power lay dormant beneath a weak state, one that was decentralized, diffuse, and divided. The presidents and their secretaries of state tried repeatedly to convert the nation's rising power into influence abroad, but they presided over a federal state structure and a tiny bureaucracy that could not get men or money from the state governments or from society at large. The president also had to contend with a state that impaired his ability to translate his administration's preferences into national policy; Congress could, and often did, prevent him from exercising his will. It refused to enact civil service and military reform, and the Senate rejected several annexation projects the executive branch had proposed. During this period, the power of the presidency was at a historic low: Andrew Johnson was impeached for daring to fire his secretary of war without congressional approval. Also, the unprecedented national debt after the Civil War fostered a pervasive sense of national bankruptcy and weakness that exacerbated this tension. America was an unusual great power—a strong nation but a weak state.

The 1880s and 1890s mark the beginnings of the modern American state, which emerged primarily to cope with the domestic pressures generated by industrialization. The exigencies of the growing national economy and the collapse of the congressional bid for supremacy gave the federal government a more centralized, less political, and rational structure. And as the only nationally elected officer of government, the president emerged with strengthened authority. This transformation of state structure complemented the continuing growth of national power, and by the mid-1890s the executive branch was able to bypass Congress or coerce it into expanding American interests abroad. America's resounding victory in the Spanish-American War crystallized the perception of increasing American power both at home and abroad. In keeping with the work of Robert Jervis and Aaron Friedberg, this study confirms that statesmen's perceptions of national power shift suddenly, rather than incrementally, and are shaped more by crises and galvanizing events like wars than by statistical measures. Having defeated a European great power in battle, America expanded dramatically in the years that followed, and several goals that had been under contemplation for decades—the annexation of Hawaii and Samoa, for example—became reality within months. At the moment of its greatest strength and security, having driven Spain out of the Western Hemisphere and with only an accommodating Britain as a European presence in the Americas, the United States chose to fill the resulting vacuum by expanding its influence. Because of its now-recognized status as a great power, actual threats to American security decreased from then on, and this greater security bred greater activism and expansionism. When confronted by real threats, as it occasionally was both before and after

1898, the United States usually opted to contract its interests, rather than expand to counter the enemy as defensive realism would forecast.

With the birth of the modern presidency under William McKinley came a symbiotic relationship between national executive power and foreign policy activism that has continued throughout the twentieth century. Theodore Roosevelt exploited the powers McKinley created and developed new ones as well, such as the routine use of executive agreements instead of treaties. The Progressive Era further strengthened the American state—again primarily for domestic reasons—and the great beneficiaries of this new authority were the national government and the president. Long a believer in congressional government, Woodrow Wilson became a particularly expansionist and unilateralist chief executive in matters of foreign policy.

PAST AND PRESENT

The causes of American expansion are not merely of theoretical or historical interest. As we look at the world today, the rise of new great powers is sure to cause ripples and repercussions across the globe. And the questions people ask about the new powers are the very ones we look at in this book. Upon the reunification of Germany in 1990, Lord Shawcross, an eminent British politician and jurist, warned that Europe might again be thrown into tumult if the Germans "use political power, commensurate with their economic strength."[10] At the other end of the world, the rise of Japanese economic might has created an entire subfield of specialists and policy analysts who debate whether Tokyo is getting rich in order that it get strong or will break the mold, remaining nothing more than a "global civilian power." The chief reason that China's rise seems threatening to so many is that it appears to be taking a thoroughly traditional course, expanding its power and interests in tandem.

It is a truism that in the long run, increasingly wealthy nations will have increasing worldwide influence. But the nature of their rise, the time frame in which it occurs, the areas and issues that become flash points—all these specific matters remain uncertain, and the specifics will determine the course of international relations for the next century. Properly understood and properly handled, great power transitions can be smooth. Misconstrued and mismanaged, they can have cataclysmic consequences.

[10] "The Rejoining of Germany: European Voices," *New York Times,* September 27, 1990, A8.

CHAPTER TWO

A Theory of Foreign Policy

WHY DO STATES EXPAND?

THE HISTORY of international politics is the history of the rise and fall of great powers. Most observers have focused, however, on the *effects* of shifts in international power. Thucydides, to take the earliest example, argued that the impact of Athens's ascent within the system of Greek city-states made war inevitable. The issues I raise are different. They concern the behavior of the rising state; specifically, I examine the reasons for the delayed rise of the United States and the process by which it acquired political interests abroad from 1865 to 1908. Thus I seek to explain foreign policy, not international outcomes. The distinction is important. Recent international relations theory has been characterized by spirited and rich discussions about theories of international politics.[1] Scholars have not, however, undertaken similar analyses of theories of foreign policy. As a result the term is often used loosely, and misplaced criticism and flawed arguments abound.

The existing international relations literature has implicit within it several alternative theories of foreign policy, of which the two most useful starting points are classical realism and defensive realism. Although both theories focus—at least in principle—on the ways in which the system influences the foreign policy behavior of the state, they profoundly disagree about the nature of those systemic constraints and opportunities. Is security in the international system scarce or is it plentiful? Are states driven constantly to expand their influence or are they pushed to seek only some minimal level of security? These questions at the heart of international life are the essence of the dispute between classical realism and defensive realism, and it is these questions that this study seeks to answer. While it may appear to be an intramural, even internecine, theoretical quarrel, the debate addresses a fundamental question: how does the international balance of power shape a state's behavior?

[1] See, for example, Robert O. Keohane, ed., *Neorealism and Its Critics* (New York: Columbia University Press, 1986); Stephen D. Krasner, ed., International Regimes (Ithaca, N.Y.: Cornell University Press, 1983); and David A. Baldwin, ed., *Neorealism and Neoliberalism: The Contemporary Debate* (New York: Columbia University Press, 1993).

WHAT IS A THEORY OF FOREIGN POLICY?

Theories of various aspects of international relations can be distinguished from one another on the basis of the phenomenon that each tries to explain, or the dependent variable. A theory of international politics seeks to explain international events. Struck by the persistence of interstate violence and balances of power—what he perceives as the regular outcomes of international life—Kenneth Waltz constructs such a theory.[2] However, in accounting for international events, a theory of international politics cannot explain the motives of nations; it must instead make assumptions about them. By contrast, a theory of foreign policy explains why different states, or the same state at different historical moments, have different intentions, goals, and preferences toward the outside world.[3] A theory of foreign policy sheds light on the reasons for a nation's efforts—the search for allies, the attempt to annex a colony—but it cannot account for the results of those efforts. Whether they succeed depends on the context in which they take place, particularly other states' goals and capabilities. To explain the outcomes of international interactions—colonization, the formation of alliances—one must consult a theory of international politics. Thus while Waltz's balance-of-power theory might have predicted a Sino-Soviet split and a Sino-American rapprochement in the wake of World War II, only a theory of foreign policy could explain why the United States and China waited over twenty years to attempt this reconciliation.[4]

All theories make certain assumptions. Graham Allison, for example, assumes that bureaucracies promote policies that advance their interests and budgets. Given this predisposition of bureaucracies, he explains a nation's foreign policy as the result of the push and pull among agencies.[5] A theory of bureaucratic politics, meanwhile, explains why different bureaucracies adopt different policies, making assumptions about the preferences of decision-makers. A theory of decision-making explains these different preferences, often making certain cognitive assumptions. Explanations of Woodrow Wilson's foreign policy that are

[2] Kenneth N. Waltz, *Theory of International Politics* (Reading, Mass.: Addison-Wesley, 1979), 8–128.

[3] Among earlier works on the subject, Lloyd Jensen raises important issues with great subtlety, though not in the context of constructing a theory; see his *Explaining Foreign Policy* (Englewood Cliffs, N.J.: Prentice-Hall, 1982). See also George Modelski, A Theory of Foreign Policy (New York: Praeger, 1962).

[4] For one explanation for this delay, see John Lewis Gaddis, "Dividing Adversaries," in his *The Long Peace: Inquiries into the History of the Cold War* (New York: Oxford University Press, 1987), 147–95.

[5] Graham T. Allison, *Essence of Decision: Explaining the Cuban Missile Crisis* (Glenview, Ill.: Scott, Foresman, 1971).

rooted in his psychology and accounts of Theodore Roosevelt's imperial impulses that stress his racism are two such theories.[6]

These distinctions among theories should not be confused with the differences among "levels of analysis." Theories can be distinguished by their dependent variable, but levels of analysis are always distinguished by the cause of the phenomenon, or the independent variable.[7] Where one locates the independent variable—at the international, national, bureaucratic, or decision-making level—determines the level of analysis.[8] Waltz, for example, finds the cause for the observed pattern of international outcomes in the structure of the international system. His theory of international politics, therefore, also operates at the international level.[9] Realism's great strength, particularly as recast by Waltz, is that by emphasizing systemic causes *and* effects, it serves as the classic theory of the international system. In fact, theories of international politics that explain outcomes without reference to systemic causes, which Waltz criticizes as "reductionist," are often theories of foreign policy that have exaggerated their explanatory claims.[10] Lenin, for example, at times claims that capitalism causes colonization and war,[11] yet at other points he argues that capitalism explains only a nation's proclivity to imperialism; competition and the distribution of power explain why these impulses result in war.[12] Naturally, a change in the foreign policy goals of large numbers of states would result in a changed pattern of outcomes,

---

[6] See Alexander L. George and Juliette L. George, *Woodrow Wilson and Colonel House: A Personality Study* (New York: Dover, 1964); George Sinkler, *The Racial Attitudes of American Presidents from Abraham Lincoln to Theodore Roosevelt* (Garden City, N.Y.: Doubleday, 1971); and John Milton Cooper, Jr., *The Warrior and the Priest: Woodrow Wilson and Theodore Roosevelt* (Cambridge: Harvard University Press, 1983).

[7] Three classic statements on levels of analysis are Kenneth N. Waltz, *Man, the State, and War: A Theoretical Analysis* (New York: Columbia University Press, 1959); J. David Singer, "The Levels-of-Analysis Problem in International Relations," *World Politics* 14, no. 1 (July 1961): 77–92; and Robert Jervis, *Perception and Misperception in International Politics* (Princeton, N.J.: Princeton University Press, 1976), 13–35.

[8] This example uses Jervis's four levels of analysis.

[9] Waltz, *Theory of International Politics*, 38–58.

[10] Ibid., 60–79.

[11] Vladimir I. Lenin, *Imperialism, the Highest Stage of Capitalism* (1916; reprint, New York: International Publishers, 1939), 120–28.

[12] "[T]here can be no other conceivable basis under capitalism for the division of spheres of influence, of interests, of colonies, etc., than a calculation of the strength of the participants in the division, their general economic, financial, military strength, etc." Since growth is always uneven, relative strength will constantly change, as Lenin recognizes. "When the relation of forces is changed, how else, under capitalism, can the solution of contradictions be found except by resorting to violence." Ibid., 119, 96 (emphasis in original). Other than the phrase "under capitalism," these lines could have been written by Gilpin, Waltz, or Kennedy. Lenin never clearly explains how socialism would evade the problem of changes in power. Elsewhere he argues vaguely that economics and power politics together cause imperial wars. Ibid., 75, 86–87.

as Richard Rosecrance suggests when he argues that "trading states" are pacific, but this does not make Rosecrance's argument a theory of international politics.[13] As Waltz points out, "Because the national and international levels are linked, theories of both types [international politics and foreign policy], if they are any good, tell us some things, but not the same thing, about behavior and outcomes at both levels."[14]

A realist theory of foreign policy would begin with the systemic level, but one can locate the reason for national preferences at any level of analysis. Joseph Schumpeter, for example, constructs a theory of foreign policy at the decision-making level, arguing that the imperial tendencies of Europe's great powers in the nineteenth century had their roots in the feudal attitudes of their ruling elites.[15] Most theories of foreign policy, like that of Schumpeter, operate at low levels of analysis, ascribing state behavior to domestic politics or national culture. A good theory, however, would first examine the effect of the international system on foreign policy, for the most important general characteristic of a state in international relations is its relative standing in the international system. Theories of foreign policy that place sole emphasis on internal—cultural, bureaucratic, or individual—causes almost always make hidden assumptions about the way the international environment shapes a state's range of choices. Such theories also typically consider only those cases in which the behavior they are examining exists, thereby biasing their conclusions. Schumpeter studies only European nations that were imperial powers, failing to ask why other European and non-European countries that were dominated by elites with feudal histories did not follow an imperial path. Part of the answer surely lies in the position Europe's great powers occupied in the international system.

A theory of foreign policy must not ignore domestic politics, national culture, and individual decision-makers. But from the standpoint of social science, a first-cut theory that generalizes across regimes, cultures, and peoples is more useful than a country-specific explanation, since it can be applied to a larger number of cases. For example, focusing on a state's place in the international economic system will produce a potential explanation that is theoretically more powerful than an explanation that emphasizes a nation's unique cultural attributes. In order to achieve some balance between parsimony and accuracy, a first-cut theory can be narrowed in scope and layered successively with additional variables from different levels of analysis—regime types, bureaucratic politics,

[13] Richard N. Rosecrance, *The Rise of the Trading State: Commerce and Conquest in the Modern World* (New York: Basic Books, 1986).

[14] Waltz, *Theory of International Politics*, 122–23.

[15] Joseph A. Schumpeter, *Imperialism and Social Classes*, trans. Heinz Norden (New York: Meridian Books, 1955).

the psychological tendencies and personalities of statesmen. As Robert Keohane writes,

The larger the domain of a theory, the less accuracy we expect. . . .The domain of theory is narrowed to achieve greater precision. Thus the debate between advocates of parsimony and proponents of contextual subtlety resolves itself into a question of *stages,* rather than either-or choices. We should seek parsimony first, then add on complexity while monitoring the adverse effects this has on the predictive power of our theory: its ability to make significant inferences on the basis of limited information.[16]

A good account of a nation's foreign policy will point to the role played by systemic as well as other factors. When historians declare German statesmen the "cause" of World War I, they often mean that the leadership's views explain the country's bellicose policies; they are, first of all, explaining foreign policy, not international events. In fact, conflict among the European great powers occurred not simply because of German statesmen's preferences—Belgian statesmen might have had similar preferences, with no effect—but because of the tremendous growth in German economic and military power and the country's late arrival on a world stage dominated by Britain, France, and Russia.[17] Consider an extreme example in which the literature is rife with domestic and personality-based explanations: German expansionism from 1933 to 1945.[18] Clearly, Adolf Hitler and Nazi ideology are crucial to an understanding of German aggression, but that aggression did not arise in a vacuum. As critics of the Treaty of Versailles continually pointed out, Germany's post-1919 position in the international system

[16] Robert O. Keohane, "Theory of World Politics: Structural Realism and Beyond," in Keohane, *Neorealism and Its Critics,* 187–88.

[17] For a superb, and rare, example of a comprehensive history that covers the full range of causes, from the systemic to personal idiosyncrasies, see Paul M. Kennedy, "The Kaiser and German Weltpolitik: Reflections on Wilhelm II's Place in the Making of German Foreign Policy," in John C. G. Rohl and Nicolaus Sombart, eds., *Kaiser Wilhelm II: New Interpretations* (Cambridge: Cambridge University Press, 1982), 143–67. Among historians, Kennedy has thought most seriously about levels of analysis (though he would never use the term). See especially Kennedy, "A.J.P. Taylor and 'Profound Forces' in History," in Chris Wrigley, ed., *Warfare, Diplomacy, and Politics: Essays in Honour of A.J.P. Taylor* (London: Hamish Hamilton, 1986), 14–29; Kennedy, *The Rise of the Anglo-German Antagonism, 1860–1914* (London: Allen and Unwin, 1980); and Kennedy, *The Realities behind Diplomacy: Background Influences on British External Policy, 1865–1980* (London: Allen and Unwin, 1981).

[18] Mainstream accounts that emphasize Adolf Hitler's role include Winston Churchill, *The Second World War,* 2 vols. (London: Cassell, 1953); and Alan Bullock, Hitler: *A Study in Tyranny,* rev. ed. (New York: Harper and Row, 1962). The most sophisticated recent argument along these lines is Gerhard L. Weinberg, *The Foreign Policy of Hitler's Germany,* 2 vols. (Chicago: University of Chicago Press, 1970, 1980).

made some form of German revanchism almost inevitable.[19] Only Hitler and Nazism can explain the particularly ghastly form this revanchism took, but a good explanation of Germany's foreign policy during this period would include both the general systemic impulses and the more specific domestic, cultural, and personal ones.[20]

While the international relations literature is replete with implicit theories of foreign policy, each emphasizing a general cause for foreign policy behavior, these theories of foreign policy are rarely stated as such. To construct a first-cut theory of foreign policy, one must first pose a basic question about national behavior: under what conditions do states expand their political interests abroad?[21] Imperialism is, of course, one important way of "expanding political interests abroad," but it is not the only one. Less formal methods include protectorates, military bases, spheres of influence, and, most commonly, activist diplomacy. Political interests can thus be measured by political control over new territories, expansion of the diplomatic and military apparatus, and participation in great power decision-making. The existing international relations literature suggests two initial answers to this question: classical realism and defensive realism.

CLASSICAL REALISM: CAPABILITIES SHAPE INTENTIONS

The first hypothesis comes from the oldest school of thought on international life. For the classical realist, a nation defines its interests "in terms of power."[22] While that famous phrase is Hans Morgenthau's, it

---

[19] Farsighted analyses from the 1920s include Jacques Bainville, *Les Conséquences Politiques de la Paix* (Paris: Fayard, 1920); Thorstein Veblen, *An Inquiry into the Nature of the Peace and the Terms of Its Perpetuation* (New York: B. W. Huebsch, 1919); and John M. Keynes, *The Economic Consequences of the Peace* (London: Macmillan, 1919).

[20] See, for example, Andreas Hillgruber, *Germany and the Two World Wars*, trans. William C. Kirby (Cambridge: Harvard University Press, 1981); and Klaus Hildebrand, *The Foreign Policy of the Third Reich*, trans. Anthony Fothergill (Berkeley: University of California Press, 1973). The most famous, extreme, and wrongheaded systemic argument, which completely discounts Hitler's personality and particularly his expansionist goals, is A. J. P. Taylor, *The Origins of the Second World War*, 2d ed. (New York: Atheneum, 1985); a balanced corrective is William Roger Louis, ed., *The Origins of the Second World War: A.J.P. Taylor and His Critics* (New York: Wiley, 1972).

[21] I use the term *interests* interchangeably with national goals, preferences, and intentions because previous discussion of this issue has been dominated by the term *interests* or *the national interest*. This is not a novel attempt to divine some "objective" national interest. There are only two sensible ways to use the term: the first is to prescribe a set of wise foreign policy goals for a country, and the second is to describe what a nation's goals were at a given time. I adopt the latter approach.

[22] Hans J. Morgenthau, *Politics among Nations: The Struggle for Power and Peace*, 5th ed., rev. (New York: Alfred A. Knopf, 1978), 5.

has a distinguished pedigree. From Thucydides' assertion over two thousand years ago in the Melian dialogue that "the strong do what they have the power to do," realists have consistently explained that the nature of man and the dictates of anarchy in the international system result in what Frederick the Great called "the permanent principle of rulers": "to extend as far as their power permits."[23] *Power,* in these formulations, refers to the material resources available to a nation,[24] while *interests* refers to a nation's goals or preferences. Classical realists have written carelessly about "power-maximization," leaving unclear whether states expand for material resources or as a consequence of material resources. This explication of realism makes the latter assumption; increased resources give rise to greater ambitions. States are not resource-maximizers but influence-maximizers.[25]

The classical realist hypothesis can be formulated as follows: *Nations expand their political interests abroad when their relative power increases.* Nazli Choucri and Robert North provide a clear statement of the implications of this hypothesis: "Despite proclamations of nonintervention or even genuinely peaceful intentions, a growing state tends to expand its activities and interests outward—colliding with the spheres of influence of other states—and find itself embroiled in international

[23] Thucydides, *History of the Peloponnesian War,* trans. Rex Warner, rev. ed. (New York: Penguin Books, 1972), 402; Frederick's remark is quoted in Felix Gilbert, To the Farewell Address (Princeton, N.J.: Princeton University Press, 1961), 90.

[24] The measure of National power is sometimes confined to military strength, but often—particularly with regard to the issues this study discusses—it is gauged using aggregate material indicators such as GNP, percentage of world trade, and population. The key for classical realism is that these elements of power are usually highly fungible; economic power can, when necessary, easily be converted into military power. As Waltz writes, "Power is much more fungible than Keohane allows. As ever, the distinction between strong and weak states is important. The stronger the state, the greater the variety of its capabilities. Power may be only slightly fungible for weak states, but it is highly so for strong ones." Waltz, "Reflections on *Theory of International Relations:* A Response to My Critics," in Keohane, *Neorealism and Its Critics,* 333.

[25] Thus when Benjamin J. Cohen writes that "for both the firm and the state the rational solution is to broaden its range of options—to maximize its power position," it is clear that he is positing that a state continually attempts to maximize its influence. See his *The Question of Imperialism: The Political Economy of Dominance and Dependence* (New York: Basic Books, 1973), 240–41. Influence is, of course, not an end in and of itself. States possess preferences that vary widely, and the roots of those preferences may lie in domestic-level causes. Influence is a means to pursue one's ends, and all nations seek the ability to impose their preferences. It should be stressed that influence-maximization is just an assumption and is, therefore, not always accurate: states may occasionally choose not to expand their influence even when they possess the ability to do so. The question to ask is not whether a given assumption is true or false, for exceptions abound. The more relevant question to ask is, how useful is the assumption? Would another assumption yield more accurate predictions? And, as this study will show, the assumption of influence-maximization is indeed useful.

conflicts, crises and wars. . . .The more a state grows, and thus the greater its capabilities, the more likely it is to follow such a tendency."[26] Robert Gilpin explains the dynamic correlation between power and interest: "The Realist law of uneven growth implies that as the power of a group or state increases, that group or state will be tempted to try to increase its control over the environment. In order to increase its own security it will try to expand its political, economic, and territorial control, it will try to change the international system in accordance with its particular set of interests."[27] After surveying the international system from 1500 to the present, Paul Kennedy makes an empirical claim with similar conclusions: "[T]he historical record suggests that there is a very clear connection *in the long run* between an individual Great Power's economic rise and fall and its growth and decline as an important military power (or world empire)."[28]

Classical realism has often been caricatured as maintaining that nations and their leaders are power-hungry jingoists, thrusting onto the international arena anywhere and everywhere. Although the hard version of realism predicts that rising, powerful states will expand, it argues that they will pursue their ends in a rational way, measuring risks, opportunities, costs, and benefits.[29] The best solution to the perennial problem of the uncertainty of international life is for a state to increase its control over that environment through the persistent expansion of its political interests abroad—but only when the benefits exceed the costs. As a nation's power increases, the costs of expansion drop and the benefits increase. As Gilpin writes, "A more wealthy and more powerful state (up to the point of diminishing utility) will select a larger bundle of security and welfare goals than a less wealthy and powerful state."[30] It will not expand anywhere, anytime, nor will it expand only when threatened by dangerous great powers. On the contrary, classical realism predicts that a rising power will expand at advantageous moments against weaker neighbors.

---

[26] Nazli Choucri and Robert C. North, *Nations in Conflict: National Growth and International Violence* (San Francisco: William H. Freeman, 1975), 1.

[27] Robert Gilpin, *War and Change in World Politics* (Cambridge: Cambridge University Press, 1981), 94–95.

[28] Paul M. Kennedy, *The Rise and Fall of the Great Powers: Economic Change and Military Conflict from 1500 to the Present* (New York: Random House, 1987), xxii.

[29] *Costs* refers to the usual material costs, military and economic. Benefits are more complex, since statesmen naturally see benefits in what they have done, but should include tangible benefits like bases and ports and also—more warily—intangible benefits of prestige and glory.

[30] Gilpin, *War and Change*, 22–23.

DEFENSIVE REALISM: THE SEARCH FOR SECURITY

Realists have always been of two minds as to the cause of national ambition. For defensive realists, the expansionist urge derives not from increased power, but from insecurity. John Herz explains the logic of this view: "In such a condition [of anarchy], a feeling of insecurity, deriving from mutual suspicion and mutual fear, compels [states] to compete for even more power in order to find more security. . . .I believe that this dilemma, and not such (possibly additional) factors as 'aggressiveness,' or a desire to acquire the wealth of others, or general depravity of human nature, constitutes the basic cause of what is commonly referred to as the 'urge for power.' "[31] The human condition is perilously insecure, and the more anarchic and nonhierarchical the circumstances, the greater the drive for security.[32] The hypothesis, then, is that *nations expand their political interests when they become increasingly insecure.*[33] The logic of this theory contrasts markedly with classical realism. While the latter implies that states expand out of confidence, or at least out of an awareness of increased resources, the former maintains that states expand out of fear and nervousness. For the classical realist, states expand because they can; for the defensive realist, states expand because they must.[34]

British historians Ronald Robinson and John Gallagher explain that England's "scramble for Africa" in the late nineteenth century was motivated by just such concerns.

---

[31] John H. Herz, "The Security Dilemma in the Atomic Age," in his *International Politics in the Atomic Age* (New York: Columbia University Press, 1959), 231; see also Herz, "Idealist Internationalism and the Security Dilemma," *World Politics* 2, no. 2 (January 1950): 157–80; and *Herz, Political Realism and Political Idealism* (Chicago: University of Chicago Press, 1951).

[32] According to Hobbes, the insecurity of the state of nature is so unbearable that man will accept tyranny rather than live under conditions of anarchy. The anarchy of international life does not similarly push the state to accept a global Leviathan because the state shelters man, easing his insecurity. See John H. Herz, "The Territorial State in International Relations," in his *International Politics in the Atomic Age,* 62–64; and Stanley Hoffmann, "Rousseau on War and Peace," in his *The State of War* (New York: Praeger, 1965).

[33] See Barry Buzan, *People, States, and Fear: An Agenda for International Security Studies in the Post—Cold War Era,* 2d ed. (Boulder, Colo.: Lynne Rienner, 1991), 294–327.

[34] Robert Jervis may fall into this category of realist: though his classic essay on the security dilemma is a theoretical statement about international politics, not foreign policy, its central argument—that systemwide insecurity heightens the level of international conflict—reflects similar thinking. See his "Cooperation under the Security Dilemma," *World Politics* 30, no. 2 (January 1978): 167–214.

No expansion of commerce prompted the territorial claims. . . . Nor were ministers gulled by the romantic glories of ruling desert and bush. Imperialism in the wide sense of empire for empire's sake was not their motivation. Their territorial claims were not made for the sake of African empire or commerce as such. They were little more than by-products of an enforced search for better security in the Mediterranean and the East. It was not the pomps or profits of governing Africa which moved the ruling elites, but the cold rules for national safety handed on from Pitt, Palmerston, and Disraeli.[35]

Similarly, statesmen from Cardinal Richelieu to Winston Churchill to Dean Acheson have explained their decisions to intervene abroad as acts of "necessity" and "compulsion."[36]

More recent scholars have adopted this perspective as well, though they have used its assumptions somewhat differently. These scholars argue that the systemic cause of state expansion is the state's attempt to "cause" or "buy" security. They criticize the central assumption of classical realism and argue variously that declining nations tend to be more aggressive; that when (technologically and geographically) the defense has the military advantage, nations are likely to feel secure and act benignly; and that state behavior is best explained as a response to external threats. In general, states are more likely to expand if they are "security poor," less likely to do so if they are "security rich."[37]

---

[35] Ronald E. Robinson and John Gallagher, with Alice Denny, *Africa and the Victorians: The Official Mind of Imperialism,* 2nd ed. (London: Macmillan, 1981), 462–63.

[36] Richelieu cited in John H. Elliott, *Richelieu and Olivares* (Cambridge: Cambridge University Press, 1984), 123; Churchill cited in Peter Gretton, *Former Naval Person: Winston Churchill and the Royal Navy* (London: Cassell, 1968), 151, 152–59; Acheson cited in Arnold Wolfers, Discord and Collaboration: Essays on International Politics (Baltimore: Johns Hopkins Press, 1962), 14.

[37] I think this is a fair summary. As Jack Snyder himself notes with respect to my earlier essay, "Realism and Domestic Politics: A Review Essay," *International Security* 17, no. 1 (Summer 1992): 177–98, "Though Zakaria is critical of the notion of defensive realism, he captures the essence of the concept very astutely." See Jack L. Snyder, "Myths, Modernization, and the Post-Gorbachev World," in Richard Ned Lebow and Thomas Risse-Kappen, eds., *International Relations Theory and the End of the Cold War* (New York: Columbia University Press, 1995), 123 fn. 7. The important works of the modern defensive realist school include Stephen Van Evera, "Causes of War" (Ph.D. dissertation, University of California, Berkeley, 1984); Van Evera, "The Cult of the Offensive and the Origins of the First World War," *International Security* 9 (Summer 1984): 58–108; Van Evera, "Why Cooperation Failed in 1914," *World Politics* 38 (October 1985): 80–118; Barry R. Posen, *The Sources of Military Doctrine: France, Britain, and Germany between the World Wars* (Ithaca, N.Y.: Cornell University Press, 1984); Posen and Van Evera, "Reagan Administration Defense Policy: Departure from Containment," in Kenneth A. Oye, Robert J. Lieber, and Donald Rothchild, eds., *Eagle Resurgent? The Reagan Era in American Foreign Policy* (Boston: Little, Brown, 1987); Stephen M. Walt, *The Origins of*

REFINING AND COMPARING THEORIES OF FOREIGN POLICY

Naturally, neither defensive realism nor classical realism can completely explain a state's foreign policy: they represent, in a focused and testable form, merely "candidate solutions" to that puzzle, two starting points for a theory of foreign policy.[38] As a theory, each rests on assumptions, which are radical simplifications of reality, and even good assumptions are unlikely to be universally true. But good assumptions are useful in constructing simple theories with strong predictive power. For example, the assumption that congressmen vote based on party affiliation is a good one: relying on little information, it simply and elegantly accounts for a large number of congressional votes. By contrast, a bad theory contains assumptions that lead to weak or tautological explanations. The notion that congressmen's votes are determined by economic class may contain some truth, but it is difficult to define economic class, ascertain the number of such classes, fit each congressman into one, and judge when a bill particularly favors one class. Thus a vague assumption produces a theory that can be "massaged" to account for any one of several voting patterns. A good theory is composed of (1) meaningful predictions that can, in theory if not in practice, be falsified,[39] and (2) parsimonious statements with strong explanatory power.[40]

Alliances (Ithaca, N.Y.: Cornell University Press, 1987); Walt, "The Case for Finite Containment," *International Security* 14 (Summer 1989): 5–50; Jack S. Levy, "Declining Power and the Preventive Motive for War," *World Politics* 40 (October 1987): 82–107; Jack L. Snyder, *The Ideology of the Offensive: Military Decision Making and the Disasters of 1914* (Ithaca, N.Y.: Cornell University Press, 1984); and Snyder, *Myths of Empire: Domestic Politics and International Ambition* (Ithaca, N.Y.: Cornell University Press, 1991).

[38] Harry Eckstein, "Case Study and Theory in Political Science," in Fred Greenstein and Nelson W. Polsby, eds., *Handbook of Political Science,* vol. 7. (Reading, Mass.: Addison-Wesley, 1975), 91.

[39] Much of the complex debate within the philosophy of science over falsification concerns the status of a theory that has been proven erroneous. The proposition here—that theoretical statements are clearest when formulated in a manner that allows for falsification—is generally accepted. Thomas Kuhn characterizes a sophisticated Popperian view as follows: "To be scientific a theory need be falsifiable only by an observation statement not by an actual observation." See his "Logic of Discovery or Psychology of Research," in Imre Lakatos and Alan Musgrave, eds., *Criticism and the Growth of Knowledge* (Cambridge: Cambridge University Press, 1970), 14; see also Lakatos, "Falsification and the Methodology of Scientific Research Programmes," ibid., 91–197; and then Kuhn's points of agreement with Lakatos in Kuhn, "Reflections on My Critics," ibid., 239–41, 257–59. The classic statement on falsification is Karl Popper, *The Logic of Scientific Discovery* (New York: Basic Books, 1959).

[40] Harry Eckstein sets out four rules for constructing theories: regularity, reliability, foreknowledge, and parsimony. Both hypotheses that I test are framed as statements implying regularity. See Eckstein, "Case Study and Theory," 88–89.

The current formulation of the hypotheses on a state's foreign policy leaves two points unclear. First, who speaks for the "nation" and perceives increases and decreases in its power and security? Second, how should a scholar objectively measure these attributes? The first problem is easily addressed by the traditional assumption that "central decision-makers" have the authority to conduct a nation's foreign policy. Clearly, many factors enter into a state's foreign policy, but since statesmen are ultimately responsible for all such decisions, any domestic pressures are reflected in their discussions and actions.[41]

The second question is resolved by abandoning objective measures of power and security in favor of the perceptions of policymakers. Discrepancies between theoretical predictions and the historical record often arise because both statesmen and scholars have great difficulty objectively measuring these terms. We cannot consistently predict what perceptions a certain reality produces. Perceptions of power and insecurity vary too widely and idiosyncratically to be systematized. As Robert Jervis writes, "we cannot even establish correlations, let alone seek general causes."[42] Therefore, the theories elaborated above should predict the relationship between the perceptions of statesmen—rather than objective measures—and state policy. When central decision-makers perceive—by whatever cognitive processes, whether correctly or incorrectly—a rise in power (classical realism) or a decline in security (defensive realism), the hypotheses predict that they will expand their nations' political interests. Such a modified hypothesis would, for example, put aside the question of whether the United States is objectively in decline or not, and instead posit that defensive realism predicts that if central decision-makers *believe* the United States is becoming increasingly insecure, they will try to expand American political interests abroad.

This modification of the original hypotheses to account for the perceptions of central decision-makers also has implications for the study's

---

[41] Some protest that determining the perceptions of decision-makers is impossibly difficult, but the entire field of diplomatic history is predicated on this very method. Political scientists and historians routinely evaluate evidence to ascertain statesmen's perceptions of threats, deterrence, defense dominance, and interdependence, among other concepts. As Alexander George and Timothy McKeown explain, "The social nature of decision making implies that actors must communicate with each other in making decisions; that the content of these communications will reveal much about the attention focus, the decision rules, and the behavior of actors (even if it cannot be taken at face value); and that this communication is often accessible to researchers. . . . the conclusions that emerge from the case study are less a product of the subjective state of the researcher than is often supposed." See their "Case Studies and Theories of Organizational Decision Making," in *Advances in Information Processing in Organizations,* vol. 2 (Greenwood, Ill.: JAI Press, 1985), 37.

[42] Jervis, *Perception and Misperception,* 7–8.

research design: it suggests that large-scale national comparisons based on objective measures of power and threat are less valuable than structured, focused comparisons that elucidate statesmen's perceptions of and responses to their nation's place in the international system. Aggregate-data studies and game-theoretical approaches have, by assuming national preferences, acknowledged the difficulty of ascertaining them.[43] Detailed historical research, however, runs the risk of resulting in rich descriptions that contribute little to our understanding of general causes and consequences. Most appropriate is a combination of the two approaches in a series of comparative case studies, uniting the generalizable power of a large sample with the nuances and judgment that can come only from in-depth research. The set of cases must be large enough to enhance the external validity and robustness of the results, but it cannot be so large as to make detailed research impossible. By culling from a forty-three-year period in American history the fifty-four specific opportunities to expand that decision-makers perceived, this study attempts to strike a balance.[44]

THE ERRORS OF DEFENSIVE REALISM

Although it expresses an important truth about international life, defensive realism is theoretically sloppy. When formulated in general terms, it is difficult to falsify, even in theory. And when formulated more narrowly, the hypothesis is fairly weak, generating a host of crucial exceptions that proponents must then explain away, invoking various auxiliary hypotheses. More serious still is the theoretical flaw at the heart of this narrower version of defensive realism: the theory misconstrues the way in which the structure of the international system affects state behavior.[45]

Let us begin with the more general formulation of defensive realism. The idea that states expand their interests in search of security has a

[43] Glenn Snyder and Paul Diesing's sophisticated study using game theory acknowledges the difficulty of defining state interests without actually observing state behavior. Bruce Bueno de Mesquita adopts an aggregate-measure approach: he assumes that states are utility-maximizers; makes suppositions about how distance, alliances, and uncertainty affect a nation's expected utility; and then predicts outcomes. See Glenn H. Snyder and Paul Diesing, *Conflict among Nations: Bargaining, Decision Making, and System Structure in International Crises* (Princeton, N.J.: Princeton University Press, 1977); and Bruce Bueno de Mesquita, *The War Trap* (New Haven, Conn.: Yale University Press, 1981).

[44] See the classic by Alexander George, "Case Study and Theory Development: The Method of Structured, Focused Comparison," in Paul Gordon Lauren, ed., *Diplomacy: New Approaches in History, Theory, and Policy* (New York: Free Press, 1979).

[45] I have published some of these ideas in Zakaria, "Realism and Domestic Politics."

convincing ring to it. But security is a malleable concept that is more difficult to operationalize than most terms in international relations. Almost any foreign policy act, from modest measures aimed at survival to ambitious steps leading to world empire, can be (and has been) explained as a part of the search for safety. History provides many examples of patently hegemonic goals that were allegedly pursued to preserve a nation's security. It is difficult to think of Napoleon's expansion as motivated by insecurity, yet he claimed it was just that.[46] The leaders of Wilhelmine Germany and imperialist Japan believed that their nations' security dictated their expansionist policies; they had to "expand or die."[47] Consider the logic of mid-Victorian British policy. The key to England's great-power status was India, the jewel in the crown of the British Empire. India's security required British control of the Suez Canal, which meant the annexation of Egypt; for Egypt to be safe the upper Nile valley had to be secure, which meant that the Sudan had to be annexed, and so on. Robinson and Gallagher's analysis demonstrates again and again the vacuity of the concept of "security": "[T]hese once remote and petty interests in the Sudan, Uganda and the northern hinterlands of Zanzibar were changing into safeguards of Britain's world power."[48] If all these adventures can be explained as a search for security, is there any behavior that cannot?

Moreover, the defensive realist hypothesis is impossible to falsify in large part because it relies on dubious evidence: the self-serving testimony of decision-makers. Statesmen have a vested interest in claiming that their policies are attempts to bring security, not pursuits of ambition. By asserting that their policy is the only viable option, they undercut the opposition. As Robert Jervis points out,

> The subjective feeling of determinacy is interesting and may lead decision makers unnecessarily to restrict their search for alternatives, but it does not show that other decision makers in the same situation would have acted in the same way. . . .when scholars claim that a situation permitted no policy other than the one that was adopted, it may be that at least part of the

[46] Pieter Geyl, *Napoleon, For and Against* (New Haven, Conn.: Yale University Press, 1962), 252.

[47] Even the scholarly accounts most sympathetic to these states' security claims recognize this problem. See James Crowley, *Japan's Quest for Autonomy* (Princeton, N.J.: Princeton University Press, 1966); David P. Calleo, *The German Problem Reconsidered: Germany and the World Order, 1870 to the Present* (Cambridge: Cambridge University Press, 1978); and Michael W. Doyle, *Empires* (Ithaca, N.Y.: Cornell University Press, 1986). The best analysis of this problem is in Jervis, "Cooperation under the Security Dilemma."

[48] Robinson and Gallagher, *Africa and the Victorians*, 288–89.

reason why the circumstances appear overwhelming in retrospect is that they were claimed to be so by decision-makers.[49]

Since decision-makers routinely claim to be acting in the name of security, explanations based on security beg the question: why do some states define security expansively while others conceive of it in more limited terms?

Recasting the hypothesis by emphasizing expansion as a response to specific threats, rather than simply a search for security, does not entirely solve the problem. Since threats are clearer and more easily identifiable and emanate from specific nations or groups of nations, they can be measured more objectively.[50] But a state's foreign policy ultimately rests on a reading of the other side's intentions, which still renders the notion of threat quite malleable in the hands of statesmen. As refined, the defensive realist hypothesis finesses debates about objective measures of a nation's security, asserting that if statesmen believe their nation is threatened, they will attempt to expand political interests abroad.

More recent attempts to refine defensive realism, particularly that of Jack Snyder, avoid the problems outlined above, but they sacrifice much of the theory's explanatory power. For these scholars, the nature of the international system dictates that a state possess limited external interests, maintain a small military, and pursue a restrained foreign policy. States expand for security, and history has repeatedly demonstrated that "security [is] plentiful,"[51] balancing swiftly occurs to counter expansion, and technology and geography usually favor defenders. Anything beyond a moderate, incremental foreign policy is unnecessary and counterproductive.[52] In practice, of course, states do try to expand beyond these objective security requirements, but defensive realism refuses to attribute these efforts to systemic factors. The system pushes states toward moderate behavior only; anything else must be explained at some other level of analysis. The result is that as a first-cut theory, defensive realism accounts for very little foreign policy. Indeed, according to the theory, most major powers in modern history are exceptions to the rule, and much scholarship has striven to explain supposedly anomalous be-

---

[49] Jervis, *Perception and Misperception*, 21.

[50] Stephen Walt has persuasively argued that states usually form alliances on the basis of threats. See his *Origins of Alliances*, especially 21–26.

[51] Ibid., 49.

[52] See Posen, *Sources of Military Doctrine*, 67–69; Stephen Walt, "The Search for a Science of Strategy," *International Security* 12, no. 1 (Summer 1987): 140–66; and Snyder, *Myths of Empire*, 1–31.

havior that is, as Snyder admits, "common" and "widespread" in history.[53]

Rather than assume that the uniform behavior of great powers, whether expansion or overexpansion, is in some large measure a result of their similar power positions in the international system, defensive realists regard it as pathological, offering explanations that revolve around domestic deformities—militaristic general staffs, strategic myth-makers, imperialistic cartels—that lead the state to pursue foolish paths.[54] While neorealism is often loosely depicted as leaving domestic politics out, many defensive realists in fact have displayed the opposite tendency, using domestic politics to do all the work in their theories. Faced with anomalies of their own making, defensive realists have confirmed Robert Keohane's observation that "when confronted with anomalies, theorists will create auxiliary theories."[55] Imre Lakatos terms such projects theoretically "degenerative."[56] Not surprisingly, these auxiliary theories that discover allegedly uniform domestic defects within all great powers are unconvincing, because they must find similarities at the domestic level across a wide spectrum of regimes.

The underlying flaw of defensive realism is its poor translation of Waltzian system-level theory into a theory of foreign policy. Waltz explains that balances of power will form against any state behavior ranging from a minimal attempt to ensure survival to a maximal attempt at expansion.[57] (See fig. 2.1.) He suggests that the international system affects states in two ways: "socialization" and "competition and selection." Socialization leads states to become more alike, i.e., functionally undifferentiated; competition and selection generate an international order in which some nations "do better than others."[58] Defensive realism assumes that state behavior falls close to the "minimal" end of Waltz's spectrum. According to defensive realism's interpretation of the socialization process, all states glean the same lessons from history—balancing confronts aggressors, the costs of expansion quickly exceed the benefits, defenders often have the advantage—and thus all shun anything more than minimal security. But the theory misconstrues the manner in which

---

[53] Snyder, *Myths of Empire*, 1, 8, 9, and in general 1–10.

[54] Van Evera, "Cult of the Offensive"; Snyder, *Ideology of the Offensive*; Snyder, *Myths of Empire*. Historians who adopt similar views include Hans-Ulrich Wehler, *The German Empire, 1871–1918* (Leamington Spa/Dover: Berg Press, 1985); and Arno J. Mayer, *Political Origins of the New Diplomacy: 1917–1918* (New Haven, Conn.: Yale University Press, 1959).

[55] Keohane, "Theory of World Politics," 185.

[56] Lakatos, "Falsification," 117–18.

[57] Waltz, *Theory of International Politics*, 118.

[58] Ibid., 74–77; Waltz, "Response to My Critics," 330–32.

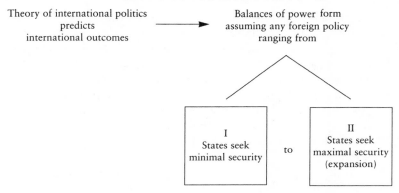

Fig. 2.1. Structural Realism

the structure of the international system influences states' decisions. Waltz's concept of socialization does not mean that the international system teaches states defensive realist wisdom.

The international system affects its constituent states' strategies much as the market affects firms' plans. Under market competition, some firms choose not to engage in risky short-term profit-taking and instead pursue long-term strategies that generate smaller short-term profits but are more secure. Firms may adopt different tactics and schemes, but one need not cast aside the theoretical assumption, basic to the economic logic of the market, that firms attempt to maximize profit.[59] Similarly, in the anarchic, nonhierarchical international environment, states are driven by the system's competitive imperative: if a state does not attempt to maximize its influence, then another will seize the opportunity in its stead. The structural-functional logic of the international system

[59] Despite numerous attacks, constraints, and layering on the concept of profit-maximization, economists still believe it is "certainly the place to start." See Stanley Fischer and Rudiger Dornbusch, *Economics* (New York: McGraw-Hill, 1983), 139–41; and William Baumol and Alan Blinder, *Economics*, 5th ed. (San Diego: Harcourt, Brace, 1991). For attempts to start from profit-maximization and then add more complex assumptions, see Oliver Williamson, "A Dynamic Theory of Inter-firm Behavior," in Bruce M. Russett, ed., *Economic Theories of International Relations* (Chicago: Markham, 1968). On "satisficing," see R. Joseph Monsen, Jr., and Anthony Downs, "A Theory of Large Managerial Firms," in Russett, *Economic Theories of International Relations*, 343–62; Michael Nicholson, *Oligopoly and Conflict* (Liverpool: Liverpool University Press, 1972), 29–30; and Martin Shubik, *Strategy and Market Structure* (New York: Wiley, 1959), 285–324. On "joint profit-maximization" in an oligopolistic market, see George Stigler, "A Theory of Oligopoly," in Russett, *Economic Theories of International Relations*, 189–90.

requires the assumption of maximizing behavior on the part of its units. The results are not always salutary in either economics or international relations, thanks to "the tyranny of small decisions." "It is an inherent characteristic of a consumer-sovereign, market economy that big changes occur as an accretion of moderate-sized steps, each of them the consequence of 'small' purchase decisions—small in their individual size, time perspective, and in relation to their total, combined ultimate effect. Because change takes place in this fashion, it sometimes produces results that conflict with the very values the market economy is supposed to serve."[60]

Kenneth Waltz's own writings are confused and contradictory on these issues. He continually cites the example of profit-maximization in the market as a parallel to state behavior. He chooses, however, to equate profit-maximizing behavior not with influence-maximizing but with state "survival."[61] Yet in distancing himself from the discredited concept of power (meaning influence)-maximization, Waltz at the same time makes clear, in his earlier writings, that the opposite—influence-minimization—is implausible: states can never have limited conceptions of their security.[62] Thus the urge to survive produces the same results as influence-maximizing. Because of anarchy, uncertainty, and differential growth rates, the notion of absolute security implicit in Waltz's concept of survival is unachievable; states can never abandon their efforts. Similarly, John Herz's description of the effects of insecurity on state behavior ends up resembling the predictions of a classical realist: "Striving to attain security from such attack, [states] are driven to acquire more and more power in order to escape the impact of power on others. This, in turn, renders the others more insecure and compels them to prepare for the worst. Since none can ever feel entirely secure in such a world of competing units, power competition ensues, and the vicious circle of security and power accumulation is on."[63] Absolute security is impossible, and whatever the cause, the result is influence-maximization. As Arnold Wolfers notes, in these explanations the "Mad Caesar" has simply been replaced by the "Hysterical Caesar."[64] Regardless of his motivation, he remains a "Caesar," relentlessly pursuing great influence.

---

[60] Alfred E. Kahn, "The Tyranny of Small Decisions," *Kyklos* 19, no. 1 (1966), reprinted in Russett, *Economic Theories of International Relations,* 537; on relating "market failure" to international relations, see Robert O. Keohane, *After Hegemony* (Princeton, N.J.: Princeton University Press, 1984), 82–83.

[61] Waltz, *Theory of International Politics,* 74–76, 117–19, 136–37.

[62] Waltz, *Man, the State, and War,* 37–38, 227.

[63] Herz, "Idealist Internationalism," 157–58.

[64] Wolfers, *Discord and Collaboration,* 84.

Defensive realists have confused the effects of the international system on states with the lessons they believe states *should* learn from that system's operation.[65] But "lessons" unfold over long time spans and are highly subjective. Outside of the imperatives of survival that the system forces on states, such long-term historical lessons have always been quite idiosyncratic. Many students of international history have pointed out that nations rarely learn any one lesson from specific events, that what each nation learns is never the same as what another learns, and that each state applies these lessons in a different manner.[66] If all states really learned from history that rapid balancing greets aggression, buck passing would become rampant: since states would expect a balance to form against an expansionist power regardless of their individual behavior, any given state would become a free-rider, unwilling to expend blood and money in the cause. Defensive realists' understanding of the socialization process would thus make balancing less common than neorealism claims.[67]

One may agree with the defensive realists that states should learn certain lessons from history, but good theory explains how the world works, not how it should work. By smuggling in normative assumptions about state behavior, defensive realism ends up regarding much foreign policy as abnormal and then explaining it away by attributing abnormality to the parties guilty of expansion. Ironically, one detects in this school of thought many of the idealistic assumptions that realists have traditionally scorned: states can be easily satisfied, nations can properly learn the "correct" lessons from the past, and state expansion (and international conflict) is not part of the normal state of affairs but instead the result of domestic disorders. One wonders, if the diseases were cured, the military bureaucracies, mythmakers, and cartels abolished, would defensive realism predict that states would pursue enlightened self-interest, never trigger balancing coalitions, and bring about perpetual peace?

[65] Benjamin Frankel nicely captures the flaws of defensive realism in "The Reading List," *Security Studies* 5 (Autumn 1995): 185–87.

[66] See Ernest R. May, *"Lessons" of the Past: The Use and Misuse of History in American Foreign Policy* (New York: Oxford University Press, 1973); May and Richard E. Neustadt, *Thinking in Time: The Uses of History for Decision-Makers* (New York: Free Press, 1986); Yuen F. Khong, *Analogies at War: Korea, Munich, Dien Bien Phu, and the Vietnam Decisions of 1965* (Princeton, N.J.: Princeton University Press, 1992); and Michael E. Howard, *The Lessons of History* (New Haven, Conn.: Yale University Press, 1991), 6–49, 177–201.

[67] Thomas J. Christensen and Jack L. Snyder, "Chain Gangs and Passed Bucks," *International Organization* 44, no. 3 (Summer 1990): 137–68.

THE FLAWS OF CLASSICAL REALISM

The classical realist contention that a nation's relative capabilities determine its intentions is a simple, powerful hypothesis. It "suggests that [a state's] adaptation to changes in relative power should be essentially continuous. The path described by state policy is therefore likely to be a smooth and straight line with no lags and zigzags."[68] And it is easily falsifiable, for whenever a nation that grows in power does not expand its political interests abroad, a discrepancy arises between the realist prediction and reality. Herein lies its great weakness: history furnishes many examples of rising states that did not correspondingly extend their political interests overseas. But as classical realists have often themselves noticed, many of these discrepancies involve policymakers' misjudgments about their country's relative power.[69] Once the crude version of classical realism has been altered to account for the problem of perception, this criticism is largely addressed.

The many attempts to narrow the gap between the predictions of classical realism and reality resemble the defensive realists' efforts to account for the exceptions to their theory, though the former's more cynical assumption generates fewer anomalies. Over the years, scholars have inserted various factors that qualified the direct correlation between increasing resources and expanding interests. Hans Morgenthau slipped in "the restraining influence of a moral consensus . . . that kept in check the limitless desire for power."[70] However, identifying the instances when restraint and moral consensus break down—Morgenthau maintains this happened in France in 1792 and in Germany in 1933— can, of course, be done only after the fact, thereby limiting the theory's predictive power. During the Enlightenment, the "interest theorists" offered increasingly detailed equations by which to calculate scientifically the "true interests" of a state, factoring in wealth, geography, mass psychology, and domestic politics.[71] In that tradition, Morgenthau and other modern realists often explain the gap by turning to the "national interest," the allegedly objective goals of a given state. The "national interest" is defined not simply as the maximization of national influence but rather as "the rational pursuit, within certain moral limitations, of

[68] Aaron L. Friedberg, *The Weary Titan: Britain and the Experience of Relative Decline, 1895–1905* (Princeton, N.J.: Princeton University Press, 1988), 14.

[69] Edward V. Gulick, *Europe's Classical Balance of Power* (New York: W. W. Norton, 1967); Friedberg, *The Weary Titan*.

[70] Morgenthau, *Politics among Nations*, 53, 239.

[71] See the chapters on the "interest theorists" in Friedrich Meinecke, *Machiavellism: The Doctrine of Raison d'Etat and Its Place in Modern History*, trans. Douglas Scott (Boulder, Colo.: Westview, 1984).

the power objectives of the state."[72] When states pursue their national interest, they foster moral consensus and the continuation of the status quo. States that exceed the national interest are revolutionary destabilizers. Once again, identifying which states are rational and which revolutionary can be done only in hindsight.

Whether by varying the "national interest" or inserting factors like statesmanship and moral restraint, these attempts to salvage classical realism were flawed because they were ad hoc and retrospective, attempting to explain away inconvenient historical cases that did not conform to the theory's forecasts. Basing the theory on statesmen's perceptions of rises in relative power preserves the basic logic of classical realism and is in accord with the theory's spirit, which emphasizes the intellectual problems of statesmanship and the need for careful judgments about national power.[73] Realists have often argued against simple numerical measures of power, claiming that national leaders often rely on pivotal events, most often wars, to assess a nation's standing.[74] Kenneth Boulding has suggested that such events create national "images" that affect the perceived place of states in the international system.[75]

Critics of classical realism view the gap between history and the simplistic version of the theory as evidence of a theoretical flaw. They charge that classical realism, with its assumption of influence-maximization, is incompatible with Waltz's balance-of-power theory; how could such states, they argue, be satisfied with a mere balance?[76] But this criticism is misguided, for it infers intentions from outcomes, committing what social psychologists call "the fundamental attribution error."[77]

[72] Morgenthau, *Politics among Nations*, 240. This distinction is also made in Henry Kissinger, *A World Restored: Metternich, Castlereagh, and the Problems of Peace, 1812–22* (Boston: Houghton Mifflin, 1957).

[73] Friedberg, *The Weary Titan*, 9–12.

[74] "The test of a Great Power is . . . the test of strength for War," writes A. J. P. Taylor in *The Struggle for Mastery in Europe, 1848–1918* (Oxford: Oxford University Press, 1954), xxxiv.

[75] Kenneth E. Boulding, "National Images and the International System," *Journal of Conflict Resolution* 3, no. 2 (1959): 120–31.

[76] Keohane, "Theory of World Politics," 174.

[77] The "fundamental attribution error" refers to the tendency to infer the attributes of units by observing the behavior of the system. Several famous social-psychology experiments document this error. Perhaps most vivid was Stanley Milgram's experiment in which "normal," "good" people could, when placed in the appropriate environment, engage in painful, sadistic behavior. See Stanley Milgram, "Behavioral Study of Obedience," *Journal of Abnormal Psychology* 67 (1963): 371–78. For the main theoretical statements about "attribution errors," see Lee Ross, "The Intuitive Psychologist and His Shortcomings: Distortions in the Attribution Process," in Leonard Berkowitz, ed., *Advances in Experimental Social Psychology* (New York: Academic Press, 1977), 184–86; and Edward E. Jones and R. E. Nisbett, "The Actor and the Observer: Divergent Perceptions of

War cannot be explained by the assertion that states are by nature aggressive; even a bellicose state will travel down the path toward hostilities only under certain conditions.[78] Outcomes in the international system—war, peace, balances of power—result not from the attributes and preferences of a single country, but from the interaction of several states within an international context. The eighteenth-century world was characterized by moderation and the balance of power, even though Frederick the Great attempted ceaselessly to maximize Prussia's influence. So, also, one cannot infer from the statement "balances of power form" that states are "minimizing" power. The two statements are drawn from theories explaining different dependent variables. Balances of power are international outcomes caused by the effect of several unintended actions by states. It is perfectly compatible, for example, to say that firms attempt to maximize profits, but that the result of the uncoordinated actions of firms in a market is a lowering of prices. Power-maximizing is a national tendency and cannot alone explain international outcomes like war or balances of power. Theories of foreign policy, like classical realism, try to explain not international outcomes but rather national preferences.

Defensive realism makes a similar error: it sees bad international outcomes—disruptions in the balance of power—and infers from these the existence of a bad state, one with some domestic deformity, within the system. But the situation in which states find themselves vis-à-vis their fellows is the most powerful force shaping international outcomes. Often it is unclear, certainly to national leaders, whether a state's expansion will trigger a balancing coalition or whether its actions are in fact part of a balancing process. Was Britain's climb to world empire in the nineteenth century an act of aggression that led to Germany's balancing in the early part of the twentieth century, or was England itself balancing against Napoleonic France and the Holy Alliance? The tragedy of international relations, as theorists from Thucydides to Rousseau to Waltz have understood, is that it does not take bad states to produce bad outcomes.

Balance-of-power theory assumes that state interests range from attempts at minimal security to attempts to maximize influence or interests. A realist theory of foreign policy must be constructed starting with one of those two assumptions about state behavior. Classical realism's assumption, drawn from the maximalist end of the spectrum, is neither true nor untrue. Many states do not maximize their influence con-

---

the Causes of Behavior," in Edward E. Jones et al., *Attribution: Perceiving the Causes of Behavior* (Morristown, N.J.: General Learning Press, 1971).

[78] Waltz, *Theory of International Politics,* 60–79.

stantly, as can be seen from the fact that after a change in leadership or an international crisis states often intensify their efforts at expansion or pursue détentelike policies. But, similarly, many firms do not maximize profits consistently, and firms also have changes in management that lead to sudden changes in profitability. This does not mean that maximizing behavior is a bad starting assumption.

Classical realism's basic assumption is superior to that of defensive realism because it leads to propositions that are elegant, easily falsifiable, and thus powerfully predictive. They serve as the foundation for an excellent first-cut theory of foreign policy that can be refined and modified on the basis of both deductive and inductive insights. However, classical realism's great strength—extreme parsimony—also weakens its explanatory power, for even a cursory look at several periods in history reveals that in the short and middle term, states often deviate from its predictions. Thus both classical and defensive realism generate exceptions. Classical realism, however, embodies a logic—a state's capabilities shape its intentions—that can be modified to make it more accurate without great loss of parsimony. The resulting theory is called state-centered realism.

STATE-CENTERED REALISM

Although classical realism correctly focuses on the nation-state as the principal actor in world politics, it inadvertently obscures an important distinction. Statesmen, not nations, confront the international system, and they have access to only that fraction of national power that the state apparatus can extract for its purposes. Therefore, according to the hypothesis of what I call state-centered realism, statesmen will expand the nation's political interests abroad when they perceive a relative increase in state power, not national power. By continuing to emphasize power as the critical variable, state-centered realism preserves the overall logic of classical realism, but its greater sophistication regarding the measurement of power creates a more accurate theory without any real loss of parsimony.

Classical realism has always been sensitive to the distinction between the state, meaning the central government, and the nation, meaning that broader entity comprising the economy, society, and population that the state controls to varying degrees.[79] The concept of the autonomous state

[79] The state is "an organization, composed of numerous agencies led and coordinated by the state's leadership (executive authority) that has the ability or authority to make and implement the binding rules for all the people as well as the parameters of rule making for

has its roots in the emergence in the seventeenth century of *raison d'état*—"the idea that the state was more than its ruler and more than the expression of his wishes; that it transcended crown and land, prince and people; that it had its particular set of interests and a particular set of necessities based upon them."[80] Realists in the continental European tradition such as Otto Hintze and Leopold von Ranke drew the distinction between states and societies boldly and theoretically. For Hintze, the state was not a perfect reflection of society because of the former's role in the international system: "the state is not merely a government internally but a sovereign power externally." The creation of the modern state was grounded in "the requirements of the nation as a whole, that is, the conditions of a rapidly and radically transformed political existence, thrust from national tranquility onto the stage of world history."[81] The well-known phrase *der Primat der Aussenpolitik* was used by von Ranke to explain state structure, assigning its primary cause to external pressures.[82] In Max Weber's view, the state was more than a mere arena for social contestation. Its essential characteristic was its monopoly over coercive power within defined territorial boundaries; the state was a set of administrative and legal bodies through which it could exert its will over its citizenry.[83] Examining Morgenthau and Carr, a recent essay notes that while the idea is not rigorously articulated in realism, "an implicit notion of the state that is at once separate from and interactive with society can be detected."[84]

However, much of modern American social science has followed either system-centered or society-centered approaches that ignore the

other social organizations in a given territory, using force if necessary to have its way." Joel Migdal, *Strong Societies and Weak States: State-Society Relations and State Capabilities in the Third World* (Princeton, N.J.: Princeton University Press, 1988), 19.

[80] Gordon A. Craig and Alexander L. George, *Force and Statecraft: Diplomatic Problems of Our Time*, 3d ed. (New York: Oxford University Press, 1995), 5.

[81] Otto Hintze, "The State in Historical Perspective," in Reinhard Bendix, ed., *State and Society: A Reader in Comparative Political Sociology*, 2nd ed. (Berkeley: University of California Press, 1973), 156, 161.

[82] Otto Hintze, "Military Organization and the Organization of the State," in *The Historical Essays of Otto Hintze*, ed. Felix Gilbert (New York: Oxford University Press, 1975), 180–215; Leopold Ranke, "A Dialogue on Politics," reprinted in Theodore H. Von Laue, *Leopold Ranke: The Formative Years* (Princeton, N.J.: Princeton University Press, 1950), 152–80.

[83] Max Weber, "Bureaucracy and Political Leadership," in Bendix, *State and Society*, 296–308; David Beetham, *Max Weber and the Theory of Modern Politics* (London: Allen and Unwin, 1974); Theda Skocpol, "Bringing the State Back In: Strategies of Analysis in Current Research," in Peter B. Evans, Dietrich Rueschemeyer, and Theda Skocpol, eds., *Bringing the State Back In* (Cambridge: Cambridge University Press, 1985), 7–8.

[84] G. John Ikenberry, David A. Lake, and Michael Mastanduno, "Toward a Realist Theory of State Action," *International Studies* Quarterly 33 (December 1989): 460.

state's capacity to act independently of social and systemic forces.[85] System-centrism is particularly prevalent among scholars of international relations who have been heavily influenced by structural realism. As a rigorous theory of international politics that seeks to predict broad patterns of international outcomes, structural realism centers on the system, consciously dismissing state structure and thereby adding to its generalizability. The need for theoretical parsimony has typically led scholars to examine relative national power rather than state power.[86] For similar reasons, scholars have by and large chosen to measure power rather than decision-makers' perceptions of power, a factor that would complicate the theory somewhat and render its measures less objective.[87] Realism's emphasis on the state as distinct from the nation has been limited primarily to the "second-image reverse" argument—external pressures shape a state's internal structure—that stems from Hintze.[88] As a recent article concluded, "We do not yet have a realist theory of the state and domestic politics, merely simplifying assumptions about them."[89]

In the past two decades, social scientists—primarily in the fields of comparative politics, American politics, and international political

[85] See G. John Ikenberry, David A. Lake, and Michael Mastanduno, "Introduction: Approaches to Explaining American Foreign Economic Policy," in Ikenberry, Lake, and Mastanduno, eds., *The State and American Foreign Economic Policy* (Ithaca, N.Y.: Cornell University Press, 1988), 1; and Skocpol, "Bringing the State Back In," 4–7. A recent literature review concluded that earlier scholars "tend to focus on government conceived of as a collection of individuals performing specific functions, or they limit themselves to circumscribed institutions within the state, such as the Presidency or Congress. They rarely view the state as an administrative apparatus where administration means the extraction of resources, control and coercion, and maintenance of the political, legal, and normative order in society." See Karen Barkey and Sunita Parikh, "Comparative Perspectives on the State," *Annual Review of Sociology* 17 (1991): 524.

[86] See, for example, Bruce Russett, ed., *Peace, War, and Numbers* (Beverly Hills, Calif.: Sage, 1972); and Wayne H. Ferris, *The Power Capabilities of Nation-States: International Conflict and War* (Lexington, Mass.: Lexington Books, 1973).

[87] See William C. Wohlforth, "The Perception of Power," *World Politics* 34, no. 3 (April 1987): 353–81; Wohlforth, *The Elusive Balance: Power and Perceptions during the Cold War* (Ithaca, N.Y.: Cornell University Press, 1993); and Friedberg, *The Weary Titan*.

[88] The literature documenting these second-image reverse effects is immense. See, for example, Charles Tilly, ed., *The Formation of National States in Western Europe* (Princeton, N.J.: Princeton University Press, 1975); Brian M. Downing, *The Military Revolution and Political Change: The Origins of Democracy and Autocracy in Early Modern Europe* (Princeton, N.J.: Princeton University Press, 1992); Peter Gourevitch, "The Second Image Reversed: The International Sources of Domestic Politics," *International Organization* 32 (1978): 881–911; and Karen A. Rasler and William R. Thompson, *War and State Making: The Shaping of Global Powers* (Boston: Unwin and Hyman, 1989).

[89] Michael C. Desch, "War and Strong States, Peace and Weak States?" *International Organization* 50, no. 2 (Spring 1996): 238.

economy—have begun to assess the role of the state as an independent actor, drawing on Weber and Hintze.[90] And modest studies have successfully layered a variable concerning the structure and power of the state onto systemic analysis.[91] State-centered realism is an attempt at a marriage between this recently resuscitated tradition and the field of international security.[92] It seeks to bring the state back into realism. It recognizes that statesmen encounter not only pressures from the international system but also constraints that are the consequence of state structure, chiefly the degree to which national power can be converted into state power. But state-centered realism clearly preserves the central tenet of classical realism that power explains foreign policy. Thus state-centered realism predicts that *nations try to expand their political interests abroad when central decision-makers perceive a relative increase in state power.*

State power is a function of national power and state strength. The stronger the state, the greater its ability to extract national power for its ends. This variable is a continuum that must be measured along several axes. The first is state scope: how broadly does the state define its responsibilities? A minimal state generally confines itself to internal order, external defense, basic infrastructure, and the like, while a maximal state expands state responsibilities to include functions such as the adjudication of civil disputes, the redistribution of wealth, and extensive infrastructure development.[93] Ignored by the concept of state scope is the equally important concern of who offers that definition of the state's duties: in other words, is the state autonomous or does its formulation

---

[90] Gabriel Almond argues that the renewed statist perspective is hardly distinctive, but Eric Nordlinger's critique convincingly shows that while Almond's claim for the state-specific contributions of earlier social science has some merit, it is also overstated. See Gabriel A. Almond, "The Return to the State," *American Political Science Review* 82, no. 3 (September 1988): 853–74; and "The Return to the State: Critiques," ibid., 875–85.

[91] One of the earliest attempts to return the autonomous state to a position of prominence and to suggest "that the absence or presence of a well-developed concept of state relates to and identifies important empirical differences" is J. P. Nettl, "The State as a Conceptual Variable," *World Politics* 20, no. 4 (July 1968): 559–92. More recent efforts include Stephen D. Krasner, "Domestic Constraints on International Economic Leverage," in K. Knorr and F. N. Trager, eds., *Economic Issues and National Security* (Lawrence: Regents Press of Kansas, 1977); Krasner, *Defending the National Interest: Raw Materials Investments and U.S. Foreign Policy* (Princeton, N.J.: Princeton University Press, 1978); Peter J. Katzenstein, ed., *Between Power and Plenty: Foreign Economic Policies of Advanced Industrial States* (Madison: University of Wisconsin Press, 1978); Katzenstein, "International Relations and Domestic Structures: Foreign Economic Policies of Advanced Industrial States," *International Organization* 30, no. 1 (Winter 1976): 1–45; and Evans, Rueschemeyer, and Skocpol, *Bringing the State Back In.*

[92] A notable exception is Desch, "War and Strong States," 237–68.

[93] Ibid., 241.

and pursuit of its goals simply reflect societal interests?[94] The concepts of state autonomy and state scope together form one set of important questions about state objectives.

The second dimension of state strength concerns its central policy-making apparatus: does the state possess sufficient capacity and cohesion to carry out its wishes? While the general underpinnings of great-state capacity are sovereignty, stability, and a loyal and skilled bureaucracy, two important factors stand out. One is the state's ability to extract wealth; as Theda Skocpol argues, "A state's means of raising and deploying financial resources tells us more than could any other single factor about its existing (and immediately potential) capacities to create or strengthen state organizations, to employ personnel, to coopt political support, to subsidize economic enterprises, and to fund social programs."[95] The other is the degree of centralization of decision-making power within the state. Is there severe competition among bureaucratic agencies, among the branches of government, between the federal and local governments? Without centralized decision-making and without access to material resources, no state can be considered strong. Thus at one end of the spectrum lie those states that are cohesive, autonomous, wealthy, and maximal, and at the opposite end lie those that are divided, society-penetrated, poor, and minimal.[96]

As noted earlier, one important school of thought believes the modern state arose in response to external challenges: in Tilly's well-known phrase, "war made the state."[97] Another approach views the state as the product of internal pressures, particularly the transition from feudalism.[98] Both share the view that structural reform occurs only in response to crisis and that therefore, institutional change is episodic rather than incremental.[99] As we shall see, primarily in chapter 4, the initial rise of the American state in the post—Civil War era came about largely to cope with the internal pressures generated by industrialization.[100] More-

[94] Skocpol, "Bringing the State Back In," 9–15.

[95] Ibid., 16–17.

[96] Naturally, this neat analytic division is not so neat in practice. Real states have mixed and uneven capacities across issue areas, but this hardly negates the logical link between state structure and policy outcomes. An uneven state is less powerful than a uniformly strong state but more powerful than a uniformly weak state.

[97] Charles Tilly, "Reflections on the History of European State-Making," in his *Formation of National States*, 42.

[98] Barkey and Parikh, "Comparative Perspectives on the State," 529–30.

[99] Ikenberry proposes several reasons on both the micro and macro levels as to why institutions are so resistant to change and can be transformed only under duress. See G. John Ikenberry, "Conclusion: An Institutional Approach to American Foreign Economic Policy," in Ikenberry, Lake, and Mastanduno, *American Foreign Economic Policy*, 223.

[100] Desch, "War and Strong States," 242, 245, 247–48, attempts to argue otherwise; but

over, those pressures never erupted in a single crisis, or even a series of crises, that prompted reform. The American state grew incrementally and continuously in the second half of the nineteenth century.[101] This is not meant to deny the essential truth of the observation that war has a tremendous impact on state-building. Certainly, World War II had a fantastic effect on the growth of the American state. This study merely seeks to emphasize the importance of the second half of Tilly's dictum—"and the state made war"—for the state can, as the example of the late-nineteenth-century United States shows, develop independently of military necessity. And that growth can in turn shape a state's foreign and military policy.

This study examines American foreign policy in the late nineteenth century in light of changes in state structure. Clearly, when compared to European states, the United States remained fairly weak until World War II, and arguably even since then. (Its diplomacy was also less activist when compared to European states of roughly comparable power.) However, when one considers state strength as a continuum, it is the shifts along that continuum that are crucial.[102] Thus the following three chapters will track the transformation of the American state in the second half of the nineteenth century along the four major variables discussed above—scope, autonomy, coherence, and capacity—and the effects on the nation's foreign policy. In the American case, the least attractive of major central institutions from a statist perspective is Congress, which is so susceptible to the influence of private interests. Thus shifts in authority and capacity from the legislative to the executive branch result in greater state autonomy and constitute a move closer to the statist end of the continuum. Although in practice the different components of the executive branch are often indistinguishable, since the president occupies the position at the top of the administrative hierarchy, the presidency is, in principle, less statist than the bureaucracy because, as an elected office, it is less insulated from societal influence. A state is, then, structurally stronger if authority is lodged in the bureaucracy rather than either Congress or the presidency.[103] As noted

---

his evidence is not at all persuasive, for he conveniently ignores those aspects of U.S. state-building that occurred outside the context of America's military excursions.

[101] Stephen Skowronek refers to the reforms that occurred before 1900 as mere patchwork, as opposed to the reconstitution of America's government system that followed. But they were, nevertheless, significant changes that laid the groundwork for later reform. See Stephen Skowronek, *Building a New American State: The Expansion of National Administrative Capacities, 1877–1920* (Cambridge: Cambridge University Press, 1982).

[102] For a similar point, see Ikenberry, "Institutional Approach," 221.

[103] Richard F. Bensel, *Yankee Leviathan: The Origins of Central State Authority in America, 1859–1877* (New York: Cambridge University Press, 1990), 106–10.

above, the empirical research will conclude that Congress still wielded great power in the latter half of the nineteenth century, and the bureaucracy was weak relative to both Congress and the president. The important point, though, is that authority and capacity began to shift in a statist direction, even as the bulk of that authority remained in arenas permeable to societal interests.

However, analysis of administrative structure is not sufficient because of the United States' federal system. The centralization of authority in the central state as opposed to either private citizens or state and local governments produces a more coherent set of national policies. Thus measures that move authority from the state to the federal level or give the federal government control over private activities represent a more statist approach. Finally, to use the terms *state* or *statesmen* or *central decision-makers* in any meaningful analytic sense, as in the proposed classical and defensive realist theories of foreign policy, is to refer to the executive branch.[104] Although the legislative and judicial branches have enormous impact on the formation of national policy, the degree to which these other branches have input determines the autonomy and coherence of the state.

Although it is true that domestic politics and international politics are "somehow entangled but our theories have not yet sorted out the puzzling tangles," this lack of progress is due in part to the ambitious nature of the project: a theory that accounted for both domestic and foreign policy would likely be so complex that it would not really be a theory. It would describe reality rather than explain it.[105] By contrast, state-centered realism has a more modest and attainable goal: it attempts to explain foreign policy, not domestic policy and not the combination of the two. Without sacrificing much parsimony, state-centered realism introduces a domestic variable that interacts with systemic forces, producing a spare but accurate realist theory of foreign policy.

CONCLUSIONS: THEORY AND PRACTICE

States may indeed sometimes expand their interests in search of security. Of greater concern to this essay is whether that concept can be clarified and formulated as a useful theoretical statement. As we have seen, statesmen have invoked security to justify all foreign policy behavior, including even blatant imperial grabs. The defensive realist hypothesis—that statesmen will expand political interests abroad when they

---

[104] See Krasner, Defending the National Interest.

[105] See Robert Putnam, "Diplomacy and Domestic Politics: The Logic of Two-Level Games," *International Organization* 42, no. 3 (Summer 1988): 427.

perceive an increase in threats—alleviates some of these concerns, but not all. Threats are more measurable than security, but the notion of threat, like security, is extraordinarily malleable, and statesmen have a vested interest in portraying expansion as necessary for the survival of the nation. These, however, are only problems of operationalization and execution, of defining the terms in a useful way and garnering data to match them. The hypothesis can still be tested, with care that the independent and dependent variables are not both caused by some other phenomenon, that the two variables do not covary. Though it remains vague, the alleged link between threats and expansion is a persistent one in the theory of international relations, and testing this relationship would certainly be useful.

In its pure form, classical realism is simple and powerful. Yet it is also a crude null hypothesis from which one can easily measure deviations; its very simplicity makes it unlikely to prove useful for actual predictions. If we modify it and add one simple constraint to the key variable of national power, many of the discrepancies between the theory and reality fall away. Statesmen, not states, are the primary actors in international affairs, and their perceptions of shifts in power, rather than objective measures, are critical. A second constraint greatly adds to the accuracy and detail of the hypothesis without greatly restricting its parsimony. Statesmen can exploit the power resources of their nation only as transmitted through the state structure: foreign policy is thus the product of state power. This hypothesis, which I term state-centered realism, is still quite demanding, generating more expansionist predictions than fashion dictates at present.

The two final hypotheses, which serve as the basis for this study, are:

1. State-centered realism: *Nations try to expand their political interests abroad when central decision-makers perceive a relative increase in state power.*

2. Defensive realism: *Nations try to expand their political interests abroad when central decision-makers perceive an increase in threats.*

The study treats these two hypotheses as competing theories. After all, theories are not judged against perfect knowledge or complete predictive power, but rather against contending explanations. When examining the historical cases selected, therefore, I will ask how successful each theory is in explaining events and will suggest the rank or explanatory weight that each theory should be accorded. These theories compete only in the sense that just one can be the starting point for analysis, answering the following question: if you wanted to predict the foreign policy behavior of a rising state, what one factor would you begin with, state power or the level of external threat? As historical explanations,

these theories are neither competing nor mutually exclusive: a full understanding of all aspects of a specific state's foreign policy will require
some combination of the two.

The specific period under study—American foreign policy from 1865
to 1908—provides an excellent set of critical cases for both state-centered realism and defensive realism. This period presents a thorny problem for state-centered realism: after the Civil War, the United States was
widely recognized as among the world's great economic powers, but its
interests remained those of a minor power. Defensive realism appears to
have a ready answer: surrounded by two vast oceans and weak neighbors, and protected by the British Royal Navy, which ruled the seas
without challenge, the United States enjoyed tremendous economic
growth in an international environment devoid of threats to its security:
no threats, no expansion. Of course, this explanation is partly true, but
is it the best first-cut theory, or is the simpler claim that capabilities
influence intentions perhaps a better starting point? The United States is
often considered the least "normal" of the great powers: isolationism is
often viewed as fundamental to the country's political tradition and national character. Its cases of expansion are hence "least-likely" cases for
state-centered realism. If the theory can explain why the United States
acquired interests abroad, that explanation would surely apply to the
other great powers, all of which demonstrate a much clearer connection
between rising power and rising influence. Conversely, America's extremely secure geographic position makes its cases of nonexpansion
"most-likely" cases for defensive realism. If the benign international environment in which the United States found itself does not explain its
isolationism, defensive realism's hypotheses will probably have difficulty
explaining other great power nonexpansion.[106] If state-centered realism
can explain the transformation in American statecraft during this period, it will have succeeded in a difficult set of cases. And if defensive
realism cannot account for the behavior of an objectively secure country, it will have failed an easy test.

[106] This is not a sure path to a general theory, but it provides a method by which to
choose among the almost limitless cases in history against which one might test such
theories. See Eckstein, "Case Study and Theory," 124–32.

CHAPTER THREE

Imperial Understretch

POWER AND NONEXPANSION, 1865–1889

ON MAY 10, 1867, the secretary of state of the United States of America was moved to write a poem. One of America's most distinguished statesmen and politicians, William Henry Seward was no ordinary diplomat. He had been governor of New York and a close runner-up for the Republican Party's presidential nomination in 1860, and upon election as president, Abraham Lincoln had appointed him secretary of state. Throughout the Civil War, Seward had been Lincoln's closest adviser as well as a skilled diplomat, deftly maneuvering to keep Great Britain and France from allying with the Confederacy. With that terrible conflict now in the past, the secretary prophesied in verse about his nation's future:

> Our nation with united interests blest,
> Not now content to poise, shall sway the rest;
> Abroad our empire shall no limits know,
> But like the sea in boundless circles flow.[1]

Seward had long discoursed on the growing power of the American economy. From his unique vantage point, he had watched the country mobilize for war, and he was quick to understand what was less apparent to many of his countrymen: in terms of material resources, the United States had come of age as a great power, and it now needed to develop interests commensurate with its power. The poem hardly exaggerated Seward's hopes for the limitless expansion of American influence. One month after that fit of inspiration, he urged Connecticut's legislators to support his expansive vision:

> The people of the United States have now before them a prospect the most glorious that ever dawned upon any nation . . . one whole and indissoluble republic extending from the Atlantic to the Pacific Ocean, aye and approaching the shores of Japan and China, from the Gulf of Mexico on the South to the Arctic Ocean. [Loud Applause] . . . and if you will but give us

[1] Quoted in Joseph Gerald Whelan, "William Henry Seward: Expansionist" (Ph.D. dissertation, University of Rochester, 1959), 95.

the support . . . I will extend the picture a little further and show you the flag of the United States waving on Plymouth Rock in the east and at the same time throwing forth its folds from the golden gate in the west and from castellated towers in the tropics, to the northern pole. [Great Applause.][2]

Of course, nothing like this happened during Seward's tenure. His dream of a mighty and influential United States with worldwide interests was to remain just that until it was partially fulfilled three decades later and wholly consummated ninety years after the conclusion of the American Civil War.

AMERICA'S ASCENT

The United States had been growing steadily in both population and wealth over the first half of the nineteenth century and by the 1850s had begun the takeoff toward sustained economic growth and industrialization that would carry it to the forefront of the global economy over the course of the century. Only in the decades after the Civil War, however, did economic growth reach a truly stunning pace.[3] By one calculation, the United States grew at an average rate of 5 percent per year between 1873 and 1913.[4] This extraordinary rise manifested itself in almost every sector of the economy. Between 1865 and 1898, American wheat production increased 256 percent, corn 222 percent, and sugar 460 percent. In industrial sectors growth was even greater: coal production rose 800 percent, steel rails 523 percent, and railway track mileage 567 percent. "In newer industries the growth, starting from near zero, was so great as to make percentages meaningless." Petroleum production, for example, rose from three million barrels in 1865 to fifty-five million barrels in 1898.[5] Despite several severe depressions, particularly those of the mid-1870s and early 1890s, America's prosperity and seemingly inexorable economic progress fostered the country's

[2] Ibid., 96–97.
[3] Economic statistics from this period should, of course, be treated with great caution. But one would not expect consistent biases to appear across countries and time periods. As was earlier argued, the greater issue for this study is change in the global distribution of wealth, the relative rise and decline of countries. Although scholars may disagree over exactly how much the American economy grew in the second half of the nineteenth century, all such studies produce the same relative rankings.
[4] D. J. Coppock, "The Causes of the Great Depression, 1873–1896," *The Manchester School of Economic and Social Studies* 29, no. 3 (1961): 205–32.
[5] David M. Pletcher, "Economic Growth and Diplomatic Adjustment," in William H. Becker, Jr., and Samuel F. Wells, Jr., eds., *Economics and World Power: An Assessment of American Diplomacy since 1789* (New York: Columbia University Press, 1984), 120.

reputation as a place of boundless opportunity, attracting millions of adventurous Europeans to its shores. Thanks to this steady immigration and what Representative Andrew Kennedy termed the "American multiplication table," the population doubled between 1865 and 1900.

Power in international life, however, is measured in relative terms. As Joseph Chamberlain cautioned around the turn of the last century, while Britain experienced and debated its relative decline, "the essential thing to keep in mind . . . [is] that the greatness of a nation is not measured by a comparison with its own past, but by its relative position in the councils of the world."[6] America was a burgeoning and prosperous nation, but was it growing faster than other countries? In fact, its meteoric rise was even more staggering in relative terms. While the United States grew at a rate of 5 percent per year, Great Britain was averaging growth of only 1.6 percent. By 1885 the United States had surpassed Britain, gaining the single largest share of world manufacturing output. One year later it replaced Britain as the world's greatest steel producer.[7] In terms of energy consumption, which some have identified as the best measure of a country's economic strength, the United States overtook Britain by 1890, and by 1900 it was consuming more energy than Germany, France, Austria-Hungary, Russia, Japan, and Italy combined.[8] Add to these statistics the vast natural resources of a large, rich country, and an industrious and growing population second in size only to that of Russia among the great powers, and one understands why, in retrospect, "[t]he United States seemed to have *all* the economic advantages which *some* of the other powers possessed *in part,* but *none* of their disadvantages."[9]

A nation's interests, like its power, should be judged in relative terms, and in this light, a glaring disparity between America's strength and its paltry influence abroad becomes apparent. After thirty years of heady growth, America's political interests—its territorial acquisitions and protectorates, defense forces, foreign legations, and alliances—were tiny compared to those of countries with comparable resources (Britain, France, Germany, Austria-Hungary, Russia, Italy, and later Japan). As

[6] Quoted in Aaron L. Friedberg, *The Weary Titan: Britain and the Experience of Relative Decline, 1895–1905* (Princeton, N.J.: Princeton University Press, 1988), 72.
[7] F. H. Hinsley, ed., *The New Cambridge Modern History,* vol. II, *Material Progress and World-Wide Problems, 1870–1898* (Cambridge: Cambridge University Press, 1970), 50.
[8] Paul Kennedy argues that energy consumption is the best measure of economic strength "since it is an indication both of a country's technical capacity to exploit inanimate forms of energy and of its economic pulse rate." Paul M. Kennedy, *The Rise and Fall of the Great Powers: Economic Change and Military Conflict from 1500 to the Present* (New York: Random House, 1987), 201.
[9] Ibid., 243.

Norman Graebner has noted, "the contrast between the United States as a potentially first-class military power and the United States as an active and predictable component in a worldwide balance of power presented a profound dichotomy."[10] The ultimate measure of international influence in the late nineteenth century, a time of colonial competition and imperialism, was political control over foreign lands. Between 1865 and 1890, the United States acquired forsaken Alaska and the tiny Midway Islands and gained basing rights in Samoa. During the same period, Britain and France each acquired over three million square miles of new colonies. The American army was tiny, with an active force of twenty-five thousand in 1890—ranking it fourteenth in the world after Bulgaria, even though by this date the United States was the richest nation in the world. The state of the American navy was so unusual for a country with long coastlines that it was an object of ridicule in Europe. (After touring America in 1890, Oscar Wilde had his "Canterville Ghost" react with surprise when told by an American that her country had "no ruins and no curiosities." " 'No ruins! no curiosities!' replied the Ghost; 'you have your navy and your manners.' "[11]) The U.S. Navy was the smallest among the major powers, just behind that of Italy, and the Italian army, smallest among the European powers, was still eight times the size of America's; American industrial strength, however, was thirteen times that of Italy.[12]

America's diplomatic apparatus was in even worse shape than its defenses. In all but a few important countries, the United States was represented by honorary ambassadors and ministers. The State Department itself was a tiny affair, housed in a few rooms and run by two assistant secretaries of state, a few junior officers, and a host of clerks.[13] Messages between Washington and most other foreign capitals were few and far between. The United States attended hardly any international conferences, participated in no joint decision-making, and of course brokered no alliances. As a result, America was treated like a second-rank power, on a par with countries that possessed a fraction of its material resources. When in 1880 the Sultan of Turkey decided to pare down his diplomatic corps, he eliminated his missions to Sweden, Belgium, the Netherlands, and the United States. Around the same time, a

[10] Norman A. Graebner, "World Power: The McKinley Years," in his *Foundations of American Foreign Policy: A Realist Appraisal from Franklin to McKinley* (Wilmington, Del.: Scholarly Resources, 1985), 314–15.

[11] Oscar Wilde, "The Canterville Ghost," in *The Writings of Oscar Wilde*, vol. 4, *Lord Arthur Savile's Crime and Other Stories* (London: Keller-Farmer, 1907), 131.

[12] Kennedy, *Rise and Fall of the Great Powers*, 202–3.

[13] Zara Steiner, *The Times Survey of Foreign Ministries of the World* (London: Times Books, 1982), 576–78.

German envoy in Madrid offered to take a pay cut rather than be transferred to Washington and endure such a demotion. None of the diplomats in Washington were ambassadors: no European power considered America sufficiently important to warrant a diplomat of that rank until 1892.[14]

Clearly, the United States might have closed this gap between its power and its interests, and many Europeans initially expected that with the end of the war between the states, the United States would assume its place among the world's great powers. European statesmen believed the Civil War represented a watershed from which there could be no turning back. Benjamin Disraeli explained in the House of Commons that the war would produce "a different America from that which was known to our fathers and even from that which this generation has had so much experience. It will be an America of armies, of diplomacy, of Rival States and maneuvering Cabinets, of frequent turbulence, and probably of frequent wars."[15] Imagining that they were witnessing the birth of a new great power that would compete with their countries for global resources, European diplomats began to reevaluate their policies toward the United States: Russia hoped to ally with the United States and increase its pressure on Britain's colonies, and Bismarck similarly saw the potential for American expansion to the north with all the ensuing complications for Britain. The British, of course, were the most concerned about America's rise: a great naval power across the Atlantic could only be a rival.[16] But it soon became clear the United States would not be converting its rising power into political activism overseas.

THE HISTORIANS AND AMERICAN EXPANSION

American influence abroad was so minimal in the second half of the nineteenth century that many historians have skipped over the period in their accounts, beginning their discussion of American expansionism with the 1890s.[17] Even those scholars who recognize the presence of expansionist sentiment throughout the post—Civil War period have assumed that the United States did not have the resources to play an important role in global affairs before the 1890s. Yet a recent review of

---

[14] Ernest May, *Imperial Democracy: The Emergence of America as a Great Power* (New York: Harcourt, Brace and World, 1961), 3, 5–6.

[15] Quoted in Belle Becker Sideman and Lillian Friedman, eds., *Europe Looks at the Civil War* (New York: Orion Press, 1960), 233.

[16] Kenneth Bourne, *Britain and the Balance of Power in North America, 1815–1908* (Berkeley: University of California Press, 1967), 251–312.

[17] See, for example, May, *Imperial Democracy.*

the literature on late-nineteenth-century American diplomatic history concluded that "precious few" scholars would deny that "the United States became a world power of the first rank by century's end."[18]

Part of the reason for this inattention to the disparity between U.S. power and interests may lie in the varying definitions of power. Like many others, Ernest May identifies 1898 as the birth of the United States as a great power, by which he means a nation with worldwide influence.[19] Given that definition, May is certainly correct. Thomas Bailey, on the other hand, defines a great power as a nation with significant material resources and dates America's emergence as a great power to the early nineteenth century.[20] Although Bailey exaggerates America's relative economic power, he adds an important component to the notion of a great power. Once one's definition of a great power includes both resources and interests, the historical puzzle of the United States in the second half of the nineteenth century becomes readily apparent. Allowing for a time lag of about a decade, powerful states nearly always develop interests commensurate with their capabilities. Yet although the United States emerged from the Civil War as one of the most powerful industrial nations in the world and overtook all countries but Britain by the mid-1880s, its interests overseas remained largely the same as before its economic takeoff.

Until the 1950s, most historians argued that the expansion of the 1890s was an aberration in the history of U.S. relations with the outside world. For some, the United States was "a nation of happy beings" too busy rebuilding after the Civil War, pioneering the West, and focusing on industry to concern themselves with foreign affairs, while others explained American isolationism as the result of internal turmoil in the years following the war between the states.[21] For these "discontinuity"

---

[18] Edward P. Crapol, "Coming to Terms with Empire: The Historiography of Late-Nineteenth-Century American Foreign Relations," *Diplomatic History,* 16, no. 4 (Fall 1992): 587. For other reviews of the historical literature, see Robert L. Beisner, *From the Old Diplomacy to the New, 1865–1900,* 2d ed. (Arlington Heights, Ill.: Harlan Davidson, 1986), 13–31; Jerald A. Combs, *American Diplomatic History: Two Centuries of Changing Interpretations* (Berkeley: University of California Press, 1983); Hugh De Santis, "The Imperialist Impulse and American Innocence, 1865–1900," in Gerald K. Haines and J. Samuel Walker, eds., *American Foreign Relations: A Historiographical Review* (Westport, Conn.: Greenwood Press, 1981), 65–90; and James A. Field, Jr., "American Imperialism: The Worst Chapter in Almost Any Book," *American Historical Review* 83 (1978): 644–68.

[19] May, *Imperial Democracy,* 263–70.

[20] Thomas A. Bailey, "America's Emergence as a World Power: The Myth and the Reality," *Pacific Historical Review* 30 (February 1961): 165–79.

[21] Samuel Flagg Bemis, *A Diplomatic History of the United States* (New York: Henry Holt, 1936); Dexter Perkins, *America and the Two Wars* (Boston: Little, Brown, 1944).

historians, the roots of the American expansionist drive lay in numerous domestic factors: social Darwinism, yellow journalism, popular frenzy, weak leadership, the crisis of the early and mid-1890s.[22] Rooted in a different tradition, the realists come to remarkably similar conclusions. Norman Graebner blames American expansion on the move to "moral abstraction" rather than "the political realism that had circumscribed previous American diplomacy"; with the Spanish-American War, "the nation began to discard its precise and limited approaches of the nineteenth century, conducted through diplomacy and power." Like Samuel Flagg Bemis and Ernest May, Graebner and his fellow realists emphasize the discontinuity in American foreign relations in the late nineteenth century and stress the importance of domestic variables.[23] These historians compared the 1890s to the previous three decades and noted a marked shift. Whether they believed that the activism of the 1890s marked the emergence of a new world power or was a temporary deviation from the tradition of isolationism, historians agreed that it had little in common with the preceding decades.

The advent of the Wisconsin school challenged the discontinuity interpretation of American expansion. Drawing on the work of Charles Beard in the 1920s, William Appleman Williams and his students, particularly Walter LaFeber, explained American foreign policy as a series of increasingly systematic efforts to help American business make inroads abroad.[24] This study disagrees with most of Williams's demoniza-

[22] See Julius W. Pratt, *Expansionists of 1898: The Acquisition of Hawaii and the Spanish Islands* (Chicago: Quadrangle Books, 1964); and Richard Hofstadter, "Cuba, the Philippines, and Manifest Destiny," in Daniel Aaron, ed., *America in Crisis: Fourteen Crucial Episodes in American History* (New York: Alfred A. Knopf, 1952). A later source that emphasizes the domestic roots of American expansion, focusing on popular pressure rather than shifts in elite ideology, is May, *Imperial Democracy*. Although May attempts, in the introduction to the 1991 edition, to portray *Imperial Democracy* as a response to the realists, who, he argues, believe that "decisions driven by popular enthusiasm or sentimentality have been *characteristic* in the history of U.S. foreign relations," in fact realist historians characterize American diplomacy *after the 1890s* in that way.

[23] See Graebner, "World Power," 313–55. For earlier examples of realist thinking on the subject, see George F. Kennan, *American Diplomacy, 1900–1950* (Chicago: University of Chicago Press, 1951); and Robert E. Osgood, *Ideals and Self-Interest in American Foreign Policy: The Great Transformation of the Twentieth Century* (Chicago: University of Chicago Press, 1953).

[24] See William Appleman Williams, *The Tragedy of American Diplomacy* (New York: The World Publishing Company, 1959), 23–44. In *The Roots of the Modern American Empire: A Study of the Growth and Shaping of Social Consciousness in a Marketplace Society* (New York: Random House, 1969), Williams identified the agrarian sector as the force behind the drive for market expansion, tracing the movement back to the idealized yeoman farmers of Thomas Jefferson. Williams and the Wisconsin school have their roots in the work of Charles A. Beard, particularly his *The Idea of National Interest: An Analytical Study in American Foreign Policy* (New York: Macmillan, 1934). Walter LaFeber

tion of business and some of LaFeber's conclusions, which exaggerate both the power and conspiratorial nature of business and imply that American statesmen's concerns to expand their country's economic interests abroad were somehow unique and immoral. But it is greatly indebted to the Wisconsin school's pathbreaking emphasis on economics, on the continuity of American foreign policy in the late nineteenth century, and on the importance of ideas that had been germinating since the end of the Civil War and of expansionist policies pursued by leaders such as William Henry Seward. However, even LaFeber, the best scholar in this tradition by far, is uninterested in the relative nonexpansion of the post—Civil War years. His *The New Empire* devoted seven times as much space to the decade of the 1890s as to the preceding twenty-five years.[25]

The debate between the traditionalists and the revisionists raged, eventually culminating in works that strove to achieve a synthesis of the two approaches.[26] Despite the criticisms lodged against the revisionists, most scholars that followed paid significant attention to the economic factors that earlier historians had often ignored (or at least downplayed) and, less frequently, to the pre-1890s roots of American expansion.[27] The 1980s and 1990s have not produced new broad interpretive works.[28]

---

was the first to offer a sustained exposition of the ideas Williams had first laid out in *The Tragedy of American Diplomacy;* see LaFeber, *The New Empire: An Interpretation of American Expansion, 1860–1898* (Ithaca, N.Y.: Cornell University Press, 1963). Over the past thirty years, LaFeber has moderated his revisionism, but the basic elements remain; see his *The American Search for Opportunity, 1865–1913,* vol. 2 of *The Cambridge History of American Foreign Relations,* ed. Warren I. Cohen, (Cambridge: Cambridge University Press, 1993).

[25] Another prominent revisionist work is Thomas J. McCormick, *China Market: America's Quest for Informal Empire, 1893–1901* (Chicago: University of Chicago Press, 1967). See also Edward P. Crapol and Howard Schonberger, "The Shift to Global Expansion, 1865–1900," in William Appleman Williams, ed., *From Colony to Empire: Essays in the History of American Foreign Relations* (New York: John Wiley and Sons, 1972), 136–202.

[26] For critiques of the revisionist thesis, see Beisner, *From the Old Diplomacy to the New,* 16–24; Tony Smith, *The Pattern of Imperialism: The United States, Great Britain, and the Late-Industrializing World since 1815* (New York: Cambridge University Press, 1981), 144–54; and Robert B. Zevin, "An Interpretation of American Imperialism," *Journal of Economic History* 32, no. 1 (March 1972): 316–60.

[27] See Beisner, *From the Old Diplomacy to the New,* 72–95; Charles S. Campbell, Jr., *The Transformation of American Foreign Relations, 1865–1900* (New York: Harper and Row, 1976); Joseph A. Fry, "In Search of an Orderly World: U.S. Imperialism, 1898–1912," in John M. Carroll and George C. Herring, eds., *Modern American Diplomacy* (Wilmington, Del.: Scholarly Resources, 1986), 1–20; and David Healy, *U.S. Expansionism: The Imperialist Urge in the 1890s* (Madison: University of Wisconsin Press, 1970).

[28] See Crapol, "Coming to Terms with Empire," 573–97. Crapol suggests new paths for the study of American imperialism, but he acknowledges that historians have so far fash-

Historians have offered various explanations for American inactivity abroad in the second half of the nineteenth century that account for important aspects of American behavior. But they often contradict widely accepted propositions regarding foreign policy in general and American foreign policy in particular. For example, some historians argue that America was war-weary in 1865 and therefore uninterested in imperialist ventures.[29] Yet historians often note that nations expand their interests abroad after a war, translating their military strength into political influence, as many European statesmen expected the United States to do in 1865.[30] Explanations for both American and Soviet behavior immediately after World War II often stress this desire to negotiate from strength.[31]

Some, in a variation on Frederick Jackson Turner's frontier thesis, argue that America's vast western lands precluded "land lust" until the closing of the frontier in the 1890s.[32] Russia, however, is an even larger country, and the wide availability of land there hardly checked its imperial drive. Moreover, proponents of this argument confuse societal expansion and state expansion. Societal expansion is the settlement by private individuals of territories already acquired by the state. State expansion is the acquisition of new foreign lands, or of political control of those lands, by the state, often through interstate negotiations aided by the diplomatic and military apparatus. The lands that were settled after the Civil War in the "great westward expansion" had all been acquired

ioned only "an acceptable synthesis" (597). In the 1980s, historians explored various important aspects of U.S. foreign relations—the role of gender and racism, the spread of American cultural hegemony—but they have not brought a major reassessment of the period. See, for example, Patricia R. Hill, *The World Their Household: The American Women's Foreign Mission Movement and Cultural Transformation, 1870–1920* (Ann Arbor: University of Michigan Press, 1985); Michael Hunt, *Ideology and U.S. Foreign Policy* (New Haven, Conn.: Yale University Press, 1987); and Emily S. Rosenberg, *Spreading the American Dream: American Economic and Cultural Expansion, 1890–1945* (New York: Hill and Wang, 1982). Historians seem generally to have followed De Santis's advice in 1981 to "take a slice-of-life approach to this period rather than to design new architectonic movements to the causes of American imperialism." De Santis, "Imperialist Impulse," 83.

[29] Geoffrey Blainey, *The Causes of War,* 3d ed. (New York: Free Press, 1988).

[30] Bourne, *Britain and the Balance of Power,* 251–312.

[31] See, for example, John Lewis Gaddis, *Strategies of Containment: A Critical Appraisal of Postwar American National Security Policy* (New York: Oxford University Press, 1982), 71–83, on U.S. foreign policy in the late 1940s and the creation of what Dean Acheson termed "situations of strength." See also Melvyn P. Leffler, *A Preponderance of Power: National Security, the Truman Administration, and the Cold War* (Stanford, Calif.: Stanford University Press, 1992).

[32] Frederick Jackson Turner, "The Significance of the Frontier in American History," *Annual Report, 1893* (Washington, D.C.: American Historical Association, 1894), 199–227; LaFeber, *The New Empire,* 10–16; Williams, *Modern American Empire,* 271–89.

or conquered by 1853 as a consequence of actions by the American government. The famous Indian wars of the period were really hundreds of tiny skirmishes occupying very little of the federal government's time, energy, or money and requiring a tiny standing army.[33] That American citizens were engaged in a flurry of settlement activity in the latter half of the nineteenth century does not explain why the American state did not follow the example of previous emerging economic powers and expand its political interests abroad until the Spanish-American War.

The national security approach mirrors the views of some policymakers and explains expansion as a response to potential or existing threats from European powers. (Both the traditionalist and revisionist schools acknowledged this factor, although they did not consider it the primary motivation for American policy.)[34] Tony Smith concludes that while economic factors were clearly important, a better explanation for U.S. policy toward Latin America is preemptive imperialism, which sets policy "in a region of importance to the United States when a potentially hostile great power might create a sphere of influence for itself there."[35] This approach, which shares much with the logic of defensive realism, fails to appreciate European behavior was viewed as benign in the 1870s and 1880s, then threatening in the 1890s in large part because the United States began to define its interests more broadly. The real question is why the United States adopted a more expansive definition of its interests and hence its security over that period.

Still other diplomatic historians maintain that domestic factors account for nineteenth-century American isolationism. There the agreement stops: some emphasize the American national character, others internal upheaval that distracted Americans from foreign affairs. But

[33] In the twenty years following the Civil War, the cost of these engagements was, on average, less than a million dollars per year. To put this figure in perspective, by 1880 the federal government was running a $100 million surplus. Arthur M. Schlesinger, *Political and Social History of the United States, 1829–1925* (New York: Macmillan, 1925), 268.

[34] For an explication of the national security approach, see Melvyn P. Leffler, "National Security," in Michael J. Hogan and Thomas G. Paterson, eds., *Explaining the History of American Foreign Relations* (New York: Cambridge University Press, 1991), 202–13.

[35] Smith, *The Pattern of Imperialism*, 152, 154. In *America Invulnerable: The Quest for Absolute Security from 1812 to Star Wars* (New York: Summit Books, 1988), James Chace and Caleb Carr seek to explain the history of American foreign policy from the national security perspective. Even their version of American foreign relations, however, shows the weakness of the approach; regarding the U.S. involvement in the 1895 British-Venezuelan border dispute, they write, "The possibility of British aggression in Latin America [was] still an American nightmare, despite evidence that Britain's now enormous imperial responsibilities had long since precluded such adventurism" (121). See also Williams, *Modern American Empire*, 236–68, for a discussion of the redefinition in the 1880s of America's security perimeter from an economic perspective.

domestic trouble is often used, even by the same historians, to explain expansion as well. Revisionist historians have stressed the primacy of economic motivations in explaining American expansion. The severe recession of 1893 to 1897, one of the worst before the Great Depression, led, they argue, to fears of American "overproduction" and pressure for the acquisition of foreign markets.[36] While the economic tumult of those years should not be underestimated, the nation's "productive capacity was not seen primarily as an economic problem, but [as] evidence of strength and prosperity."[37] Moving beyond those four years, the broader period from 1889 to 1908 was undeniably one of great material progress.[38] Statesmen were, of course, always looking to expand the American economy, but the "depression theory" overstates the importance of particular business groups. Further, a theory that points to depressions as causing expansion must explain why the opposite occurred in the most important case of modern times—the Great Depression.

If domestic ills like depressions prevented the United States from expanding in the 1860s and 1870s, how could the very same factors have forced it to expand—in a form of "social imperialism"—during the 1890s? This contradiction, common in the literature, underscores the general problem with domestic politics arguments. Clearly, the United States was significantly more active in foreign affairs during the 1890s than in the two decades before. Many of the factors that allegedly explain American inactivity during the first period were just as strong during the second, yet American foreign policy was markedly different. Statesmen in both periods perceived distinct opportunities to expand; some of these resulted in formal attempts at expansion, while others did not. If explanations for nonexpansion in 1865–89 cannot be reversed to explain the expansion of 1890–1908, they must be considered suspect.

American foreign policy from 1865 to 1908 provides an excellent case with which to test the two general theories of foreign policy introduced earlier: state-centered realism and defensive realism. This study examines fifty-four cases of distinct opportunities to expand between 1865 and 1908—with an opportunity defined as a serious discussion within the executive branch of the U.S. government of a specific possi-

[36] See LaFeber, *The New Empire;* and Williams, *Modern American Empire.*

[37] Paul S. Holbo, "Economics, Emotion, and Expansion: An Emerging Foreign Policy," in H. Wayne Morgan, ed., *The Gilded Age* (Syracuse, N.Y.: Syracuse University Press, 1963), 202; also see Charles Hoffmann, "The Depression of the 1890s," *Journal of Economic History* 16, no. 2 (June 1956): 137–65.

[38] See E. H. Phelps Brown with S. J. Hanfield-Jones, "The Climacteric of the 1890s: A Study in the Expanding Economy," *Oxford Economic Papers* 4, no. 3 (October 1952): 266–307.

bility to extend American influence abroad. A close examination of the cases in the first period—in which nonexpansion prevailed—from 1865 to 1889 demonstrates that while both theories accord with some cases, state-centered realism explains much more American behavior. Even if one codes all ambiguous cases against state-centered realism, the theory explains fifteen of the twenty-two opportunities to expand. America's central foreign policy decision-makers—the executive branch—responded to their growing national power and attempted to expand America's interests abroad on several occasions after the Civil War. For the most part, they did not respond to threats from foreign powers by expanding their interests, as defensive realism predicts; in fact, when they felt truly threatened, they retrenched. Most of their expansionist plans failed to become state policy—they expanded only six times out of twenty-two opportunities. But the reason is precisely what state-centered realism predicts: the United States could not expand because its policymakers presided over a weak, divided, and decentralized government that provided them with little usable power.

ANTEBELLUM EXPANSION

In 1853 Secretary of State Edward Everett, among the less expansionist statesmen of his time, confidently asserted that the "Americanization" of the continent would proceed rapidly in the future. "The pioneers are on their way," he said. "Who can tell how far and how fast they will travel? Who, that compares the North America of 1753 . . . with the North America of 1853 . . . will dare to compute the time-table of our railway progress?"[39] While eighteenth-century European statesmen such as Talleyrand had assumed that a western frontier at the Allegheny Mountains would provide the newly independent settlers with ample land and security, since independence Americans had viewed the country's boundaries as temporary obstacles to fulfilling their "manifest destiny."[40] As American power grew, so did the country's ambitions, and its "natural boundary" extended accordingly: first west to the Mississippi, then south into Florida, farther west to the Rockies, south to the Rio Grande, northwest into Oregon, and then finally still farther west to the Pacific coast. In eighty years, thirteen breakaway colonies on the eastern seaboard of North America had become a vast continental nation larger than any in Europe, save Russia.

[39] Edward Everett, "Stability and Progress: Remarks Made on the 4th of July, 1853, in Faneuil Hall" (Boston, 1853), 10.

[40] On manifest destiny, see Anders Stephanson, *Manifest Destiny: American Expansionism and the Empire of Right* (New York: Hill and Wang, 1995).

In the 1850s, in the aftermath of the Mexican War, America's leaders held forth with great fervor on the virtues and necessity of expansion. President Franklin Pierce declared in his inaugural address in 1853 that his administration would "not be controlled by any timid forebodings of evil from expansion."[41] His successor, James Buchanan, announced that "expansion is the future policy of our country." Nor was expansion limited to rhetoric, for American diplomats attempted to negotiate the purchases of parts of Mexico, Cuba, and Hawaii. The American minister to Mexico even asked his hosts to "anticipate the inexorable" by selling his country six provinces that, unlike the Rio Grande, would form "a natural territorial boundary."[42] However, the nation's deep division over the future of the South's "peculiar institution" prevented the successful completion of these projects.

The Civil War resolved the dispute over slavery, and with that great obstacle to expansion eliminated, with the country unified and its economic power growing, expansionist plans might have been eagerly undertaken. American statesmen had for decades eyed several neighboring regions, but, perhaps uneasy about confronting Europe's great powers, they had always concluded that the time was not right. Madison and Monroe had both assumed that the colonies in Canada would soon fall into the United States' hands, "even against [Britain's] strongest efforts to retain them."[43] John Quincy Adams had referred to Cuba as "natural appendages to the North American continent." His minister to Spain agreed and added, "such I believe is the general opinion in the United States."[44] Adams thought it only a matter of time before the United States annexed all of North America: "[I]t is a physical, moral, and political absurdity that such fragments of territory, with sovereigns at fifteen hundred miles beyond sea, worthless and burdensome to their owners, should exist permanently contiguous to a great, powerful, enterprising, and rapidly-growing nation."[45] Armed with a strong tradition of expansionist ideology, backed by the power of immense industry-driven growth, supported by a newly unified nation, America's leaders after the Civil War should have had little trouble extending their country's borders, but they ran into a serious impediment: the structural weakness of the American state.

[41] James D. Richardson, *A Compilation of the Messages and Papers of the Presidents* (Washington, D.C.: Bureau of National Literature, 1911), 5:198.

[42] Quoted in J. Fred Rippy, *The United States and Mexico* (New York: Alfred A. Knopf, 1926), 141. See also Albert K. Weinberg, *Manifest Destiny: A Study of Nationalist Expansion in American History* (Baltimore: Johns Hopkins Press, 1935), 56.

[43] Quoted in Weinberg, *Manifest Destiny*, 228.

[44] Ibid., 65.

[45] *Memoirs of John Quincy Adams*, ed. Charles Francis Adams (Philadelphia: J. B. Lippincott, 1875), 4:438–39.

SEWARD FOILED, 1865–1869

William Henry Seward, who served as secretary of state from 1861 until 1869, greatly admired John Quincy Adams. Like Adams, he was a fervent believer in America's manifest destiny who had, as a staunch opponent of slavery, refused to sanction antebellum expansion that would have created slaveholding territories. His views on foreign policy represent a classical realist ideal type. Seward understood that power is fungible, that material wealth could be translated into international influence. As early as 1853, he noted that "the nation that draws the most from the earth, and fabricates the most, and sells the most . . . to foreign nations, must be, and will be, the great power of the earth."[46] Throughout his political career, Seward advocated policies that strengthened the industrial economy, such as large investments in America's transportation infrastructure and the import of cheap foreign labor. He understood that a strong America would be active abroad and that it would annex territory whenever opportunities presented themselves. "All prosperous nations must expand," he argued. "That expansion will be in adjacent regions if practicable; if not it will then be made in those regions however distant, which offer the least resistance."[47] For Seward, America's desire to convert its power into influence and territory was typical of a rising state; for this reason, he told his minister to Russia, both Russia and the United States could be expected to expand in the future.[48] Nor did he anticipate much of a time lag between America's economic emergence as a great power and the corresponding expansion of the country's international influence: "Empire moves far more rapidly than it did in ancient times." Given American power, Seward believed, soon "mankind shall come to recognize in [the United States] the successor of the few great states, which have alternately born commanding sway of the world."[49]

The timing of Seward's appointment to his post directing the United States' international activities also seemed opportune. Upon the close of the Civil War, the expansionist climate in the United States possessed "a vigor greater than any of the past," thanks to popular recognition of the country's enormous mobilized power.[50] The Monroe Doctrine Commit-

[46] *The Works of William H. Seward*, ed. George E. Baker (New York: Redfield, 1883), 3:616.

[47] William Henry Seward, *William H. Seward's Travels around the World* (New York: D. Appleton, 1873), 357.

[48] Seward, *Works*, 5:246.

[49] Ibid., 4:319; see also Ernest N. Paolino, *The Foundations of the American Empire: William Henry Seward and U.S. Foreign Policy* (Ithaca, N.Y.: Cornell University Press, 1973), 7.

[50] Weinberg, *Manifest Destiny,* 224. See also Doris A. Graber, *Crisis Diplomacy: A His-*

tee, one of the many nationalist groups that attracted great followings across the country, urged expansion southward—by force if necessary, as its popular jingle made clear:

> If the old-world minions on our Continent remain,
> We'll take the old familiar guns, and go with Grant again![51]

As Henry Adams, the grandson of John Quincy Adams, observed, many politicians now envisaged the ultimate acquisition of not only the entire continent, but all adjacent islands as well.[52] Seward himself was hopeful that with the war over, Congress and the public would turn their attention to foreign policy.[53] There seemed little danger that a partisan political quarrel would undermine expansion. The most outspoken jingoists after the Civil War were the same Republicans and ex-Whigs who had blocked the many Democratic expansionist initiatives before the war, and with the Republicans in control of the presidency and both houses of Congress, the party was expected to have little trouble implementing an activist foreign policy agenda.

Seward's plans for expansion were often cloaked in soaring, imprecise rhetoric. His vague, if uplifting, phrases could not serve as the basis for a coherent foreign policy: what did he mean when he said that "the borders of the federal republic shall be extended so that it shall greet the sun when he touches the tropics, and when he sends his gleaming rays towards the polar circle"?[54] On several occasions, however, and in specific terms, he portrayed as inevitable the annexation of Alaska, Canada, and Mexico. Seward also spoke of the need for island bases in both the Pacific and the Caribbean to project American power abroad and to defend the country's interests. He was so confident of the continued continental growth of the United States that he even devoted serious consideration to the new location for the capital of this far-flung empire, deciding on Mexico City as the most strategically placed site.[55]

If Seward's rhetoric was ambiguous, however, his actions were clear. From 1865 until the end of his term in 1869, Seward led vigorous

tory of U.S. Intervention Policies and Practices (Washington, D.C.: Public Affairs Press, 1959), 64–65.

[51] Quoted in Richard W. Van Alstyne, *The Rising American Empire* (New York: Oxford University Press, 1960), 161–62.

[52] Henry Adams, "The Session," *North American Review* 108 (April 1869): 639.

[53] *Foreign Relations of the United States, 1865* (hereafter *FRUS*) (Washington, D.C.: Department of State), 1:413.

[54] Quoted in Paolino, *Foundations of the American Empire*, 7.

[55] Seward, *Works*, 4:332–33; Paolino, *Foundations of the American Empire*, 9–10. Also see Edward L. Pierce, *Memoir and Letters of Charles Sumner* (1877, 1894; reprint, New York: Arno Press, 1969); also see Pierce, "Charles Sumner Vindicated: The Truth about the Treaties," *Boston Evening Transcript*, November 28, 1877.

American efforts to extend the country's borders on all these fronts and more. While not all of his "inquiries" can be deemed serious, he initiated at least some official steps toward expanding American political control in Alaska, Canada, Greenland, Iceland, Mexico, the Darien Islands, Hawaii, the Danish West Indies, Santo Domingo, Haiti, Culebra, French Guiana, Tiger Island, Cuba, Puerto Rico, and St. Bartholomew.[56] Of these, Alaska was his only success and, along with the unplanned acquisition of the Midway Islands, remained the only extension of American rule abroad for almost twenty years.

Lee had not yet surrendered at Appomattox when, in January 1865, Seward fixed his gaze on the Danish West Indies, strategically situated some forty miles east of Puerto Rico. Seward informed the Danish government that the United States wished to purchase the archipelago, comprising of St. Thomas, St. Croix, and St. John. The Danes were initially reluctant but by the end of the year decided that they could use the money. In the meantime, Seward had planned a voyage "for his health" to St. Thomas, Santo Domingo, Haiti, and Cuba that was widely perceived as an inspection of potential bases and colonies. On his return Seward sent his son, Frederick—who, conveniently, was assistant secretary of state—to purchase Samaná Bay, a potential naval base, from the Dominican government. The secretary also attempted to buy the harbor of the Môle Saint Nicolas from Haiti. When discord spread across Santo Domingo, he thought the United States should seize the opportunity to establish a protectorate there or even annex the entire island. He also signed a treaty with Colombia giving the United States control over a proposed isthmian canal, in clear violation of the 1850 Clayton-Bulwer Treaty with Great Britain. Meanwhile, other agents were also negotiating for lands in the Caribbean. George Bancroft was dispatched to Madrid to purchase the small but strategically located islands of Culebra and Culebrita off the coast of Puerto Rico. Seward discussed with the American legation in Madrid the possibility of buying Cuba and Puerto Rico from the increasingly bankrupt Spanish government. Initial talks were also held with the Swedish government over St. Bartholomew, with the French government over St. Pierre and Martinique, and with the British government over Tiger Island off the west coast of Central America.[57]

Seward's efforts were not confined to the Caribbean. He sent one of his close associates, Robert Walker, to Greenland and Iceland and had him draw up a report detailing the rich natural resources and crucial

[56] Whelan, "William Henry Seward," 101.

[57] Glyndon G. Van Deusen, *William Henry Seward* (New York: Oxford University Press, 1967), 526–34.

geographic position of the two islands; Walker even enlisted an eminent scientist in the effort.[58] But outside the Caribbean, a region of obvious strategic importance to the United States by virtue of proximity, Seward was most excited by the Pacific Ocean area, where he believed the future battle for world supremacy would take place. He had favored the acquisition of the Hawaiian islands as early as 1852, but President Millard Fillmore had not been interested. Now the secretary sought to bring Hawaii gradually and peacefully into the American sphere of influence. His first step was to negotiate a commercial reciprocity treaty, which he envisioned would foster Hawaiian dependence on the United States and eventually lead to annexation. In his instructions to the American representative in Hawaii, Seward emphasized that if reciprocity and annexation came into conflict, "annexation is in every case to be preferred."[59] Seward initiated and pursued all these plans within the first three years after the Civil War. Had they been successful, they would have led to further projects: expansion has a way of begetting further expansion.

But one after another, Seward's various efforts failed, the vast majority for a single dominant reason: constant strife between Congress and the executive branch both over plans for Reconstruction of the South and over more general issues of authority. In the end, Seward had less to fear from the Democrats than from the Republicans who controlled Congress. In the postwar period, Congress took control of virtually all aspects of national government, opposing almost every proposal—domestic and foreign—put forward by the Johnson administration. The Senate Foreign Relations Committee was headed by Charles Sumner, the fiery abolitionist from Massachusetts, who regarded the executive branch's desire to control foreign policy as a "usurpation" of congressional power. He repeatedly rejected administration nominees for diplomatic posts, permitting the appointment of only his own men. Even though he was an expansionist who believed the United States "must embrace this whole continent," Sumner rejected all but one of the administration's schemes. Compounding this interbranch warfare was the radical abolitionists' personal hatred for Seward, a feeling that was entirely mutual.[60]

Congress also easily rejected the executive's expansionist plans because of the atmosphere of "economy and retrenchment" that pervaded Wash-

[58] Benjamin M. Pierce, *A Report on the Resources of Iceland and Greenland* (Washington, D.C.: U.S. Government, 1868).

[59] Seward, *Works*, 3:373; Frederic Bancroft, *The Life of William H. Seward* (New York: Harper and Brothers, 1900), 489.

[60] David Herbert Donald, *Charles Sumner and the Rights of Man* (New York: Alfred A. Knopf, 1970), 281; Van Deusen, *William Henry Seward*, 345; Paolino, *Foundations of the American Empire*, 207.

ington. The material costs of the Civil War had been immense, and in its wake the United States found itself saddled with a national debt of unprecedented proportions: the debt, just $64,844 in 1861, had exploded to over $2.5 million by 1865.[61] Never mind that America's economy and population were growing so fast as to make the debt relatively painless. As Aaron Friedberg has pointed out with respect to Britain during a later period, the absence of calculations of GNP and of government expenditures and debt as a percentage of GNP forced statesmen to focus obsessively on absolute numbers.[62] Congress viewed Seward's schemes as costly flights of ambition that the United States could ill afford. It could have raised the money to finance the proposed purchases, but it was hardly in the mood to levy taxes for purposes that enhanced the power of the executive branch. Indeed, the atmosphere was hardly one in which to propose new taxes, for the high wartime taxes were being repealed. After two years of watching Seward scheme, the House of Representatives passed a resolution declaring that "in the present financial condition of the country any further purchases of territory are inexpedient, and this House will hold itself under no obligation to pay for any such purchase unless there is a greater present necessity for the same than now exists."[63] The structure of the American state—particularly the strict separation of the executive and legislative branches of government—thus prevented the conversion of the executive's plans into state policy as well as that of national power into state power.

The attempted annexation of the Danish West Indies was the administration's first serious expansionist effort. After Seward had convinced Johnson and the cabinet of the islands' merits, he began to negotiate the terms of annexation with Denmark, mainly the price tag and Denmark's insistence that the islands' population approve the deal. Seward haggled over the first issue and nervously agreed to the second. When the plebiscite went in favor of annexation, the treaty was formally completed, and Seward was optimistic that the Senate would pass it. Seward hoped the senators would regard the treaty as a *fait accompli* and recognize that the country was obligated to follow through on its commitment. Furthermore, General Waldemer Raasoff, the Danish minister who had negotiated the treaty, was a skillful diplomat who was highly regarded in Washington.

While the treaty was being negotiated, however, relations between the president and Congress worsened. By the time it was ready for ratifica-

[61] *Historical Statistics of the United States: Colonial Times to 1970* (New York: Basic Books, 1976), 1104.

[62] Friedberg, *The Weary Titan*, 128–29.

[63] *Congressional Globe*, November 25, 1867, 792.

tion, the Senate was considering impeachment proceedings against Johnson. Mindful of America's relations with foreign countries, Sumner decided not to reject the treaty outright but to kill it by silence and delay. He marked the treaty inactive but pending. Ordinarily, the matter would have ended there, but Seward pushed the issue to the fore again. He persuaded the Danish government to extend its deadline for ratification and asked Raasoff, now a minister in the Danish cabinet, to lobby Sumner personally. All these efforts had no effect; Sumner persisted in tabling the treaty and made it "fall through oblivion." By the time Ulysses Grant entered the White House, the plan was clearly doomed, and Grant disassociated himself from it. Grant, the Foreign Relations Committee itself, and various scholars all later pointed to the same reason the attempted annexation of the Danish West Indies had failed. Put simply, "[t]he President and the Department of State had negotiated the treaty; therefore, if for no other reason, the Senate would not consent to it."[64]

While the Danish West Indies discussions were proceeding, Johnson sent the Hawaiian reciprocity treaty to the Senate, describing it as a first step toward annexation.[65] The Senate delayed considering the treaty and after a year and a half tabled it, hoping to have quietly killed it. But again the president had the deadline extended, and he sent the Senate the new treaty in July 1868. Again the Senate delayed, and finally, in June 1870, it voted against ratification. After watching two official treaties and several unofficial proposals die through inattention and rejection on Capitol Hill, Seward mourned that Congress, concerned solely with domestic issues, "refuses . . . to entertain the higher but more remote questions of national extension and aggrandizement."[66]

This same factor felled most of Seward's other projects as well.[67] Sweden and France, both initially interested in selling their Caribbean possessions, backed away after the Danish West Indies treaty fell through. The Republican leadership of the Senate used any excuse to thwart the executive branch's plans. When the Colombian Senate signaled its desire for more money by rejecting the isthmian canal treaty, Seward hoped the U.S. Senate would still approve it or at least wait until he could renegotiate the treaty, as other countries often did with

[64] Anna L. Dawes, *Charles Sumner* (New York: Dodd, Mead 1892) 282; see also W. Stull Holt, *Treaties Defeated by the Senate: A Study of the Struggle between the President and Senate over the Conduct of Foreign Relations* (Baltimore: Johns Hopkins Press, 1933), 108.

[65] Richardson, *Papers of the Presidents*, 8:387.

[66] Quoted in Holt, *Treaties Defeated by the Senate*, 104.

[67] One exception was Tiger Island. Seward's plans to acquire it went nowhere because the British were reluctant to sell it and Seward did not want to confront them.

the United States. Although the canal project was popular and had many supporters in Congress, the Senate dropped the treaty from consideration. Similarly, the Senate simply ignored Johnson's last message to Congress proposing the annexation of Haiti and Santo Domingo; when an administration ally offered a resolution to create an American protectorate over the two countries, it was soundly defeated.[68]

Seward recognized the role that the divided U.S. governmental structure and the atmosphere of retrenchment played in defeating his plans. He observed, "The leaders of each party therefore seem to shrink from every suggestion which may involve any new national enterprise, and especially any foreign one."[69] "We have come to regard dollars more and dominion less," Seward remarked upon the defeat of the Hawaiian treaty.[70] When he tried to muster private support for the canal project, he found that businessmen and financiers were reluctant to commit such large sums for a risky venture. They thought the project ought to be financed with federal funds, but Seward knew that Congress would never appropriate the money.[71] By the end of his term, Seward was finally convinced that the combination of the perception of the United States as impoverished and the Senate's desire to control foreign policy would prevent his plans from coming to fruition. He decided to abandon his exploratory talks over Greenland, Iceland, Puerto Rico, Cuba, and all other island bases in the Caribbean. To his minister in Madrid he explained that even if Spain were ready to sell Cuba and Puerto Rico, Congress would not be willing to buy them. "How sadly domestic disturbances demoralize the national ambition," Seward sighed.[72]

The two cases of successful expansion during the Johnson administration were clearly opportunistic, stemming from the desire for international influence, not from foreign threats. These efforts became national policy under unique circumstances and, as the exceptions that prove the rule, highlight the structural constraints on American foreign policy at the time. The Midway Islands were not acquired as part of Seward's extensive plans. Under instructions from the Department of the Navy, a Navy officer took the islands, and since they were uninhabited and be-

[68] R. W. Logan, *The Diplomatic Relations between the United States and Haiti* (Chapel Hill: University of North Carolina Press, 1941), 316–31.

[69] Quoted in Holt, *Treaties Defeated by the Senate*, 104.

[70] Quoted in Frederick Seward, *William H. Seward* (New York: Derby and Miller, 1891), 3:369; see also Ernest R. May, *American Imperialism: A Speculative Essay* (New York: Atheneum, 1968), 101–3; and Donald, *Charles Sumner*, 416.

[71] Paolino, *Foundations of the American Empire*, 130–31; Pletcher, "Economic Growth and Diplomatic Adjustment," 151.

[72] Quoted in Van Deusen, *William Henry Seward*, 530; also see Brainerd Dyer, "Robert J. Walker on Acquiring Greenland and Iceland," *Mississippi Valley Historical Review* 27 (September 1940): 263–66.

longed to no European power, the administration did not require Senate approval of their acquisition. Thus the Midway Islands were a case of expansion by chance.

The purchase of Alaska, on the other hand, was a more protracted affair.[73] Since the administration of James Polk, presidents and cabinets had entertained the possibility of acquiring "Russian-America." After the Crimean War, with Russian finances under severe strain, Grand Duke Constantine, head of the Admiralty and the czar's brother, described these provinces to Foreign Minister Gorchakov as barren, indefensible, and of no use to Russia. Better to sell them to the Americans, he recommended in 1857, than to have them fall to British forces in North America in the event of another conflict with London. Constantine suggested taking advantage of the U.S. Treasury surplus to bolster his country's finances.[74] The Civil War arrested these developments, but with the war over both countries once again showed interest in a deal.

In 1866 the czar agreed to invite America to buy his lands west of Canada. His minister to America, Edouard de Stoekl, was instructed to inquire in Washington and not to accept less than $5 million. By March 1867, negotiations between Seward and Stoekl began in earnest. Knowing the limits of Seward's power, Stoekl suggested that negotiations take place with congressional leaders present, but Seward rejected the suggestion and insisted that the whole affair be kept secret. After initial talks, Seward presented the cabinet with an agreement to offer Stoekl $7 million. The cabinet agreed unanimously. Stoekl, however, knew how eager Seward was for the land and kept haggling until his counterpart finally offered an additional $200,000. Stoekl wired his government for its approval. On the evening of March 29, 1867, Stoekl called on the secretary of state at home to inform him that Russia had accepted the American offer and that he would be willing to sign a treaty tomorrow. Seward was so excited by the news that he impatiently exclaimed, "Why wait till tomorrow, Mr. Stoekl? Let us make the treaty tonight."[75] That night he summoned Charles Sumner to his house, where his son and Stoekl—Seward had rushed to the State Department—explained the agreement and urged Sumner to support its ratification in the Senate. Stoekl and the younger Seward then joined the secretary at the State Department, where the treaty was signed at four o'clock the following morning.

Seward arrived at the Capitol later in the day to urge the Senate to

[73] The best account is Ronald J. Jensen, *The Alaska Purchase and Russian-American Relations* (Seattle: University of Washington Press, 1975).

[74] Paul S. Holbo, *Tarnished Expansion: The Alaska Scandal, the Press, and Congress, 1867–1871* (Knoxville: University of Tennessee Press, 1983), 5–6.

[75] Quoted in F. Seward, *William H. Seward*, 3:348.

approve the treaty. The affair placed Charles Sumner in a quandary. An ardent continental expansionist, he had long dreamt of a North America rid of Russian and British possessions, yet he despised the administration and believed that Seward had usurped his equal authority in foreign policy by keeping the negotiations secret and presenting him with a *fait accompli*. Sumner began by refusing to have the whole Senate consider the treaty, sending it first to his Committee on Foreign Relations, where it became clear that the treaty did not stand a chance of passage. Most senators saw it as yet another of Seward's unnecessary and expensive ventures, and the debates spawned phrases still well known today: "Seward's farm," "Seward's ice-box," "Seward's folly." But in the end, Sumner decided to support the treaty, convinced that the land was economically and strategically valuable. He also felt that "a bargain once made had to be kept," especially with Russia, which enjoyed great favor in Washington for its pro-Union stand during the Civil War.[76] Sumner managed to garner a majority in the committee; the two dissenters had, only half in jest, offered to support the treaty if Seward agreed to live in the arctic province.[77] He then turned to the task of convincing his colleagues in the full Senate. Opposition there was also organized along two main themes: the expense of the purchase and hatred for the administration. Sumner persevered, having warmed to his new role as the leading expert on Russian-America, which he named "Alaska" from the Aleut word for the area. During the Senate floor debate over ratification, Sumner's efforts reached their climax with an eloquent, nearly three-hour-long plea for annexation. Thanks to Sumner's enormous political power, the Senate approved the treaty overwhelmingly.[78]

However, one more aspect of America's institutional structure threatened the executive branch's wishes: the House of Representatives could undermine the deal by refusing to appropriate the funds for the purchase. Though Seward appeared less concerned about House approval, the odds seemed significantly worse in the House than in the Senate.

[76] The Russian tilt was in fact a myth born of a misperception. In 1863 Russia sent two fleets, one to San Francisco and the other to New York. The beleaguered North saw this as a warning to Britain and France to stay out of the conflict and welcomed the ships with great fanfare. In fact, Russia had simply moved its ships out of harm's way because it feared that the contemporaneous rebellion in Poland might lead to a European war. These facts were revealed only in 1915, however, and in the immediate postwar period, Northerners felt a great debt of gratitude toward Russia. See Thomas A. Bailey, "The Russian Fleet Myth Re-Examined," *Mississippi Valley Historical Review* 38 (June 1951): 81–90; and Frank A. Golder, "The Russian Fleet and the Civil War," *American Historical Review* 20 (1915): 807–12.

[77] Donald, *Charles Sumner,* 307.

[78] Ibid., 354.

The House delayed considering the bill for over a year, indicating its intentions by passing, 93 to 43, the resolution refusing to appropriate funds for any future territories. It also unanimously passed a resolution requesting that the Judiciary Committee report as to whether the House was obligated to provide money for a treaty that had been ratified. The debate over funds for Alaska took place in the midst of the impeachment proceedings against Johnson, and Representative Ben Butler, an ardent expansionist but an even more ardent Johnson hater, led the anti-Alaska charge. Stoekl was dispirited enough to suggest to his foreign minister that Russia offer the lands to America gratis, a suggestion that was not heeded because Gorchakov assumed that the obstacle lay in American sentiment not against expansion, but against higher taxes and increased government expenditures. If he offered Alaska for free, he was sure the United States would grab it immediately.[79]

The tide turned once Seward won over Thaddeus Stevens, the powerful Speaker of the House. Stevens hated Johnson as much as anyone, but he was convinced that, once made, a deal had to be kept. He believed the House could not refuse payment for a treaty the Senate had ratified and the president had signed, a view that most congressmen grudgingly came to accept.[80] Stevens defeated Butler's attempt to transfer the treaty's hearing from the Foreign Affairs Committee to the Appropriations Committee, a move that would have surely killed it. After a heated debate that centered on the expense of the treaty, the value of the land, and the venality of the executive branch, the House passed the bill by a margin of 113 to 43. Of the forty-three who voted against the treaty, forty-one had voted to impeach Johnson. As with the Senate, the House was moved considerably by the debt it owed Russia, the only great power believed to have openly sided with the North during the Civil War. Representative James G. Blaine, who later became secretary of state, believed that had the treaty involved any other country, the deal would never have gone through.[81]

Many journalists asserted at the time—and historians have since confirmed the veracity of their claims—that without the concerted use of bribery and various political machinations, the treaty would not have passed. The scandal that ensued so poisoned the political climate that future territorial acquisitions became impossible. The *New York Tribune,* which was leading the charge for thrift in government expendi-

---

[79] Jensen, *Alaska Purchase,* 108–9.

[80] *Congressional Globe,* November 25, 1867, 792–94; *House Journal,* 40th Cong., 1st sess., 266–67; also see Holbo, *Tarnished Expansion,* 17–18.

[81] James G. Blaine, *Twenty Years of Congress: From Lincoln to Garfield,* 2 vols. (Norwich, Conn.: Henry Bill, 1884–86), 2:333.

tures and for limits on the executive branch's authority to make national policy, clearly reflected the mood in Congress:

> We believe President Johnson was guilty of a gross usurpation in taking possession of Mr. Seward's hard bargain before Congress had sanctioned the trade. And now, we trust the House will be held to have given fair notice that this assumption must not be repeated. We have the verdict— "Not guilty; but he mustn't do so again."

> Gentlemen who want to sell us Northern Mexico, Lower California, St. Thomas, St. John, Bay of Samana, and other nick-nacks! understand once and for all, that both Houses of Congress must assent or there is no valid trade! We have debt enough and none too much gold; our government costs enough, and ought not to be rendered more expensive as every outlying possession surely *will* make it. Be content, please do, with this haul, and keep your hands henceforth out of our pockets.[82]

The consummation of the purchase of Alaska proved such a Herculean task that it can be regarded only as an exception to the general pattern during Andrew Johnson's administration.

THWARTED AGAIN: GRANT AND EXPANSION, 1869–1877

Seward's repeated failures did not entirely crush the expansionists' hopes, for the election of Ulysses S. Grant in 1868 gave the cause another chance. An "instinctive expansionist," Grant had long been in favor of various plans, such as the 1854 Ostend Manifesto, that urged the acquisition of Cuba; and his secretary of state, the patrician Hamilton Fish, was also a strong proponent of American expansion.[83] As the commanding general of what was, at its peak, the largest army in the world, Grant had a keen—perhaps even exaggerated—sense of American power. And given his immense popularity as the hero of the Civil War and Fish's friendship with Charles Sumner, Grant thought he would have less trouble than his predecessor with Congress.[84] But personal friendship and respect could not alter the structural realities of the American government. This period in American history was marked by a "constant campaign" by the Senate "to establish itself as the dominant part of the government," a campaign that eventually succeeded.[85]

---

[82] Quoted in Holbo, *Tarnished Expansion*, 33.
[83] Campbell, *Transformation of American Foreign Relations*, 50.
[84] Donald, *Charles Sumner*, 372.
[85] Holt, *Treaties Defeated by the Senate*, 122.

Against this backdrop of interbranch rivalry, Grant's chances of turning his foreign affairs preferences into national policy were slim. He nevertheless made several serious efforts during his term, the most ambitious of which—and the one he tried hardest to achieve—being ratification of the treaty annexing Santo Domingo.

Grant went after Santo Domingo for a simple reason: the opportunity arose, and the costs seemed low. Like Seward, Grant followed the clear dictate of classical realism that the strong do what they can. One historian has listed the president's motives as "grab," "glory," and "power."[86] When Congress rejected a proposal in early 1869, supported by then–President Johnson, to establish a protectorate on the island, annexationists in America and Santo Domingo did not give up, and while Fish was not enthusiastic about the idea, Grant found it very appealing. After learning that the president of the Dominican Republic favored annexation and after receiving a positive report on the island from high-ranking naval officers, he sent a longtime aide, General Orville Babcock, there to prepare a report. Babcock did more than that, however: by September he returned to Washington with a protocol for the island's annexation. Grant was thrilled and, after formalizing matters through the consul, decided to present the treaty to the Senate. The key figure he had to persuade was Sumner, and so, on January 2, 1870, the president walked to the Foreign Relations Committee chairman's house on Lafayette Square to inform him of the treaty and to ask for his support. That ill-fated meeting marked the beginning of the battle of Santo Domingo, which was fought in Washington with nothing deadlier than words but set the sad course for the Grant administration and beyond. It handed the administration its first major failure, crowned the Senate as the venue for important foreign policy decisions, nearly destroyed the Republican Party, and signaled the end to attempts at formal annexation for the next twenty-eight years.[87]

Emerging from that fateful meeting, Grant believed that Sumner had promised his support. But Sumner vehemently denied the president's claim, and relations between the two quickly worsened. The administration began to take the necessary steps to strengthen its case. It arranged with the Dominican government for a plebiscite, which showed strong local support for American rule, and Grant, who was increasingly obsessed by the issue, also took the unprecedented step of personally lobbying wavering senators. He argued that the island was rich in natu-

---

[86] Beisner, *From the Old Diplomacy to the New,* 49.

[87] This struggle is dealt with comprehensively in Allan Nevins, *Hamilton Fish: The Inner History of the Grant Administration* (New York: Dodd, Mead, 1936), 249–78, 309–34.

ral resources and strategically situated for both American commerce and the navy.[88] But the administration soon realized that it lacked the two-thirds of the Senate required for ratification. The treaty's supporters let it lapse unconsidered on March 29, allowing Grant more time to lobby for his cause—which he did vigorously, making patronage appointments to satisfy the demands of borderline senators and modifying the new treaty to accommodate their concerns. But all of Grant's efforts were to no avail. Sumner was dead set against the project, and many Republicans broke with the president and followed Sumner's lead. On June 30, 1870, the treaty was defeated 28 to 28, with 16 abstentions.[89]

Senators cited three chief reasons for the treaty's defeat: the financial costs of annexation, the problems of assimilating a nonwhite populace, and the executive branch's improper unilateral attempts to initiate foreign policy. But the last was clearly the most critical. One of the shrewdest journalists in the country, E. L. Godkin, explained that the Senate's chief motive was the desire to preserve its newly acquired paramount role in government and "to gratify on every possible occasion its mania for humiliating the President and guiding the lower House."[90] Secretary of State Fish and several members of Congress privately concurred that this issue was the key to the administration's defeat.[91] Reporting on the treaty's fate, Henry Adams wrote:

> Senator Sumner again stood forward to assume the control and direction of foreign affairs. He again wielded the power of the Senate and declared the policy of the government. The President and Mr. Fish struggled in vain against the omnipotent senatorial authority, although the President went so far as to make the issue one of personal weight, and condescended to do the work of a lobbyist almost on the very floor of the Senate Chamber, using his personal influence to an extent scarcely known in American history . . . Mr. Sumner flung them both aside and issued orders with almost the authority of a Roman triumvir.[92]

In Adams's view, Santo Domingo represented but the tip of an iceberg. Congress had usurped all foreign policy powers from the executive branch: "[T]he whole internal fabric of government has been violently

[88] See *Annual Message of the President to Congress, 1870.*

[89] One historian argues that Sumner's role has been exaggerated. He maintains that Republican senators were sufficiently independent of the executive branch and the party that the treaty could, if not for Grant's personal efforts, have been defeated by an even greater margin. See Holt, *Treaties Defeated by the Senate,* 127–29.

[90] E. L. Godkin, *The Nation,* January 27, 1870, 1–2.

[91] Nevins, *Hamilton Fish;* John Sherman, *Recollections of Forty Years in the House, Senate, and Cabinet* (Chicago: Werner, 1895), 398–99; Blaine, *Twenty Years of Congress,* 461; May, *American Imperialism,* 101.

[92] Henry Adams, "The Session," *North American Review* 111 (July 1870): 58.

wrenched from its original balance." When the British ambassador asked the secretary of state for the United States' response to certain British proposals, Fish's reply was remarkably frank: "I don't know; I can't get Sumner to take up anything." The British had already concluded that Sumner "evidently directs the foreign policy of his government."[93]

America's state structure did not, of course, guarantee that the executive branch and Congress would disagree, but it ensured that when they did, a powerful Congress could wrest control of public policy from the executive branch. At times, both branches would broadly agree on a policy: such was the case with Cuba.[94] On two separate occasions during Grant's presidency, the United States, in the attempt to extend its sphere of influence to Cuba, almost went to war with Spain. Congress was, in this case, generally more hawkish than the administration, and it often pressured the somewhat more cautious Fish to confront Spain more directly. The Cuba examples clearly show that Congress was hardly isolationist during the 1870s. It simply opposed the exercise of executive leadership.

From the early years of the century, Americans thought of Cuba as a natural part of the mainland United States. Thomas Jefferson, James Monroe, Henry Clay, and John Quincy Adams all confidently asserted that Cuba would soon move into the American sphere. As Adams explained to the cabinet in 1819, "Cuba, forcibly disjoined from its own unnatural connection with Spain, and incapable of self-support, can gravitate only towards the North American Union, which by the same law of nature, cannot cast her from its bosom."[95] In 1854 President Franklin Pierce sent three diplomats to Europe to offer Spain $130 million for the island. Spain refused, and the ministers sent a secret memorandum, the Ostend Manifesto, to the president urging the United States to "wrest Cuba from Spain." But until the slavery question was settled, any further expansion was impossible. With the end of the Civil War, Secretary of State Seward was, of course, interested in acquiring Cuba. He even had a novel justification for America's claim: the island had been formed by the sands of the Mississippi as they washed into the Gulf of Mexico.[96] However, no clear opportunity arose, and when, late in his term, Seward espied an opening, he decided that congressional obstinacy made pursuing such a path futile.

When Grant entered the White House, a rebellion was already under

[93] Quoted in Donald, *Charles Sumner,* 465, 411.

[94] Except where otherwise noted, the following account draws on Nevins, *Hamilton Fish.*

[95] Quoted in Weinberg, *Manifest Destiny,* 228–29.

[96] Ibid., 234.

way in Cuba. The Americans could not accurately estimate its size, but the Spanish authorities were clearly having trouble maintaining their hold on the island. Exiles and refugees crowded into Florida with gruesome tales of Spanish brutality, engendering deep sympathy among the American press and public. The refugees tirelessly raised money for the rebels back home and sought to involve the United States in the civil war. Most leading newspapers pressed the government to intervene on the rebels' behalf; congressmen and senators usually opposed to an activist foreign policy urged the president to do the same. Within the cabinet, the secretary of war saw the civil war as an opportunity to fulfill the mandate of the Ostend Manifesto, and Grant was also sympathetic to the rebels. Fish, however, was cautious for three reasons: first, he believed—as did almost everyone—that Cuban independence would soon lead to annexation by the United States, and he doubted whether the Cubans could be assimilated into America's political and cultural system. Second, contrary to Grant and the War Department, he felt that taking on Spain with America's tattered navy would be a long and costly affair.[97] Finally, and most important, formally recognizing the rebels as belligerents under international law, a natural first step that would affirm Washington's neutrality and allow it to send ships and goods to either side, would endanger negotiations with the British over Civil War reparations. Fish was currently in the process of extracting massive concessions from Britain because it had recognized the Confederacy as a belligerent. For Washington to recognize a much weaker and less organized rebel force while asking Britain for hundreds of millions of dollars for doing the same just a decade before would have appeared as rank hypocrisy.

But Grant's expansionist instinct had been aroused, and by the middle of 1869 the reluctant secretary of state found himself negotiating with Spain for the independence of Cuba. For good measure, Grant ordered reinforcements sent to the navy's West Indies squadron. Spain suggested that the United States guarantee the amount that Cuba would pay Spain for its independence. As both parties converged on a figure of $125 million that would include Puerto Rico as well, it became clear that Madrid was actually far from ready to cede the islands; the proposal, and others like it, had merely been a stalling tactic while the Spanish squabbled among themselves. Meanwhile, in the United States, domestic pressures to act were growing increasingly intense. By February 1870, impassioned congressional pleas for recognition of the rebels were commonplace. Fish, who was being pilloried in the press as a

---

[97] Secretary of the Navy, *Annual Report, 1869* (Washington, D.C.: U.S. Government, 1869); see also Secretary of the Navy, *Annual Report, 1870.*

weak-kneed appeaser, attempted to delay any decision, but Grant was increasingly determined to act. By June 1870, the House of Representatives seemed ready to move unilaterally. Fish decided to confront Grant and persuade him that the negotiations with Britain were too important to sacrifice for Cuban independence. He threatened to resign, and Grant finally agreed to advocate publicly a nonrecognition policy. Because of the president's urging, the resolution in the House lost by a margin of 100 to 70, and the Cuban issue died down for the time being.

Fish's influence alone, though, was not enough to have reversed U.S. policy. Several factors combined to sway Grant. First was the death in September 1869 of the rebels' greatest ally in the administration, Secretary of War John A. Rawlins. More important, Charles Sumner agreed with all three of Fish's reasons for caution and kept the Senate from acting unilaterally during the crisis. Most critical, however, was the struggle over the Santo Domingo treaty, which had reached a crucial point in June 1870, absorbing all of Grant's time and attention. Grant confessed to Fish and others that his support for the Cuban rebels had less to do with the virtues of their cause than with the fate of Santo Domingo: he feared that if he were to appear weak on Cuba, he would lose votes for the Dominican treaty.[98] Thus the first opportunity to extend American influence into Cuba was narrowly lost for a confluence of reasons, mostly related to the timing of the event and the form action would take. Three years later, when the chance arose again, the negotiations with Great Britain over Civil War reparations had been concluded, Charles Sumner had been deposed as chairman of the Senate Foreign Relations Committee, and Grant was in firmer control of the Republican Party. This time, the United States failed to seize the opportunity because economic depression dampened the expansionist mood.

After the crisis of 1869–70 had receded, Spanish-American relations remained tense, as Spain alternated between concessions and crackdowns and the United States reacted with hope and then disappointment. The civil war in Cuba raged on, and Spanish brutalities continued. Fish kept negotiating with Spain and gained some concessions, such as the abolition of slavery in Puerto Rico. In late 1872 sparks flew once again when a sensitive secret memorandum from Fish to the Spanish government was leaked to the public. In blunt language, it pointed out that Spain had not carried out the reforms it claimed, nor was it in control of the Cuban situation. Fish threatened that the United States might have to alter its presently accommodating policy toward Spain.[99]

[98] Fish convinced Grant that his fear was unfounded. See Nevins, *Hamilton Fish*, 363; and Campbell, *Transformation of American Foreign Relations*, 55–56.

[99] Fish to Sickles, October 29, 1872, in *FRUS, 1872*, 581–82.

Only in the following year, however, six months into Grant's second term, were the two countries brought to the brink of war, this time by the *Virginius* affair. In November 1873 a Spanish gunboat captured a ship flying the American flag and took it to Santiago. The Cuban authorities summarily executed the captain, thirty-six crew members, and sixteen passengers; many of those shot were American. The United States exploded in anger: as the London *Times* reported, there was "an outburst of indignation from the press and the people that is ominous for Spanish rule in Cuba." Across the country, a mood of righteous fury dominated large public meetings. Fish demanded that within twelve days Spain return the survivors, formally apologize, pay reparations, prosecute the officers who ordered the executions, and salute the American flag in Santiago; if not, the United States would sever diplomatic relations. The U.S. army and navy began to mobilize and plan an initial landing of ten thousand soldiers on Cuba, and the War Department was eager to move.

One day after the deadline expired, Spain offered to release the *Virginius* with its passengers but to delay the negotiation of reparations and the salute of the flag until an investigation was held to determine if the ship was in fact American. Negotiations began, and Fish and the Spanish ambassador—both reasonable, practical men who were trying to keep their respective countries from coming to blows—hammered out a solution. Fish knew the *Virginius* was probably engaged in illegal filibustering activities and may not have even had legitimate title to American nationality. Congress was not yet in session, and Fish succeeded in wrapping up the matter before legislators arrived in Washington. The danger of war had passed yet again. While war had received greater consideration in the cabinet during the Cuban crisis of 1873 than in 1869–70, the public clamor for war had been much stronger during the earlier crisis. Indeed, had the popular and congressional mood been equally warlike in 1873, Fish's attempts to extinguish the flames would have failed.

Two factors produced a less jingoistic public temperament. First, the country had just plunged into an unprecedented financial panic and was entering the worst depression in American history to date.[100] In 1873, five thousand businesses failed, with an aggregate loss of $228.5 million. Three million wage earners out of a labor force of approximately fourteen million were thrown out of work.[101] The Grant administration

---

[100] Harold G. Vatter, *The Drive to Industrial Maturity: The U.S. Economy, 1860–1914* (Westport, Conn.: Greenwood Press, 1975); Edward C. Kirkland, *Industry Comes of Age: Business, Labor, and Public Policy, 1860–1897* (New York: Holt, Rinehart and Winston, 1961).

[101] Seymour E. Harris, *American Economic History* (New York: McGraw-Hill, 1961), 282.

was left "helpless before the storm." In this climate, few wanted to take on the burdens of war and the possible assimilation of new peoples.[102] Second, Spain had just become a republic (as it turned out, for a brief period), and Congress in particular wanted to give the new regime the benefit of the doubt. However, one should be careful not to assign too much weight to this factor, for England, widely viewed as the second most liberal and democratic country in the world, also aroused the greatest hatred in the bosom of the average American.

However, war was averted in 1873 for a broader reason as well, one that explains why the Grant administration was on the whole considerably less activist than one would have expected given Grant's, and even Fish's, expansionist ideology. The defeat in 1870 of the Santo Domingo treaty, in which Grant had had an enormous personal stake, had a chilling effect on future foreign policy. Ernest May argues that the failure of the treaty was a pivotal moment that shaped the outlook of a generation. It yielded a "lesson" against expansion that politicians would ignore at their peril; it had a "multiplier effect." Santo Domingo shaped American foreign policy much as Munich would later.[103] After the grueling passage of the Alaskan treaty, the corruption scandal that erupted in its wake, and the bitter defeat of the Santo Domingo treaty, the executive branch recognized that an ambitious foreign policy was impossible given the limits of its power. Indeed, after 1870, presidents and secretaries of state were careful not to expend political capital on bold foreign policy initiatives, and the following two decades were, for the most part, uneventful.

One exception during the Grant administration was Hawaii. In 1873 Hawaii offered to give the United States Pearl Harbor for a naval base. Fish initiated negotiations with the king of the islands, but as talks progressed, opposition in Hawaii made the cession of the harbor impossible. Motivated by fear of British encroachment, Grant and Fish did sign a reciprocity treaty that made the United States' influence on the island supreme. While myriad concerns were raised in the Senate, that body eventually approved the treaty handily for the same reasons that Grant and Fish had pushed it. The Senate did not, however, approve another expansion of American interests in the Pacific. The Grant administration presented the Senate with a treaty establishing a naval base in the harbor of Pago Pago, Samoa, but it never passed the Foreign Relations Committee.[104] Grant also tried to move forward on the popu-

---

[102] Beisner, *From the Old Diplomacy to the New,* 52–53; Nevins, *Hamilton Fish,* 673; Campbell, *Transformation of American Foreign Relations,* 59.

[103] May, *American Imperialism,* 114.

[104] George H. Ryden, *The Foreign Policy of the United States in Relation to Samoa* (New Haven, Conn.: Yale University Press, 1933), 42–52.

lar but perennially troubled issue of an isthmian canal. The Nicaraguan government rebuffed his overtures, but Grant had success with the Colombian government. In this diplomatic coup, Grant succeeded in rescuing Seward's treaty with Colombia, which had allowed the United States construction rights through the province of Panama but had so incensed the Panamanians that the treaty had to be reconsidered. But, in what had become a familiar pattern, the Senate rejected the new treaty.

THE BEGINNING OF THE END: HAYES, GARFIELD, ARTHUR, AND CLEVELAND, 1877–1889

During the 1870s, national leaders perceived tight constraints on state power. The national debt continued to paralyze Washington, the panic of 1873 and the depression that followed further aggravated concerns about government spending, internal revenues were lowered, the income tax was abolished, and there was even pressure to lower tariffs. Coupled with this extreme reluctance to extract national resources for government projects was the state's divided structure, in which the executive was faring badly. By the middle of the decade, congressional domination of American politics was secure. The Senate, in particular, was the source of almost all important public policy initiatives. "So far as Presidential initiative was concerned, the President and his Cabinet might equally well have departed separately or together to distant lands," wrote Henry Adams. Senator George Hoar concurred, averring that his colleagues would have regarded it as a "personal affront" had the White House asked them to vote for or against legislation. "If they visited the White House," he wrote, "it was to give, not to receive, advice."[105] Writing about this period in his novel *Democracy,* Adams characterized American government as being "of the people, by the people, for the Senate."[106] The conflict between the executive and the legislative branches was not strictly a partisan issue, but it certainly did not help that control of the House of Representatives moved firmly into the hands of the Democratic Party in 1872 and that the opposition also took over the Senate five years later, while Republicans controlled the presidency. The election in 1884 of Grover Cleveland, a Democrat, as president could have broken the logjam, but that same contest turned the Senate Republican.

Weak executive power translated into passivity and inaction in foreign policy. The administration of Rutherford B. Hayes (1877–81) rep-

[105] Quoted in Leonard D. White, *The Republican Era, 1869–1901: A Study in Administrative History* (New York: Macmillan, 1958), 41, 24.
[106] Henry Adams, *Democracy: An American Novel* (New York: Henry Holt, 1880).

resented the nadir of American state power and hence the low point of the expansion of American influence; some historians have called it the "dead center" of late-nineteenth-century American foreign policy.[107] Hayes was elevated to the White House without the legitimacy that a clear-cut electoral victory would have bestowed, a fact that congressional Democrats never forgot, and his tenure was marked by severe gridlock. With one exception, Hayes and Secretary of State William Evarts did not even consider involving the United States in international events.[108] Not that there weren't opportunities: previous (and subsequent) administrations saw (and would see) such incidents as invitations to expand. During Hayes's tenure, revolution engulfed Mexico, a French company signed a treaty with Colombia to build an isthmian canal across Panama, and Chile went to war against Peru and Bolivia. In each case, the United States viewed instability in these areas as a minor irritant to American commerce that involved no important security interests. Having watched the defeat of Grant's foreign initiatives, Hayes, a much less popular president, restricted his policies to helping American trade and travel—the only business of the State Department that directly involved American voters and therefore the only one with congressional support. As the depression led businessmen in some sectors to look beyond the domestic market to those in foreign lands, trade promotion became the principal activity of the State Department in the 1870s.[109]

The one exception to this pattern of inactivity involved Samoa.[110] In 1877 a tribal chief from Samoa journeyed to Washington to seek American annexation or at least protection of his island. He met with Frederick Seward, still assistant secretary of state and still frustrated by the inability of the American government to fulfill his father's vision. Seward was delighted at this opportunity and, recognizing that Congress would simply dismiss either of the chief's preferred options, negotiated a treaty in which the United States would acquire a naval and coaling station at Pago Pago in return for Washington's "good offices" in the event of trouble between Samoa and any other nation. Strangely, the Senate approved the treaty unanimously in executive session, leaving no rationale on record to explain why, after rejecting a virtually identical

[107] David Pletcher, *The Awkward Years: American Foreign Relations under Garfield and Arthur* (Columbia: University of Missouri Press, 1962).

[108] Brainerd Dyer, *The Public Career of William M. Evarts* (Berkeley: University of California Press, 1933), 185–238.

[109] This aspect of American diplomacy is highlighted in LaFeber, *The New Empire;* and Williams, *Modern American Empire.*

[110] Ryden, *Foreign Policy of the United States in Relation to Samoa,* 188–200.

treaty just six years earlier, it moved so quickly now.[111] Even after the
Senate ratified the treaty, however, the House of Representatives refused
to allot any funds to build a coal yard at Pago Pago.

The Hayes administration marked a watershed in late-nineteenth-
century American foreign policy. With its close, several powerful constraints on state power loosened, and the direction of foreign policy
shifted slowly but discernibly. The minor opportunity was that for a
period of two years (1881–83), the House of Representatives moved
back into the hands of the Republican Party. The more important
change regarded the most fungible source of power: money. By the
early 1880s, American statesmen realized that, despite several tax cuts,
the Treasury was still yielding surpluses, year after year. In 1880 the
surplus passed $100 million. They could have reduced tariffs, thereby
eliminating most of the surplus, but strong domestic constituencies—
many of them Republican—favored protecting indigenous industries.
Politicians searched for issues that the federal government could spend
money on—"surplus financiering," in the words of its critics. Concerns over the national debt and fears of large government expenditures persisted among Democrats, but the large recurring surplus gradually altered even their views on government spending. As the decade
wore on, Congress abandoned the assumption that the government
could not afford to spend money outside of bare necessities, and it
grew receptive to increased spending in certain areas, particularly the
U.S. Navy. These surpluses combined with the professionalization of
the bureaucracy and a less divided government to result in the rise of
"the new navy."[112]

Chester Arthur was an unlikely man to initiate grand policy changes.
A little-known Republican politician, he was named vice president by
James Garfield to satisfy an important faction within the party. Garfield
was assassinated shortly into his first term, and Arthur suddenly and
unexpectedly became president (1881–85). Confounding expectations,
Arthur proved to be a reformer, and he was the first president to press
for naval expansion.[113] Secretaries of the Navy William Hunt and William Chandler began lobbying Congress for a larger navy from 1881
on. Hunt's reasoning was simple and related quite straightforwardly to

[111] *Journal of the Executive Proceedings of the Senate* (Washington, D.C: U.S. Government, 1901), 21:220–1.

[112] The best accounts of this buildup are in Harold and Margaret Sprout, *The Rise of
American Naval Power* (Princeton, N.J.: Princeton University Press, 1939), 165–202; and
John D. Long, *The New American Navy* (New York: Outlook, 1903).

[113] For a good overview, see Justus D. Doenecke, *The Presidencies of James A. Garfield
and Chester A. Arthur* (Lawrence: Regents Press of Kansas, 1981).

America's growing resources: "We have been unable to make such an appropriate display of our naval power abroad as will cause us to be respected." He explicitly compared the relationship between America's economic power and its manifest influence with that of other great powers: "It is a source of mortification to our officers and fellow countrymen generally, that our vessels of war should stand in such mean contrast alongside those of other and inferior powers."[114] Chandler reasoned, similarly, that a larger navy "quickens the nation's powers and infuses life and vigor into its international relations."[115] Both Hunt and Chandler initially asked not for a "new" navy but for a bigger version of the old one—coastal guns, harbor mines, and ships designed to raid enemy commerce and, at most, deflect enemy attacks. Within a few years, however, neither Congress nor the intellectuals and navy professionals known as the navalists were content with more of the same; they instead sought to expand both the size and purpose of the American navy. After three or four years of mixed results, they succeeded in moving the navy, in one scholar's terms, from a "defensive-defense" posture to an "offensive-defense" one.[116] The new forward maritime strategy relied on bigger, heavily armed ships. This change was neither consciously mapped out nor, until 1889, fully implemented, but it marked the beginnings of a shift in American strategy that would become widely noticed by the turn of the decade.

Though the Arthur administration made an important start, congressional follow-through was inconsistent. In 1883 the lame-duck Congress completely accepted the administration's proposals, approving three new armor-plated cruisers, one clipper, and four (partially built) monitors. The new House of Representatives elected the previous fall, however, had a Democratic majority and soon found fault with the administration's plans. By the time Arthur left the presidency, his new navy amounted to little more than the completion of the 1883 buildup. Even in Congress, however, the intellectual climate had changed, for a bigger navy was seen as essential to a growing nation's prestige. Representative E. John Ellis argued in 1882 that "if we ever expect to have our proper rank among the nations of the earth, we must have a navy." Another congressman asked his colleagues to stop pretending that the new ships were being built for coastal defense and to "take up the question of a navy competent to take the sea as an aggressive power."[117] The

[114] Secretary of the Navy, *Annual Report, 1881,* 3.

[115] Secretary of the Navy, *Annual Report, 1882,* 32.

[116] Mark Russell Shulman, "The Emergence of American Sea Power: Politics and the Creation of a U.S. Naval Strategy, 1882–1893" (Ph.D. dissertation, University of California, 1990), 204–56.

[117] Quoted in Robert Seager, "Ten Years before Mahan: The Unofficial Case for the

House Naval Affairs Committee declared that "there is an immense moral power in a fifteen knot ship."[118] This navy would serve not simply to protect America, but to pursue "affirmative policies" such as establishing American influence in South America and "subjugating" Mexico.[119]

Arthur's secretary of state, Frederick Frelinghuysen, spent most of his time assisting businessmen with their exploration of foreign markets. He turned down offers of bases and protectorates from the Haitian and Venezuelan governments and specifically explained that he did not want "outlying territories." Chandler's recommendation that the United States acquire coaling stations in the Caribbean, South America, Liberia, East Africa, and Korea went nowhere. But the terms of the conversation had changed, and voices within the administration implicitly called for a return to the goals of the postwar expansionists. A minor, though symbolically striking, example was the United States' decision to participate in the Berlin Conference of 1884, a classic meeting of the great European imperialists to resolve the growing struggle over the Congo.

Two issues involving American interests that appeared once again on the administration's agenda were Hawaii and the isthmian canal. The former was simply a matter of renewing the reciprocity treaty of 1875, which had expired in 1882. Important business opposition delayed the negotiations, and Frelinghuysen and the Hawaiian minister in Washington signed the new treaty in 1884. The Senate took even longer to consider the treaty, approving it over two years later, when President Grover Cleveland put his support behind it. True to its desire to assert control over policy, irrespective of consistency, the Senate, which usually pushed the administration not to take on obligations, bases, or territories in foreign lands, insisted that the United States be granted exclusive basing rights at Pearl Harbor. Hawaii agreed, and the treaty went into effect in January 1887.

Arthur and Frelinghuysen were deeply concerned with French plans to finance an isthmian canal in Panama. They assumed that once a European great power provided the funds for such a strategically valuable project, the canal would fall into its hands. American companies had tried but failed to raise the capital on their own, and Congress refused to charter an American company or even to pass a resolution expressing support for the project. Added to these difficulties was the Clayton-

New Navy, 1880–1890," *Mississippi Valley Historical Review* 40, no. 3 (December 1953): 501–2, 504.

[118] Quoted in Shulman, "Emergence of American Sea Power," 227.

[119] Seager, "Ten Years before Mahan," 506.

Bulwer Treaty with Great Britain, which prohibited an exclusively American canal. Frelinghuysen decided to initiate negotiations with Nicaragua, an alternate site for the canal. On December 1, 1884, he signed a treaty with the Nicaraguan government, in violation of the Clayton-Bulwer Treaty, granting the United States permission to construct a canal, in return for which Washington would protect Nicaragua's territorial integrity. But this was too much, too fast for the Senate, which refused to approve the treaty. Arthur persisted and was granted assurances that the body would reconsider the treaty during the next president's term, but his successor was Grover Cleveland, an isolationist and antiexpansionist by temperament. Cleveland withdrew the treaty because, in his view, it would have entailed an "entangling alliance."

The election of Cleveland (1885–89) could have brought the fledgling assertiveness of American foreign policy to a dead halt. Cleveland was a committed isolationist who had campaigned in opposition to imperialism and expansion. The president often harked back to the advice of George Washington's Farewell Address in decrying alliances, and he clearly slowed the pace of the expansion of interests that Arthur had resuscitated. Cleveland refused to promote Arthur's Nicaragua canal treaty, which, along with reciprocity treaties with Mexico and several South American countries, died for want of Senate approval. He withdrew from Senate consideration the Berlin Conference treaty that guaranteed an open door for U.S. interests in the Congo. But while Cleveland retarded the speed and aggressiveness of U.S. foreign policy, the overall direction did not change. One cynical scholar maintains that the audiences who listened to Cleveland and Secretary of State Thomas F. Bayard's moralistic lectures "readily detected through the high moral tone a sharp eye for the national interest."[120] Cleveland supported Hawaiian reciprocity and even accepted an amendment that gave the United States a coaling and naval station in Pearl Harbor. The British consul general in Honolulu correctly appraised the importance of this move, noting that this expansion of American influence there would make the loss of Hawaiian independence inevitable.[121]

The most tangible evidence of the shift in American foreign policy was the continued naval buildup. Orders were now placed with Republican industrialists rather than Democratic ones, but the pace actually quickened.[122] Between 1885 and 1889, the Democratic House of Repre-

[120] Campbell, *Transformation of American Foreign Relations,* 77. On Cleveland's foreign policy in general, see also Richard E. Welch, Jr., *The Presidencies of Grover Cleveland* (Lawrence: University Press of Kansas, 1988), 157–201.

[121] Campbell, *Transformation of American Foreign Relations,* 71.

[122] Allan Nevins, Cleveland's hagiographer, tries to give Cleveland credit for the origins of the new navy. See Nevins, *Grover Cleveland: A Study in Courage* (New York: Dodd, Mead, 1932), 217.

sentatives and president, both supposedly antinavy and antiexpansionist, authorized the construction of thirty ships of various classes, including the nation's first battleships, and carried on the strategic shift toward a more offensive naval posture.[123] The aggregate displacement of
the new vessels was 100,000 tons, and the price tag was not insignificant: the battleships alone cost at least $2.5 million each. The *New
York,* an armored cruiser authorized in 1888, eventually cost nearly
$4.5 million, or 1 percent of federal revenues. The authorization of the
ill-fated battleship *Maine* in 1886 marked "the tipping of the balance"
toward offensive forces as coastal defenses became an increasingly small
and obsolete part of the new American fleet.[124] In the debates and discussions surrounding the naval buildup, both the administration and
Congress justified the increased expenditure by comparing the U.S.
Navy with the larger fleets of other great powers as well as second-rank
regional powers like Chile, Brazil, and Argentina.[125] By 1890, American
grand strategy had been transformed: Secretary of the Navy Benjamin
Tracy had made his famous plea for a battleship fleet, and Alfred
Thayer Mahan had powerfully explained the underlying reasons. But
the previous decade had laid the groundwork, both intellectually and
materially, for the new American navy.

THREATS AND RESPONSES, 1865–1889

The record of U.S. foreign policy during this period confounds defensive
realism's central prediction that states expand to confront threats from
abroad. In fact, when faced with a serious threat—one that people at
the time and since would regard as serious—American statesmen reacted in precisely the opposite fashion: they were usually cautious, often
retrenching American interests rather than expanding them. Moreover,
the history of American foreign policy between the Civil War and 1890
demonstrates the malleability of the concept of threat and thus the
weakness of the defensive realist explanation for expansion. Whenever
American leaders decided to expand their country's interests abroad,
they quickly discovered foreign threats to the area in question and—
sometimes out of genuine belief, sometimes to manipulate the debate—
justified their policies as dictated by the nation's dangerously vulnerable

---

[123] The 1884 election brought the Senate into Republican hands, but the naval buildup
continued unabated since the Republicans were far more enthusiastic about a large, modern navy than the Democrats. Moreover, shifts in the Senate were less important for the
future of the navy since the House was the relevant body for funding bills.

[124] Shulman, "Emergence of American Sea Power," 255.

[125] "Increase of the Naval Establishment," *House Report No. 993,* 1886, 1–23; *Congressional Record,* July 24, 1886, 7476.

position. As McGeorge Bundy, John F. Kennedy's national security adviser, said when he admitted that American intervention in Vietnam was not motivated by the Viet Cong attack at Pleiku or any other specific crisis, "Pleikus are streetcars. If you are waiting for one, it will come along."[126]

The first general pattern—that the United States did not confront genuine threats but instead accommodated them—is reflected in the U.S. response to the threat Britain and its colonies in North America posed. Since the middle of the twentieth century, historians have commonly asserted that through most of the previous century, the United States enjoyed a tacit alliance with Great Britain and was, in particular, protected from the vagaries of the world by the virtually omnipotent Royal Navy. This interpretation of nineteenth-century history would certainly have stunned American statesmen of the late nineteenth century, who without question regarded Britain as the greatest threat to the United States and its interests, and the Royal Navy, in particular, as the single greatest threat to the physical safety of the country. This reaction could hardly be considered peculiar, since the United States had fought two wars with England in the last century and a half—the last of which it lost resoundingly as the Royal Navy sailed up the east coast, shelling Washington and setting fire to the White House.

At the close of the Civil War, anti-British sentiment in the United States was at its peak. London was widely perceived as having allied itself with the Confederacy in both word and deed. Directly north of the United States lay a large, visible, and constant reminder of British power. Some expansionists, who had long eyed Canada, believed that a fully mobilized United States had the perfect opportunity to act. A marching song popular with Yankee regiments explicitly expressed this idea:

> Secession first he would put down
> Wholly and forever,
> And afterward from Britain's crown
> He Canada would sever.[127]

This sentiment was shared by enough important American politicians and journalists to worry the British. In 1865, when the House of Commons debated measures for the defense of Canada, virtually every member assumed that America would take the slightest opportunity to move north. A pamphleteer explained that the conditions for opportunistic

[126] Quoted in Robert Jervis, *Perception and Misperception in International Politics* (Princeton, N.J.: Princeton University Press, 1976), 14.
[127] Quoted in Joe Patterson Smith, "The Republican Expansionists of the Early Reconstruction Era" (Ph.D. dissertation, University of Chicago, 1933), 16.

expansion were ripe: "Canada is quite defenseless, and what is more indefensible. The United States have an enormous army and navy which will soon be idle and in want of employment. They want something to reunite them, and they imagine a foreign war would have that effect." In Canada, Archbishop Conolly of Halifax made a similar classical realist assumption: "No nation has ever had the power of conquest that did not use it or abuse it, at the very first favorable opportunity."[128]

But none of these predictions was fulfilled, in large part because no matter how popular the cause, neither the president nor his secretary of state believed Canada was worth the prospect of a conflict with mighty Britain. Not that Seward did not want to annex Canada—in his earlier imperialist writings and speeches he had always referred to Canada as part of the United States' destiny. He may even have encouraged the Irish Fenian Brotherhood to conduct raids across the northern border between 1866 and 1870 in the belief that it would place the annexation of Canada on the agenda between the United States and Great Britain. However, Seward always took pains to make clear that he would not attempt to wrest Canada forcibly from Britain. Any union between the two North American nations had to be "free and spontaneous" and with "the fullest consultation with the government of Great Britain."[129] When Seward raised the matter with the British and found them unreceptive, he quickly dropped it. This approach differs strikingly from his dogged determination to acquire tiny islands in the Caribbean in which he had a much more recent and less-developed interest.

Seward and his successor Hamilton Fish maintained this cautious approach in the face of popular and even senatorial sentiment to the contrary. At the outset of Fish's tenure, Charles Sumner delivered an extravagant speech on the *Alabama* claims negotiations between Britain and the United States. He claimed that Britain's neutrality and construction of several Confederate cruisers—the most notorious of which had been the *Alabama*—had done $125 million of direct damage to the North and $2 billion of indirect damage. It was assumed, as Sumner later stated explicitly, that Britain would repay this absurd figure by ceding Canada to the United States. Grant and Fish were both expansionists, and both were particularly enthusiastic about a union with Canada. But like Seward, they—mainly Secretary Fish—recognized that a conflict with Britain would be enormously costly.[130] By raising the stakes so dramatically, Sumner had unintentionally sobered the discussion of the issue, and much of the casual anti-British rhetoric gave way to caution. In

[128] Ibid., 23.
[129] Van Deusen, *William Henry Seward*, 536–37.
[130] Nevins, *Hamilton Fish*, 218.

Henry Adams's words, "It was not until England began to scold that our people began to hesitate." Britain's permanent under secretary in the Foreign Office noted that expansionist Americans often "draw in their horns" when they face a foe with whom "bluster and bully" alone will not work.[131]

The United States similarly "drew in its horns" when facing another great power to its south. Taking advantage of American weakness during the Civil War, Napoleon III revived his plans for a French imperial presence in North America and proceeded to send an expeditionary force to Mexico. In April 1864 his puppet, Archduke Maximilian of Austria, "accepted" the Mexican throne. Seward had always regarded Mexico as vital to American interests, and, as noted earlier, his dreams of a continental American empire had envisioned Mexico City as its capital. But with the Civil War still raging, Seward responded to this threat with caution and inaction. Congress, however, was quick to anger, passing a resolution declaring that a monarchy established in North America by a European state violated American policy and must not be tolerated. In the U.S. Army, generals were ready to enlist with Benito Juárez's anti-French force to drive out Maximilian.[132] Yet Seward kept quiet, toning down his occasional public rhetoric in official conversations. Most strikingly, this great expansionist never once mentioned the Monroe Doctrine in reference to the Mexico issue. Seward recognized that given the nation's weakness, he could only wait until the Civil War was over to respond to this threat. Once the war ended, however, Seward's attitude changed markedly. He informed the French government that the United States wanted France out of Mexico. Many army generals, including Grant and Lew Wallace, wanted to move against Mexico, and Congress was also calling for action. Again Seward advocated caution, and with firm but patient diplomacy he was able to remove the French presence on the continent by 1867.[133] When in 1866 a weaker potential European adversary, Austria, explored the possibility of sending troops to aid Maximilian, Seward's diplomacy was significantly more aggressive; and with an eye to France, he issued a thinly veiled threat of war to the Austrian government.[134] One should, however, note that Seward's decision not to challenge the French presence in North America was in large part due to the great turmoil wrought in the United States by the Civil War. Faced with the Confederate threat to national unity, the Union government had little choice but to turn a

---

[131] Quoted in Donald, *Charles Sumner,* 387.

[132] Ibid., 357.

[133] Van Deusen, *William Henry Seward,* 368–70, 488–95.

[134] See Stephen J. Valone, "'Weakness Offers Temptation': William H. Seward and the Reassertion of the Monroe Doctrine," *Diplomatic History* 19, no. 4 (Fall 1995): 583–99.

blind eye to such threats that were minor in comparison, making this case somewhat ambiguous.

But the general trend is clear: the places where Seward chose to attempt expansion belie the notion that his efforts were a response to any threats. He consciously avoided areas where European great powers had interests, choosing instead weak, isolated areas; the uninhabited islands of Midway represent an appropriate, though somewhat exaggerated, example. Gideon Welles, Andrew Johnson's fiery secretary of the navy and a committed expansionist, noticed that Seward's efforts were not aimed at countering particular threats and thus failed to see the value of Seward's coveted West Indies bases. As historian Ernest Paolino concludes in his careful study of Seward, "The argument that Seward's interest in purchasing coaling stations was primarily military is further weakened by the absence of a proximate threat from any foreign power then holding possessions in the area."[135] Grant's plans mirrored Seward's and are susceptible to the same criticism. Defensive realists might counter that although they posit that countries are sure to expand in response to threats, countries might nevertheless expand during periods of relative security. During such times other factors will predominate. The United States profited from a virtually threatless international environment in the late nineteenth century, they might argue, and its expansionist impulses were motivated by other factors. But if the defensive realist theory of foreign policy can simultaneously claim that threats cause expansion and the lack of threat can also cause expansion, then the theory is impossible to prove false and its predictive power is minimal.[136]

Once the plans for expansion were set, threats appeared without fail. Though most of the reasons presented for the purchase of Alaska dealt with that region's natural resources, Seward and Sumner both argued that the area was highly vulnerable to British power. While this was certainly true, since Canada did border the territory, Britain had displayed no interest in Alaska, not even once it learned that America was to be its new owner. From a geopolitical point of view, keeping two European powers—Britain and Russia—on the continent to occupy one

[135] Paolino, *Foundations of the American Empire*, 119–21; Gideon Welles, *Diary of Gideon Welles, Secretary of the Navy under Lincoln and Johnson* (Boston: Houghton Mifflin, 1911), 3:95–96.

[136] In other words, such a defensive realist argument would imply that threats are only a sufficient cause of expansion, not both necessary and sufficient. But there are numerous sufficient causes for expansion, from domestic interest groups to nationalist mythmaking to threats. As I argued earlier, the defensive realist position captures a portion of the truth about international relations. The key question is to identify causes that are both necessary and sufficient.

another might have been a better strategy from a threat perspective. Grant's discovery of supposed foreign threats was still more dramatic. After the Senate had rejected his treaty to annex Santo Domingo, Grant decided to renew the struggle with a new, secret reason why annexation was now imperative: "[A] European power stands ready to offer two millions of dollars for the possession of Samana Bay alone." It did not work; the Senate rejected the treaty again. No documents have come to light that would substantiate Grant's claim, nor was the bay transferred to any European power.[137]

The naval buildup in the 1880s was, of course, accompanied by a discussion of the threats the nation faced.[138] The United States was portrayed by pronavy writers and politicians as "ringed by hostile states bent on laying waste its coastal cities and destroying the national wealth concentrated there." Harrowing images of British gunships shelling New York and San Francisco were regularly drawn, and the navies of Chile, Brazil, and even China were soon added to the list of enemies. The historiography of the War of 1812 was debated and rewritten so that the lessons would accord with the need for a large navy. The best example of these exaggerated, if not downright fraudulent, scare tactics is the "Chilean Myth." Chile was cited even more frequently than Great Britain as the nation most likely to plunder the American coast. Until the discussion of the new navy, Chile had been widely regarded—by the very same people who later spoke fearfully of it—as "insolvent," "powerless," and ruled by "idiots, seeking self-destruction." Its possession of a few British ironclads could hardly challenge America's hegemonic position in the Western Hemisphere, let alone its physical safety. The more convincing reason for the naval buildup, and one made with equal clarity, was to add military muscle to American foreign policy.[139]

While threats and fears of insecurity clearly played some role in spurring America's expansion of interests abroad, they rarely were the prime motivation. As a recent historical survey concludes, "[T]he dramatic extension of America's overseas involvement and commitments in the past hundred years has reflected a growth of power rather than a decline of security."[140] When genuine threats existed, as in the case of the British in Canada and the French in Mexico, American statesmen—who were by nature and in other areas jingoistic, even foolhardy—turned

[137] Nevins, *Hamilton Fish,* 328–30; Donald, *Charles Sumner,* 451–52.

[138] See Seager, "Ten Years before Mahan," 502–6.

[139] See Mark Russell Shulman, "The Influence of Sea Power upon History: Rewriting the War of 1812," *Journal of Military History* (Summer 1992).

[140] John A. Thompson, "The Exaggeration of American Vulnerability: The Anatomy of a Tradition," *Diplomatic History* 16, no. 1 (Winter 1992): 43. On the presence of this tradition in the late nineteenth century, see especially 24–25.

cautious and patient. On both occasions, despite prodding from Congress and the army, they opted for what John Calhoun had earlier termed "masterly inaction."

CONCLUSION

This careful examination of the opportunities to expand American interests abroad after the Civil War, both those taken and those refused, demonstrates the power of state-centered realism. As table 3.1 shows, its hypothesis accounts for fifteen of the twenty-two cases. (Those labeled "other" are cases in which the cause was too varied to validate any one theory.) Between 1865 and 1889, American foreign policy slowly reacted to the country's augmented material resources and was characterized by increasing and opportunistic expansionism; when opportunities were not seized, the cause was a weak state structure that could not translate executive-branch schemes into government policy. These results conflict substantially with defensive realism's belief that the primary force motivating a nation's foreign policy is its response to threats. That theory's claim that the more benign the surrounding international environment, the less expansionist a state is challenged by the United States of this period, a state that was relatively secure but nevertheless pursued an increasingly ambitious foreign policy. When the United States did not expand, the reason had less to do with the absence of threat than with the weakness of the American state. And when the United States did face real threats, it chose not to expand.

A simple counterfactual clarifies the role of state structure in explaining America's inactivity during the post–Civil War period. Had the United States had a state structure similar to that of every other great power at the time—a stronger central government and a parliament with the executive and legislative branches fused—it is almost certain that many of the executive's plans would have become national policy. The United States would have acquired, during the utterly threatless era of 1865–77 alone, close to a dozen bases, coaling stations, and entire islands with subject populations. This initial expansion would surely have resulted in greater expansion in the next decade as the stability of neighboring areas became a vital concern.

This study's emphasis on state structure is different from explanations that rely on domestic or party politics. Expansion was not thwarted because one party was for it and the other against, nor did internal troubles generally distract politicians. The structure of the American state ensured that central decision-makers, who respond most directly to the pressures of the international system, were unable to translate

TABLE 3.1
America's Opportunities to Expand, 1865–1889

Period	Case	Outcome	Hypothesis Validated
1865–1869	1) Hawaii	NE	SCR
	2) Greenland and Iceland	NE	SCR
	3) Danish West Indies	NE	SCR
	4) Alaska	E	SCR
	5) Midway Islands	E	SCR
	6) Santo Domingo	NE	SCR
	7) Haiti	NE	SCR
	8) Isthmian canal	NE	SCR
	9) Canada	NE	SCR
	10) Mexico	NE	SCR
1869–1877	11) Santo Domingo	NE	SCR
	12) Cuba I	NE	Other
	13) Cuba II	NE	Other
	14) Hawaii	E	DR
	15) Isthmian canal	NE	Other
	16) Samoa	NE	Other
1877–1889	17) Samoa	E	DR
	18) Hawaii	E	SCR
	19) Nicaragua canal	NE	Other
	20) Venezuela	NE	SCR
	21) New navy	E	SCR
	22) Berlin Conference	NE	SCR

Note: NE = nonexpansion; E = expansion; SCR = state-centered realism; DR = defensive realism; Other = cause too varied to code as either state-centered realism or defensive realism

national power into national influence because they presided over a weak federal government that had enormous difficulty extracting resources, particularly for expenditures that did not directly benefit congressional constituents. The division between the legislative and executive branches allowed Congress to thwart the executive's plans. Congress was not blindly antiexpansionist, but it was blindly antiexecutive. It adopted a belligerent posture regarding Mexico and Canada because the executive branch had been more conciliatory;[141] Charles Sumner had

---

[141] Joe Smith argues persuasively that even the initial hotheaded, anti-British attitude of Congress in 1865 was motivated by a desire to take control of foreign policy from an executive branch that it feared had grown too powerful during the Civil War. See Smith, "Republican Expansionists," 120.

been markedly pro-British until he found a cutting-edge anti-British issue with which to seize control of foreign policy. This irony was not lost on Seward, who pointed out that those arguing for the annexation of Canada were the same legislators who had opposed all territorial acquisitions proposed by the Johnson administration.[142]

Seward could only fret about his inability to shape national policy. In his day, the federal government was more a patchwork of patronage positions and programs than a professional bureaucratic apparatus, and Congress was the ringleader of this big tent. By the late 1880s, however, the balance of power had shifted in two ways. First, the congressional bid for supremacy had exhausted itself and was clearly petering out, and second, the growth of the national economy was creating the need for a national, professional bureaucracy. Both of these developments strengthened the office of the president, better enabling him to convert any plans he might have into national policy and resulting in a more expansionist American foreign policy.

[142] Van Deusen, *William Henry Seward*, 509.

CHAPTER FOUR

The Rise of the American State, 1877–1896:

THE FOUNDATION FOR A NEW FOREIGN POLICY

IN 1883 an ambitious graduate student in political science at the Johns Hopkins University began writing a critical study of American government. Johns Hopkins, then not yet ten years old, was a hotbed for all kinds of ideas, many of them imported from Germany and England, about political institutions and structures. The young scholar, Woodrow Wilson, had been reflecting on these issues since his undergraduate days at Princeton and had published some preliminary thoughts in an article four years earlier.[1] His book, *Congressional Government*, was published in 1885. Its argument was as simple as it was dramatic. Congress had indisputably become the most powerful branch of American government—"the predominant and controlling force, the center and source of all motive and of all regulative power"—but it was poorly structured for this preeminent role.[2] For the U.S. government to function with efficiency, responsibility, and accountability, Congress's de facto power would have to be made de jure. Wilson proposed that executive powers be transferred into the hands of a cabinet chosen by and accountable to Congress. The president, according to this scheme, would serve as a kind of republican monarch, faithfully executing the laws Congress passed but no more.

Congressional Government was a great success, in both the academic and the broader intellectual worlds. Tens of thousands of copies were sold, and the book went into multiple printings. However, in the fifteenth edition of the book, published in 1903, Wilson let his readers know that, quite frankly, he had made a mistake. The central assumption—that Congress was omnipotent—had turned out to be wrong. Changes in the political landscape between 1885 and 1901 had, he ad-

---

[1] Thomas Woodrow Wilson, "Cabinet Government in the United States," *International Review* 7 (August 1879): 146–63. In a strange quirk of history, the editor of *International Review* at the time was Henry Cabot Lodge. Forty years later, the two men would clash in perhaps the most famous struggle between the legislative and executive branches.

[2] Woodrow Wilson, *Congressional Government: A Study in American Politics* (reprint, Gloucester: P. Smith, 1973), 31.

mitted in a new preface, "put this volume hopelessly out of date."[3] The president, Wilson declared in 1908, was now supreme: "His is the only national voice in affairs. Let him once win the admiration and confidence of the country, and no other force can withstand him, no combination of forces will easily overcome him. His position takes the imagination of the country. He is the representative of no constituency but the people. When he speaks in his true character he speaks for no special interest. If he rightly interpret the national thought, and boldly insist upon it, he is irresistible."[4] Wilson practiced what he preached. His dream as a student at Princeton had been to be elected a senator from Virginia, and he even practiced signing his name in that fashion. Soon after his change of mind, however, he began charting his course to the White House.

In writing *Congressional Government,* Wilson made a mistake not uncommon to political scientists: he built a general theory upon recent, ephemeral trends. Wilson was eight years old when Lincoln died; while he was growing up, the occupants of the White House were Andrew Johnson, Ulysses Grant, Rutherford Hayes, James Garfield, and Chester Arthur. It was the high tide of congressional power. Yet even as he completed his treatise, Grover Cleveland won the 1884 election and the Senate's power was beginning to wane. The very success and popularity of *Congressional Government* was a manifestation of the widespread fear of an all-powerful legislature, a sentiment that would soon turn the balance of power in the opposite direction.[5] The presidencies of Cleveland, William McKinley, and Theodore Roosevelt had by 1908 completely transformed the configuration of power in American government.

[3] Ibid.

[4] Woodrow Wilson, *Constitutional Government in the United States* (New York: Columbia University Press, 1908), 68.

[5] In America, Samuel Huntington explains, "power remains strong when it remains in the dark; exposed to the sunlight it begins to evaporate." Huntington calls this America's "power paradox" and makes a similar argument about post—World War II presidential power. In the 1950s and early 1960s, Richard Neustadt called for greater presidential authority, detailing to great acclaim the severe constraints that had emasculated the presidency. In fact, as the popularity of Neustadt's work indicated, the power of the presidency was on the rise. More than a decade later, when Arthur M. Schlesinger, Jr.'s *Imperial Presidency* became a best-seller, the presidency was actually in the process of sinking into real weakness. Schlesinger's book was so popular precisely because so many were concerned about the excesses of the executive and were striving to weaken it. See Samuel P. Huntington, *American Politics: The Promise of Disharmony* (Cambridge: Harvard University Press, 1981), 75–76; Richard E. Neustadt, *Presidential Power: The Politics of Leadership* (New York: Wiley, 1960); and Arthur M. Schlesinger, Jr., *The Imperial Presidency* (Boston: Houghton Mifflin, 1973).

STATE STRUCTURE AND FOREIGN POLICY

Between the late 1870s and the late 1890s, America's political structure changed dramatically as two key institutions gained strength: the federal government and the presidency. The scope of the government's role in society grew as new industries and technologies arose and as business became increasingly national; the existing set of state regulations became obsolete, and the federal government slowly expanded to meet this need. Civil service reform began to free the country's administrative structure from the stranglehold of patronage, resulting in a state that was relatively more autonomous and therefore more capable of responding to international systemic pressures. And the increasing strength of the presidency, an office some would soon see as an "elective monarchy," created a far more cohesive state and permitted a more coherent U.S. policy on both the domestic and international fronts. With these developments, particularly through more developed and more autonomous bureaucratic structures, the state's capacity—its ability to harness the power of the nation to fulfill its ends—grew.

Although few historians would question the particulars of this account of the development of the American state, the larger interpretive conclusion—that the U.S. national government functioned rather differently in the mid-1890s than in 1877—would strike many as a bold claim. Students of American political development generally believe that the late nineteenth century did not bring a fundamental change in the American state. Both before and after the Civil War, the American state was dominated by the principal parties, and although the mid-1890s saw a major realignment, the system remained largely intact. During this period, "the government's most pervasive role was that of promoting development by distributing resources and privileges to individuals and groups," and, in "the policy equivalent of patronage," the parties channeled these benefits to their supporters. According to the standard view, although the post—Civil War state expanded the scope of its activities, government still primarily served a distributive function; "not until the early twentieth century did social and economic developments permanently enlarge governmental responsibilities by strengthening both regulation and administration."[6] While the standard account cor-

---

[6] Richard L. McCormick, "The Party Period and Public Policy: An Exploratory Hypothesis," in his *The Party Period and Public Policy: American Politics from the Age of Jackson to the Progressive Era* (Oxford: Oxford University Press, 1986), 203–4, 209, 213, and see generally 197–227. Other prominent examples of the standard view are William Nisbet Chambers and Walter Dean Burnham, eds., *The American Party Systems: Stages of Political Development* (New York: Oxford University Press, 1967); and Leonard

rectly notes the great influence of the parties throughout this period, it ignores those developments that slowly eroded the control of the parties over the administrative structures and led to increasing state autonomy.[7] It is time to take the American state of the late nineteenth century a good deal more seriously.

The growing strength of the nineteenth-century American state had significant effects on American foreign policy. When a state can more easily extract national resources and when its decision-making is more centralized and unified, statesmen can respond more directly to international systemic pressures. The development in the United States of what John Brewer calls "the fiscal-military state"—greater powers for the federal government, increased tax revenues, and a strengthened executive—resulted in a foreign policy in the 1890s and 1900s that more accurately reflected, and more directly exploited, America's growing national power.[8] During the Progressive Era, between around 1902 and 1919, the American state grew still stronger, and the country's foreign policy expanded its scope and force even more. Just as Roosevelt profited from the strengthened institutions that Cleveland and McKinley had bequeathed to him, Woodrow Wilson benefited from Roosevelt's contributions to the development of the state. But the important shift in state power that laid the groundwork for the Progressives began in the 1880s with a corresponding trend in the foreign policy of the late 1890s and early 1900s.

This study is concerned only with such relative shifts in American state power. The American state would grow more powerful in the decades that followed, especially after the New Deal and World War II, and the rise of the American state was qualitatively weaker in every sense than the growth of its European counterparts. During the period under study, the power of the American state never equaled that of the French or German states. In fact, because of the relative weakness of the American state even in 1908 or 1917, while American foreign policy was more activist than in the past, it was still passive and reactive compared to the foreign policies of Europe's great powers. The period 1889

D. White, *The Republican Era, 1869–1901: A Study in Administrative History* (New York: Macmillan, 1958).

[7] Stephen Skowronek calls the government of the late nineteenth century "the state of courts and parties," but this widely quoted phrase is somewhat misleading. Skowronek's work catalogues the growing strength of the state during this period at the expense of the party system, and this study draws heavily on his research. See his *Building a New American State: The Expansion of National Administrative Capacities, 1877–1920* (Cambridge: Cambridge University Press, 1982).

[8] John Brewer, *The Sinews of Power: War, Money, and the English State, 1688–1783* (London: Unwin Hyman, 1989), xvii.

to 1908 witnessed far more American activity in international affairs, but the era as a whole can still be characterized as underexpansionist.

While one of these trends is linear—the national government has over time consistently gained power at the expense of the states—the second is more complex. The structure of the American state ensures that should Congress choose to exercise its constitutionally mandated powers, it can at any time create a divided regime and cause a disjuncture between international pressures and national policy. As Lord Bryce observed, "Congress has been the branch of government with the largest facilities for usurping the powers of the other branches, and probably with the most disposition to do so."[9] Relations between the executive and legislative branches have exhibited a cyclical pattern. During the 1860s and 1870s, congressional power prevented (one might say saved) the United States from acquiring an empire in the Caribbean. After the intervening Progressive Era blitz of presidential power, Congress reasserted its authority, thwarting Woodrow Wilson's plans for the postwar world and making clear to his Republican successors that activism abroad would not garner congressional support and was, therefore, not viable. As Arthur Schlesinger has pointed out, the pattern is not entirely cyclical, for the congressional reaction "never quite cut presidential power back to its earlier level."[10] The presidency has grown stronger over the last century, particularly during the Cold War, but even this overwhelming power shift cannot erase what Wilson called "the literary theory of the constitution." Sometimes for better, sometimes for worse, Congress can—and does—block executive proposals, generating a disparity between international structural pressures and national policy. As Alfred Thayer Mahan wrote in 1897, "any project of extending the sphere of the United States, by annexation or otherwise, is met by the constitutional lion in the path."[11]

Finally, and most important, international pressures did not cause the rise of the American state. Historians and political scientists alike recite with reverential devotion Charles Tilly's dictum that "war made the state, and the state made war." Scholarship has understandably focused on the first half of that sentence; war and other international pressures

[9] James Bryce, *The American Commonwealth* (London: Macmillan, 1891), 2:711.

[10] Schlesinger, *The Imperial Presidency*, 68; see also his *The Cycles of American History* (Boston: Houghton Mifflin, 1986). Michael Desch makes a similar point, noting the two-steps-forward-one-step-back pattern of American state strength. See Michael C. Desch, "War and Strong States, Peace and Weak States?" *International Organization* 50, no. 2 (Spring 1996): 244–46.

[11] Quoted in Walter LaFeber, *The American Search for Opportunity, 1865–1913*, vol. 2 of *The Cambridge History of American Foreign Relations*, ed. Warren I. Cohen (Cambridge: Cambridge University Press, 1993) 236.

have indeed had a powerful effect on state-building in Europe. But the second phrase is also true, if not as important. To say that "the state makes war" is, in a sense, trivial. Understood more broadly, however, it implies that the more powerful a state, the more likely it is to adopt an activist diplomatic and military policy. The idea that state structures affect policy outcomes has a distinguished pedigree, and it lies at the heart of a renaissance in scholarship that has over the last two decades revived the concept of the autonomous state.[12]

During the late nineteenth century and the Progressive era that followed, the American state grew primarily in response to pressures generated by industrialization. In contrast to the European states, which developed largely to cope with external pressures, the American state came to the fore during a period that lacked rising threats, and the documentary record reflects no clear link between international pressures and the building of the American state. The two wars at either end of the period under study—the Civil War and the Spanish-American War—left only slight impressions on the American state. The fiscal-military state that arose in America in the 1890s, albeit in weak form, also developed in Britain during its "isolationist" period after the Glorious Revolution of 1688, and, as John Brewer brilliantly demonstrates, this change in state structure set the stage for England's rise to world power by the late eighteenth century.[13] National power can be converted into international influence, but the state first requires the mechanisms and institutions that make this conversion possible.

THE AMERICAN STATE, OR THE ABSENCE THEREOF

"In framing a government," James Madison famously declared in *The Federalist,* No. 51, "you must first enable the government to control the governed; in the next place oblige it to control itself." The American theory and practice of government, however, have been far more concerned with the dangers of untrammeled government than with the dangers of inefficient government. In Samuel Huntington's words, "When an American thinks about the problem of government-building, he directs himself not to the creation of authority and the accumulation of power but rather to the limitation of authority and the division of

[12] See chapter 2.

[13] Brewer, *Sinews of Power.* Brewer acknowledges that war and international competition were strong influences on the development of the English state, but he points out that the state was also built for many internal reasons and that, once created, it became capable of waging war. To highlight one process is not to deny the existence of the other.

power."[14] Both the dimensions of state power mentioned above reflected this attitude: state governments were made strong enough to prevent the federal government from becoming all-powerful, and the federal government itself was divided into three separate, equal branches "all claiming the absolute power of the people."[15] During the nineteenth century, the complicated system of checks and balances created a government of shared functions and divided power. Economic policy, for example, was the preserve of state and local governments, several federal executive agencies, the Senate, and the House of Representatives, and each could adopt its own economic policy that was wholly incompatible with that of another branch. In contrast, European states had, by the eighteenth century, created functionally specialized agencies, and ultimate power had come to rest largely in one branch of government. "Thus America perpetuated a fusion of functions and a division of power, while Europe developed a differentiation of functions and a centralization of power."[16]

While many of the basic features of the European states were formed in the eighteenth century to extract national resources for the purpose of defense, industrialization demanded still further state-building during the nineteenth century. As the population, production, and capital of the nations of Europe grew, the organizational aspects of these societies expanded as well. With large-scale industrialization, factories and companies became truly massive undertakings. As Geoffrey Barraclough explains:

> In the steel industry, for example, the introduction of the blast furnace meant that the small individual enterprise employing ten or a dozen workmen quickly became an anachronism. Small scale family businesses, which were typical of the first phase of industrialism, were in many cases too narrowly based . . . nor had they always the means to finance the installation of new, more complicated and more expensive machinery. . . . [R]ationalization and unified management was a spur to the large-scale concern and to the formation of trusts and cartels; and the process of concentration, once begun, was irreversible.[17]

The new industrial economy also resulted in the mass concentration of people in urban centers. To cope with the problems of industrialization—the power of big business, the rights of consumers, urban development, poverty, health, and hygiene—the governments of Europe had to accept ever-expanding tasks, and with these new responsibilities

[14] Samuel P. Huntington, *Political Order in Changing Societies* (New Haven, Conn.: Yale University Press, 1968), 7.

[15] Skowronek, *Building a New American State*, 22.

[16] Huntington, *Political Order in Changing Societies*, 110.

[17] Geoffrey Barraclough, *An Introduction to Contemporary History* (New York: Basic Books, 1964), 50–51.

came, of course, new powers. This change was most clear in the two largest industrial economies of Europe, England and Germany. In England, Joseph Chamberlain's radical protectionist program marked the end of "pure" laissez-faire. In Germany, Otto von Bismarck's social legislation of the mid-1880s fundamentally altered the relations between government and society, imposing on the state a responsibility for the protection of its citizens' welfare.[18] "The Government in its modern sense . . . ," wrote A. V. Dicey in 1905, "involving the development of an elaborate machinery of administration and enforcement, was a necessary outcome of the new industrial society."[19]

The American governmental structure has always had its share of critics who have asserted that this institutionalized division ensures inefficiency and gridlock. The earliest and most distinguished was Alexander Hamilton, who argued during the constitutional debates in Philadelphia for both a more powerful central government and a more powerful president.[20] In Hamilton's opinion, if America were to achieve the economic prosperity of Europe, greater responsibilities and power would have to be placed in the hands of the national government and, in particular, the presidency. Throughout his career in public life, he struggled to expand the government's powers over every aspect of American life, from taxation and banking to military affairs and public projects. His plans met with some success, but it was short-lived: few survived after his death. The Supreme Court under Chief Justice John Marshall probably did more to nationalize the country than any other institution of its time. Senator Daniel Webster was a staunch supporter of a national economy and defended the National Bank often. And though he sought to make Congress the directing force in his plans for "internal improvements," Henry Clay adopted Hamilton's centralizing spirit. But despite the leadership of these powerful and articulate statesmen, Hamilton's vision remained largely unfulfilled through much of the nineteenth century. Jefferson's agrarian myth of the yeoman farmer and Andrew Jackson's populism and localism were more appealing to a people that had recently escaped the grip of Europe's strong states.[21] As Stephen Skowronek puts it, "Those who sought to build the central

[18] F. H. Hinsley, "Introduction," in Hinsley, ed., *The New Cambridge Modern History,* vol. II, *Material Progress and World-Wide Problems, 1870–1898* (Cambridge: Cambridge University Press, 1970), 11–34.

[19] Quoted in Barraclough, *Introduction to Contemporary History,* 125.

[20] See Lynton K. Caldwell, *The Administrative Theories of Hamilton and Jefferson: Their Contribution to Thought on Public Administration* (New York: Russell and Russell, 1944); also see Henry Cabot Lodge, *Alexander Hamilton* (Boston: Houghton Mifflin, 1898), 50–84.

[21] See Bernard Bailyn, *The Origins of American Politics* (New York: Alfred A. Knopf, 1968), 3–58.

state apparatus in early America ended up building minority parties instead."[22]

The Civil War created a sense of nationalism and solidarity, and "the old individualism yielded in a hundred ways to disciplined association."[23] But it did not give rise to a permanent fiscal-military state—to large bureaucracies that would handle taxation and revenue collection, government expenditures, and military organizations. The North's war machine was dismantled and the army and navy demobilized within a year after the war. Other institutions took longer to take apart, leading to the impression of a boom of government activism in the late 1860s followed by a bust in the 1870s. In fact, the period is more aptly described as one of demobilization in spurts, coupled with the initial attempts at reconstruction, which collapsed by 1876. Because of the large national debt, some wartime tariffs and taxes were kept in place for a few years, but they too were soon reduced or eliminated. Even during Reconstruction, government employment did not grow substantially in either the civilian or military sectors, and the climate of "retrenchment" was pervasive. The institutional shift of power toward the national government and the president that had occurred during the war proved ephemeral. Lincoln's wartime powers spurred Congress to enfeeble the office under his successors. Leonard White has described the postwar years as "the culmination of Jacksonian theory and practice."[24] War may often make the state, but the greatest industrial war of the nineteenth century did not have that effect in America.[25]

NATIONALIZING THE GOVERNMENT

The atmosphere immediately after the Civil War was dominated by intense battles between the president and Congress, the radical Republicans and the Democrats, and the North and the South. The efforts to integrate the South into the new American nation manifested "the interplay between the war-born ideals of a strong central government and

[22] Skowronek, *Building a New American State,* 22.
[23] Allan Nevins, *Ordeal of the Union,* 8 vols. (New York: Scribner, 1957–71), 2:viii. On the expansion of the state during the Civil War, see Richard F. Bensel, *Yankee Leviathan: The Origins of Central State Authority in America, 1859–1877* (New York: Cambridge University Press, 1990).
[24] White, *The Republican Era,* viii.
[25] For the best account of the return to localism and divided government, see Morton Keller, *Affairs of State: Public Life in Late Nineteenth Century America* (Cambridge: Harvard University Press, 1977), 1–37, 85–122, 162–97. Also see David Montgomery, *Beyond Equality: Labor and the Radical Republicans, 1862–1872* (New York: Alfred A. Knopf, 1967), chap. 2; and Bensel, *Yankee Leviathan,* 1–4, 10–17.

race-blind citizenship, and more traditional American beliefs in localism, limited government, and racial inequality."[26] By the early 1870s, the latter had won. Whether Reconstruction failed because it was too harsh or because it was too mild, fail it did. The Compromise of 1877 removed federal troops from the South and reversed the nation-building enterprise of the previous decade.[27] But if the end of Reconstruction marked the end of the old state-building problem—Southern separatism—it also marked the beginning of a new one as the nation quickly outgrew its administrative structure.[28] Post—Civil War America was rapidly becoming a great industrial economy and society, and its government was ill equipped to handle that transformation.

More important, in this context, than the breathtaking aggregate growth of the American economy was the national market that undergirded it.[29] As the far-flung lands of the continental United States were settled by waves of immigrants and then connected by roads, canals, railroads, post, telegraph, and telephone, the many peoples of this vast country began to constitute a single market. With the creation of mass demand came the incentives for mass production and distribution. These large-scale processes brought many advantages to businesses— economies of scale and reduced unit costs, for example—but they also required large investments in new machinery, plants, and distribution facilities. The country succeeded in meeting the demand for an infusion of capital thanks to the extraordinarily high national savings rate— around 25 percent of GNP—which kept rising through the late nineteenth century, the proliferation of new and ingenious financial intermediaries, and, finally, surplus capital from Europe that quickly found its way across the Atlantic.[30]

National firms—businesses that crossed state boundaries—were

[26] Keller, *Affairs of State*, 37–38.

[27] The classic analysis is C. Vann Woodward, *Reunion and Reaction: The Compromise of 1877 and the End of Reconstruction* (Boston: Little, Brown, 1966). Recent scholarship, chiefly by Kenneth Stampp and Eric Foner, has argued that the radical Republicans have been unjustly vilified as malevolent oppressors who wanted to occupy and rule the South. The reality was that while the North won the war, the South won the peace. See Eric Foner, *Reconstruction: America's Unfinished Revolution, 1863–1877* (New York: Harper and Row, 1988); and Kenneth M. Stampp, *The Era of Reconstruction, 1865–1877* (New York: Vintage Books, 1965).

[28] Bensel, *Yankee Leviathan*, 10.

[29] For a surprisingly balanced and competent history, see the famous muckraking journalist Ida M. Tarbell's survey of the period, *The Nationalization of Business, 1878–1898* (New York: Macmillan, 1944).

[30] Stuart W. Bruchey, *The Wealth of the Nation: An Economic History of the United States* (New York: Harper and Row, 1988), 104, and generally 100–142. Also see Harold G. Vatter, *The Drive to Industrial Maturity: The U.S. Economy, 1860–1914* (Westport, Conn.: Greenwood Press, 1975), 61–87.

spreading all over America, and national associations to promote their interests were cropping up in Washington. The National Board of Trade was founded in 1868, and the American Bankers Association in 1875. As business became national, so did labor; in 1866 the National Labor Union was formed, followed one year later by the farm group the National Grange and then in 1878 by the Knights of Labor. The process accelerated greatly in the 1880s and 1890s, as merger followed merger and trusts, cartels, and syndicates formed. Spurred in part by mass national demand, businesses grew increasingly large as they took advantage of their place in an oligopolistic market. The supreme example of horizontal and vertical integration coupled with aggressive price-fixing was the effective monopoly of John D. Rockefeller; by the 1880s his Standard Oil Company produced 90 percent of the petroleum sold in the United States.[31] A similar trend was manifest in the rise of licensing organizations through which professionals, from lawyers and doctors to barbers and blacksmiths, controlled the quantity and makeup of their colleagues. Labor organizations also grew enormously, with the American Federation of Labor, founded in 1886, becoming the most prominent. The move to national organizations took place even in the realm of agriculture; in 1880 the National Farmers' Alliance was formed, and in 1889 the Farmers and Laborers Union.[32]

The increasingly national aspect of business and labor created problems that local and state governments could not address. While the federal government remained largely aloof, businesses that operated across state boundaries were increasingly confused about which regulations they had to obey. But in this era of laissez-faire economics and localism, particularly during the 1870s, the result was an odd kind of state intervention, "a thickening of government supervision, but one that rested on traditional conceptions of public power."[33] State-building certainly occurred in the decades after the Civil War, but it was, in Skowronek's words, "state building as patchwork."[34] It may not have been neatly packaged, but the national government's power and purpose grew impressively. New national bureaucracies were founded: the Civil Service

[31] Tarbell, *The Nationalization of Business,* 74–5.
[32] Selig Perlman, *A History of Trade Unionism in America* (New York: A. M. Kelley, 1922), 180–86; and Tarbell, *The Nationalization of Business,* 121–68.
[33] Keller, *Affairs of State,* 409.
[34] According to Skowronek, this patchwork state-building gave way to "state building as reconstitution" by 1900, but his discussion indicates clearly that 1896—the date I would use—is the more proper turning point. The difference is important, for it emphasizes a point Skowronek's account illustrates clearly: most of the important changes in state structure preceded the Spanish-American War and were not caused by it. Skowronek, *Building a New American State,* 37, 167.

Commission (1883), the Bureau of Labor (1884), the Interstate Commerce Commission (1887). In Congress, dozens of new committees and subcommittees were formed, from Education and Labor to Appropriations. In 1882 Congress took from the states control of the nation's immigration policies. The business of the House and Senate was increasingly centralized and became subject to the kinds of hierarchy and organization that were moving the rest of the nation.[35] Finally, the growth of society led to the growth of national party organizations, which until the late 1890s were the most effective national political institutions and could absorb the new and increasing "social mobilization" of the American nation. "[I]t is . . . impossible to ignore the growing strength of centripetal and unifying forces," observed Lord Bryce in 1888.[36]

Expenditures and Taxation

With the end of the Civil War and Reconstruction, both of which had called for unusual amounts of federal spending, federal expenditures could have been expected to grow at their usual peacetime average, approximately 3 percent a year. But they in fact grew much faster after 1877. From $239 million in 1877, federal spending more than doubled to $505 million by 1901, reaching $694 million in 1909. In thirty-two years, federal expenditures had increased 190 percent.[37] The growth in expenditures over the thirty years between 1819 and 1849, a period that had also included one minor war, was only 100 percent.[38] The Treasury Department became the largest civilian department in the government. Its staff grew from four thousand in 1873 to almost twenty-five thousand by the end of the century, a 625 percent increase. Customs duties had provided approximately 55 percent of the federal government's income during the nineteenth century as a whole. Excise

[35] Nelson Polsby, "The Institutionalization of the House of Representatives," *American Political Science Review* 62 (1968): 144–68.

[36] Bryce, *The American Commonwealth,* 2:710.

[37] This astounding growth in federal expenditures is explained in part by the tremendous increase in pensions paid to Civil War veterans. These pensions, which accounted for approximately $20 million per year in the 1870s, had reached $150 million per annum by the 1890s. Theda Skocpol points out that the pensions were primarily a political tool of the Republican Party. See her *Protecting Soldiers and Mothers: The Political Origins of Social Policy in the United States* (Cambridge: Harvard University Press, 1992), especially 102–51.

[38] M. Slade Kendrick, *A Century and a Half of Federal Expenditures* (New York: National Bureau of Economic Research, 1955), 10–11; and on the effects of the Spanish-American War and the Mexican War, 21.

taxes were raised during the 1880s and 1890s, moving their share from 34 percent of federal revenues in 1880 to 43 percent by 1900.[39] The rise in state capacity during the late nineteenth century, although still limited in comparison to the European states, was astounding.

However, while the British government supplemented customs and excise taxes with death, property, and income taxes, these were nominal or nonexistent in America. The Civil War income tax was abolished to popular acclaim in the 1870s. The inability to reinstate a federal income tax was caused, however, less by public animosity than by the divided U.S. state structure. By the 1890s, both for reasons of equity and as a way of reducing the high tariffs, support for an income tax gained ground in Congress; in 1894 a 2 percent income tax was instituted, applying only to incomes above $4,000. But the Supreme Court, the most economically conservative branch of government at the time, had begun to flex its own muscles, and it ruled the income tax unconstitutional.[40] Once again, the United States' incoherent state structure had intervened to prevent the expansion of state capacity.

The federal government continued to finance its expenses with ad hoc levies and duties on stock sales, trade boards, and inheritances. Congress raised new tariffs in 1890, 1897, and 1909. By 1913 enough popular support for an income tax had coalesced to pass a constitutional amendment. Had the extra revenue come in earlier, it could easily have created "more" government and through that "more" foreign policy. But the American government was hardly starved for cash. As early as 1880, the U.S. Treasury enjoyed a $100 million surplus, and these surpluses appeared year after year. The problem in the United States by the 1880s was not reining in federal expenditures, as in Europe, but rather spending the ever-increasing federal revenues; the option of eliminating some revenues by lowering protective tariffs was not considered, since the Republican Party held it as dogma that that system be preserved.[41] By the late 1880s, tariffs and a growing industrial economy had essentially quenched the American state's thirst for money. The problem in the late nineteenth century was not as much the state's extractive capacity—that was sufficient—but its administrative capacity. However, the American state did not lie entirely dormant over these years: as the 1880s wore on and industrialization pressed forward, the American state began to rise from its slumber.

[39] Keller, *Affairs of State*, 308–9.

[40] Loren P. Beth, *The Development of the American Constitution* (New York: Harper and Row, 1971), 155–60; also see Sidney Ratner, *Taxation and Democracy in America* (New York: Wiley, 1967).

[41] Keller, *Affairs of State*, 316.

Regulating Business

The American economy grew rapidly in the 1870s and 1880s, but the country experienced as many panics as booms, and there were many more bankruptcies than new businesses. Due in part to the cyclical nature of capitalism, these swings were aggravated by the absence of a network of government institutions that could mediate the economy and mitigate its negative effects. Observers at the time noticed this troubling juxtaposition of, in Henry George's phrase, "progress and poverty."[42] While they might have found George's solution—communal ownership of all land—almost utopian, they certainly perceived many of the same problems: declining agricultural production, automation, distant markets connected by large transportation systems, a financial system too complicated for the average person to understand, and rising income inequality.

Much of the modest growth in government regulatory structures in the mid-1870s was simply the immediate result of new industrial activity and new technologies. As they were set up, gas, water, electric, and telephone companies came under the purview of the government. Reformers like Henry Adams, James Russell Lowell, E. L. Godkin, and Charles Eliot Norton applauded this development, which they saw as inevitable, but pushed for a more far-reaching state. They called largely for the expansion of the national administrative organizations. As Henry C. Adams, director of statistics of the Interstate Commerce Commission, observed, "Organization is the potent fact in the industrial history of the nineteenth century, and it must be used for the good of society, or society must bear the ills which it brings." Adams's influential 1886 tract, *Relation of the State to Industrial Action,* argued that "the collapse of faith in the sufficiency of the philosophy of laissez faire, has left the present generation without principles adequate for the guidance of public affairs." Adams, like many mugwump reformers, demanded that government use its power to foster "genuine" competition and promote enlightened business conduct. Most important among the government's tasks was, he believed, the regulation of the rules and rates of inherently monopolistic industries, the prime example of which was the railroad industry.[43]

---

[42] Henry George, *Progress and Poverty* (New York: Sterling, 1879).

[43] *"Relation of the State to Industrial Action" and "Economics and Jurisprudence": Two Essays by Henry Carter Adams,* ed. Joseph Dorfman (New York: Columbia University Press, 1954), 3–54. For another reformist perspective, see E. L. Godkin, *Problems of Modern Democracy,* ed. Morton Keller (Cambridge: Harvard University Press, 1966). In general, see John G. Sproat, *The Best Men: Liberal Reformers in the Gilded Age* (New York: Oxford University Press, 1968).

Because of their size, capital, and national reach, the railroads provide an excellent case through which to relate the story of the jerky expansion of the American state. After the Civil War, the railroads had speedily laid their lines across the country. With the help of the government, between 1865 and 1875 trackage more than doubled to over seventy-four thousand miles. Widespread corruption in the state subsidization of canals had discredited this form of activism before the war, but the new power and zeal of the postwar government overwhelmed any old reluctance; proponents also noted that government-sponsored railroad construction was creating an economic boom. In the ten years after 1862, the federal government gave away approximately one hundred million acres of land and $100 million in bonds and loans to the largest railroad companies. State and local legislatures added to this bounty, passing literally hundreds of proposals to aid railroad construction.[44]

With government aid came government regulation. James Garfield approvingly quoted E. L. Godkin, who observed that "the locomotive is coming into contact with the framework of our institutions. In this country of simple government, the most powerful centralizing force which civilization has yet produced must, within the next score years, assume its relations to that political machinery which is to control and regulate it."[45] The initial impetus toward regulation, however, was not nearly so philosophical. Large railroad companies had begun "pooling"—forming cartels—and price-fixing to enhance profits, raising concerns for the farmers of the west and south who were so dependent on the railroads for transport of their goods, though easterners also had reasons for wanting regulation. State legislation banning rate discrimination and unrealistic pricing might have been sufficient to end the practice. But the Supreme Court decided it would be the final arbiter of state powers over interstate business in general and the railroads in particular, and by the 1890s the federal courts had become the primary authority controlling the railroads. Although the Supreme Court had a strong bias in favor of an unfettered free market, it tended to support nationalizing railroad problems and solutions; the majority of Court decisions during the 1880s and 1890s went against the railroad companies.[46] Moreover, federal-court receivership of bankrupt lines shifted

[44] Carter Goodrich, *Government Promotion of AmericanCanals and Railroads, 1800–1890* (Greenwood, Ill.: Greenwood Publishing Group, 1960), 155–85; Edward C. Kirkland, *Industry Comes of Age: Business, Labor, and Public Policy, 1860–1897* (New York: Holt, Rinehart and Winston, 1961), 63–96; Keller, *Affairs of State,* 165–85; and for a most interesting contemporary account, see Charles Francis Adams, *Railroads: Their Origin and Problems* (New York: G. P. Putnam's Sons, 1878).

[45] Quoted in Keller, *Affairs of State,* 177.

[46] On whether this intervention was probusiness or antibusiness, whether it constituted

power away from the states toward the judiciary. Between 1884 and 1896, four hundred lines went into receivership and were being run by court-appointed receivers.[47]

As business became increasingly national in scope, conflicts between the police power of the individual states and that of the federal government grew. By 1899 the Supreme Court had found twenty-nine state laws unconstitutional on the grounds that the "commerce clause" of the Constitution designated the regulation of interstate business the responsibility of the federal government. The various trends away from localism also manifested themselves in pressures on Congress for action. The difficulties of handling the growing railroad industry within the confines of state regulations led, in large part, to the passage of the Interstate Commerce Act of 1887. The act's major purpose was to prevent pooling, rate discrimination, and other cartel mechanisms. It created the Interstate Commerce Commission (ICC), the first regulatory agency of the federal government, which was composed of five members appointed by the president with the approval of the Senate. The commission had investigative and punitive powers; it could subpoena company records and order payments of compensatory and punitive damages. It met with mixed results, constantly struggling with a Supreme Court that was both jealous of its powers and zealous in its protection of business interests.[48] Yet, with all its problems, the commission was an important step in state-building. As Skowronek says, "The commission's annual reports reveal the first notion of positive government in America emerging simultaneously in theory and practice. . . . It rejected the negative—to police, destroy, or cut and slash; rather it sought to build administrative authority in order to conserve, protect, reconcile, guide, and educate."[49]

Similar concerns about corporate cartels and pools led to the passage of the Sherman Antitrust Act in 1890. The Senate, then considered a millionaires' club, passed this vague bill 52 to 1. While the reasons for its overwhelming passage are still unclear, popular sentiment in favor of government action to regulate big business was certainly key. The enforcement mechanisms of the act proved weak, and the executive

---

judicial overreach, and whether it was weak and ineffective, see Skowronek, *Building a New American State*, 138–50; Beth, *Development of the American Constitution*, 150–52; and Keller, *Affairs of State*, 422–30. The seminal source arguing that the vast majority of regulations favored business is Gabriel Kolko, *Railroads and Regulation, 1877–1916* (New York: W. W. Norton, 1965).

[47] Keller, *Affairs of State*, 425.

[48] As Loren Beth observes, it was "remarkable" that "a laissez-faire oriented Supreme Court should have upheld" the ICC. Beth, *Development of the American Constitution*, 27.

[49] Skowronek, *Building a New American State*, 151, and generally 150–62. The ICC was revived in 1920 as the centerpiece of the Progressive Era's state-building efforts.

branch of the government, through the Justice Department, lacked the administrative reach and power to fulfill its potential. Moreover, the Supreme Court undermined the act with its 1895 decision in *U.S. v. E. C. Knight* by so narrowly defining "commerce" as to exclude manufacturing enterprises. While ideology had much to do with the Supreme Court's efforts to keep Congress and, to a lesser extent, the president ineffective, the structure of the American state certainly provided a rationale. With three equal branches, any growth in the power of one was seen as a threat by the others.

Many of the early regulatory efforts were fairly ineffective in terms of their stated mission. But even the ICC—a classic example of industry capture of a regulatory agency—added to the power of the central government. With each new piece of legislation, with each new bureaucratic organization, Congress and the states were further removed from direct control over national policy. The central government may not have acted completely autonomously as powerful businessmen, interest groups, and political parties twisted officials' arms, but its position had certainly improved vis-à-vis its chief competition. Many reformers made explicit the goal of restricting the powers of the states and Congress to the benefit of the federal administration and the courts; Henry Adams supported regulation and even state ownership of railroads because of "the great and growing incompetence so manifest in the national Congress."[50] Congress, in turn, regularly sought to nullify the Court's encroachment into what it regarded as purely administrative and regulatory affairs. The result was a seesaw pattern of state-building. But despite this struggle, or perhaps because of it, the branch of government that benefited most from the late-nineteenth-century trend toward nationalization and regulation was the presidency.

THE INFANCY OF THE IMPERIAL PRESIDENCY

One important source of support for centralization was increasing frustration with the corruption and inefficiency of the late-nineteenth-century American state and, as a result, with Congress. This "party state" appalled foreign observers as it did mugwump reformers. Friedrich Engels wrote on a visit to the United States in 1891, "we find here two great gangs of political speculators, who alternately take possession of state power and exploit it by the most corrupt ends—and the nation is powerless against those two great cartels of politicians, who are ostensi-

[50] Keller, *Affairs of State*, 179; Henry Adams, "The Government and the Railroad Companies," *North American Review* 112 (January 1871): 35.

bly its servants, but in reality dominate and plunder it."[51] Reducing the influence of the parties required professionalizing the government, for appointments had for decades been determined by party politics and congressional patronage. And the only way to reform the bureaucracy while preserving democracy was, in the view of the reformers, to strengthen the power of the president. The president was not admired for his powers of action; he became primarily a negative symbol, personifying the absence of petty favors, pork-barrel politics, and local demands.[52] While reformers trumpeted the virtues of the presidency, the congressional bid for supremacy petered out and the occupants of the White House began once again to assert presidential prerogatives. While Congress, unable to govern with the unity and dispatch required in this turbulent era, fell sharply in the public's esteem, the president became an increasingly popular figure. Lord Bryce noticed in 1882 that "the tendency everywhere in America to concentrate power and responsibility in one man is unmistakable." He predicted that despite the low point to which the office had fallen, "there may . . . be still undeveloped possibilities of greatness in store for the presidents of the future."[53]

The President versus Congress

The balance of power between Congress and the White House began shifting in the late 1870s. As Wilfred Binkley writes, "When Grant retired from the presidency, no one, in or out of the Senate, could have believed it possible that within the following decade the Executive would four times successfully challenge and decisively repulse the Senate in its pretension of control over the executive."[54] Whether or not one accepts that particular number, the growth of presidential power in the twenty years after Grant is undeniable. Leonard White lists five arenas in which Congress and the White House struggled for power, with the president winning significant victories in each: executive independence in cabinet nominations; executive independence in appointments in general; congressional attempts to dictate policy and the assertion of the president's veto power; executive independence in the

---

[51] Quoted in Skowronek, *Building a New American State*, 40. For the classic indictment, see Matthew Josephson, *The Politicos, 1865–1896* (New York: Harcourt, Brace and World, 1963).

[52] The pivotal change in the image of the presidency as a policy initiator came later, probably with Theodore Roosevelt.

[53] Bryce, *The American Commonwealth*, 2:712–13.

[54] Wilfred E. Binkley, *President and Congress* (New York: Vintage Books, 1962), 186.

dismissal of officials; and the somewhat intangible shift in policy leadership from the legislative to the executive branch.[55]

(1) The first conflict arose almost at the start of Rutherford B. Hayes's term.[56] Until Hayes, the standard presidential practice regarding cabinet appointments had been simply to ratify congressional recommendations. Many congressmen believed this power was their constitutional right. The Speaker of the House, Thaddeus Stevens, explained that "Congress was the supreme department of the Government and must be recognized as the supreme power. Members of Congress must be permitted to exercise executive duties. The legislative department must control the action of the Government, prescribe its policy, its measures, and dictate appointments to the executive, or subordinate, department."[57] Grant had meekly acquiesced to Congress on this matter. He told a journalist after his retirement, "It has become the habit of Congressmen to share with the Executive in the responsibility of appointments. It is unjust to say that this habit is necessarily corrupt. It is simply a custom that has grown up, a fact that cannot be ignored. The President very rarely appoints, he merely registers the appointments of members of Congress."[58]

Congress had assumed that Hayes, given his shaky accession to the White House, would prove as amenable to its wishes as Grant had been. But Hayes, a three-term governor of Ohio with an unblemished reputation, was determined to appoint an administration free of political hacks, whether from Grant's administration or from Congress and its circles. The list of cabinet appointees he submitted to the Senate totally disregarded the requests of several important senators. Chief among the outraged were Roscoe Conkling of New York, Simon Cameron of Pennsylvania, and James G. Blaine of Maine, all of whom wanted their cronies appointed to the prize positions. Even worse from the point of view of party hands, Hayes had not placed key Republicans in positions of power. Most appointees were simply prominent citizens with good reputations: the reformers William Evarts—Conkling's bête noire—and Carl Schurz were named secretary of state and secretary of the interior respectively. Hayes removed appointments from the realm of party politics, transforming them into a contest between the presi-

[55] White, *The Republican Era*, 28.

[56] This account can be found in Binkley, *President and Congress*, 188–91; Rexford G. Tugwell, *The Enlargement of the Presidency* (New York: Doubleday, 1960), 207–12; and Charles Smith Williams, *The Life of Rutherford B. Hayes* (Boston: Houghton Mifflin, 1914), 2:26–29.

[57] Gideon Welles, *Diary of Gideon Welles, Secretary of the Navy under Lincoln and Johnson* (Boston: Houghton Mifflin, 1911), 2:426.

[58] Quoted in White, *The Republican Era*, 24.

dency and Congress. The Senate began delaying the confirmation process and made it known that none of the nominations was likely to be approved. It even refused to accord the traditional senatorial courtesy—confirmation without inquiry—to Senator John Sherman, who had been appointed secretary of the treasury. The battle lines had been drawn.

The events that followed stunned most political observers. Public support began to gather behind the president even though he was not personally popular. Editorials in leading newspapers branded the Senate's tactics a dictatorial usurpation of power and praised the high caliber of Hayes's nominees. Telegrams and letters flooded the White House and the offices of senators and congressmen. Mass meetings were organized in major cities and resolutions were passed urging the president to stand firm. In a last-ditch effort, the Republican leadership sought an alliance with the Southern Democrats to defeat the nominations, but the Southerners were not about to cripple the presidency of a man who had pledged to end martial law in the South. The confirmations were all approved easily. "For the first time since the Civil War the Senate had been vanquished on a clear-cut issue between it and the President. The upper House had passed its zenith."[59]

(2) Emboldened by his victory, Hayes decided to press forward on an even more troublesome front and challenge the party patronage system that maintained a tight hold on most government positions.[60] He directed the secretary of the treasury to establish a commission that would investigate the corruption and waste resulting from the spoils system. Hayes then issued an executive order forbidding federal officeholders from participating in party politics. When one senior official—a fellow Republican, Alonzo Cornell of the New York Customhouse—defied this order by presiding over a Republican Party convention, Hayes demanded the resignations of Cornell and two colleagues from the customhouse, including the collector, future president Chester Arthur. They refused to resign, but Hayes sent the names of their three successors to the Senate. Hayes was again confronting the Senate over the question of the power of appointment, but this time he was stepping even more firmly on the turf of its strongest leader, Roscoe Conkling.

The port of New York was the lifeline of American government, generating well over half of all federal revenues. It employed over a thousand people and was therefore also the base of Conkling's political

---

[59] Binkley, *President and Congress,* 190.

[60] For a lively, though biased (anti-Senate), account see Josephson, *The Politicos,* 238–75; also see H. Wayne Morgan, *From Hayes to McKinley: National Party Politics, 1877–1896* (Syracuse, N.Y.: Syracuse University Press, 1969), 31–40.

power. "More than any other single office, the New York Customhouse symbolized the fusion between party and state."[61] Conkling tried to ignore the new nominations under the 1867 Tenure of Office Act, which required the Senate to approve not merely the appointment but also the dismissal of any federal officeholder, and he succeeded in delaying the confirmation process considerably. But Conkling eventually had to yield. Public opinion supported the president, and Secretary of the Treasury John Sherman, under whose jurisdiction the customhouse fell, aggressively lobbied his former colleagues in the Senate to uphold the administration's right of appointment. At the end of his tenure, Hayes viewed his triumph over the spoils system as his greatest achievement: "The end I have chiefly aimed at has been to break down congressional patronage, and especially Senatorial patronage. The contest has been a bitter one. It has exposed me to attack, opposition, misconstruction, and the actual hatred of powerful men. But I have had great success. No member of either house now attempts ever to dictate appointments. My sole right to make appointments is tacitly conceded."[62]

This victory of the executive over Congress had a reprise during the brief presidency of James Garfield.[63] Garfield, who had spent many years in the House, knew that the patronage system would not die easily, and, eager to consolidate the White House's powers, he chose to force a confrontation by nominating an archenemy of Roscoe Conkling, William Robertson, to the collectorship of the port of New York. Garfield recognized that he had thrown down the gauntlet. "This [nomination]," the president wrote to a friend, "brings on the contest at once and will settle the question whether the President is the registering clerk of the Senate or the Executive of the United States. Summed up in a single sentence this is the question: shall the principal port of entry in which more than ninety percent of our custom duties are collected be under the control of the administration or under the local control of the factional senator."[64] The factional senator in question, Roscoe Conkling, pressured his fellow senators to reject the president's nominee, and he met with some success; the Senate agreed to confirm the nominations of all except Robertson. But Garfield, advised by former senator James Blaine, now secretary of state, outwitted the Senate.[65] Before the upper

---

[61] Skowronek, *Building a New American State*, 61.

[62] Quoted in White, *The Republican Era*, 34.

[63] Justus D. Doenecke, *The Presidencies of James A. Garfield and Chester A. Arthur* (Lawrence: Regents Press of Kansas, 1981), 42–5.

[64] Quoted in Binkley, *President and Congress*, 195.

[65] This incident provides strong evidence for bureaucratic theories that posit that "where you stand is where you sit." Not only did Garfield's move from the House of Representatives to the White House convert him within weeks into a staunch defender

house could actually approve the bulk of the nominations, Garfield withdrew them, forcing the senators to vote up or down on Robertson. Much to Conkling's chagrin, the Senate approved the nomination. A frustrated Conkling sought to reverse this presidential "usurpation" of power by turning to the public for support. Both of New York's senators resigned and hoped to receive vindication of their positions through reelection. To their great shock, however, the New York State Legislature, sensing the public mood, repudiated them. The patronage power of the Senate had been dealt a serious blow.

(3) The third battle between Hayes's executive branch and Congress shifted the focus to the lower house.[66] The House of Representatives had periodically asserted its authority against Presidents Johnson and Grant. During Johnson's term, the House had vigorously debated whether to appropriate money for the purchase of Alaska, even though the Senate had ratified the treaty, and had shortly thereafter passed a resolution refusing to pay for any future purchases of territory. Now the Democratic majority sought to manipulate the House's critical role in the appropriations process to shift the power of policymaking away from the White House. It attached a rider to the 1879 Bill of Appropriations for the Army declaring that certain policies had to be discontinued or funds would be withheld. Outraged that the Democrats would abuse the rider provision to dictate policy to a department, Hayes vetoed the bill. In his veto message, the president made clear that this was not merely a partisan political quarrel, that his chief objection was to the usurpation of the executive's constitutional authority. The House had overstepped its bounds, and Hayes spelled out the danger inherent in such a precedent: "[T]he House may on the same principle determine that any other act of Congress, a treaty made by the President with the advice and consent of the Senate, a nomination or appointment to office, or a decision or opinion of the Supreme Court is a grievance, and that the measure of redress is to withhold appropriations required for the support of the offending branch of government."[67] The House refused to capitulate, but Hayes persisted, vetoing seven successive versions of the bill. Again the press and public were persuaded by Hayes's arguments and backed his case for stronger presidential authority. The House eventually withdrew the offending rider and passed the Army

---

and enlarger of presidential powers, but two senior senators, Sherman and Blaine, underwent similar transformations.

[66] See Binkley, *President and Congress*, 209–15; and Morgan, *From Hayes to McKinley*, 52–54.

[67] James D. Richardson, *A Compilation of the Messages and Papers of the Presidents* (Washington, D.C.: Bureau of National Literature, 1911), 3:531–32.

appropriations bill, saving face by withholding $600,000 of the $46 million.

While dramatic, Hayes's use of the veto was well within the postwar pattern. He exercised his veto twelve times; Arthur used it only four times, and Grant had turned to it forty-three times in his two terms. But it was Grover Cleveland who most expanded the president's veto power, striking down 301 bills in his first term alone. He transformed the veto from an emergency power used only in extreme circumstances into a device used whenever the president disagreed strongly with a bill passed by Congress. Most of his vetoes were cast for partisan reasons against pension bills for Civil War veterans, though even excluding them he rejected many more bills than the previous four presidents combined.[68] Although Cleveland often asserted his veto power for partisan purposes, he also strengthened the authority of the executive branch vis-à-vis Congress, and by targeting the pension bills, he struck directly at an important source of congressional power and patronage. Representatives and senators often passed bills providing pension benefits to specific veterans who had, after careful examination, been deemed unqualified by the Pension Bureau. By training his veto on this prominent example of congressional patronage and by using, perhaps even overusing, the veto—his successors would not be quite so cavalier—a Democratic chief executive enlarged the presidency even though he was, in terms of both party and personal ideology, committed to the opposite position.

(4) Cleveland further strengthened the executive branch by finally burying the Tenure of Office Act of 1867.[69] Though all presidents after Grant had opposed the act, none had posed a direct challenge to it until Cleveland. He ordered his departments to discontinue the practice of sending the Senate files on both appointments and dismissals. The latter, he claimed, were no concern of the legislative body. The senators and Cleveland fought each other vigorously, trading the parliamentary maneuvers Hayes and Garfield had used to such effect, but Cleveland went still further. He attacked the act directly, declaring it unconstitutional in his March 1886 message to Congress (the Supreme Court later concurred) and contending that the Senate's demand of executive-department files constituted a breach of the separation of powers. One of Cleveland's biographers characterizes his blanket assertion that the files were the personal property of the president as "the most extreme assertion of executive privilege by any peacetime president prior to Richard

<hr/>

[68] White, *The Republican Era*, 39; Richard E. Welch, Jr., *The Presidencies of Grover Cleveland* (Lawrence: University Press of Kansas, 1988), 62–65.

[69] See Tugwell, *Enlargement of the Presidency*, 239–41.

M. Nixon."[70] The political atmosphere had indeed changed: not only did Cleveland win battles over particular dismissals, but one year later Congress repealed the Tenure of Office Act.

(5) More broadly, Cleveland's struggle helped create a very different presidency at the expense of the legislative branch. Under Cleveland's leadership, the president became an initiator of national policy rather than a "mere onlooker," as he had seemed during previous postwar administrations.[71] During the Johnson and Grant presidencies, all in Washington had viewed the executive branch as a cluster of departments, with the head of each responsible to Congress. The secretaries, directors, and other administrators developed independent relationships with the corresponding congressional committees, to which they were answerable on matters of great detail. Thanks in large part to Cleveland's efforts, by the late 1880s it was becoming increasingly common to ask the White House's opinion of particular proposals, on the assumption that if the president disagreed with them, they were not likely to become law. The challenges to congressional patronage that especially Hayes and Cleveland undertook profoundly altered the public's perceptions of the legislative and executive branches, converting the postwar president into a critical participant in the policymaking process. But the movement for reform of the national bureaucracy played an equally important role in fashioning the image of the president as an honest broker in Washington. And it also greatly increased his capacity to effect change.

Civil Service Reform

Both before and after the Civil War, Congress exerted enormous influence on the executive branch chiefly through party patronage. Federal bureaucrats were beholden to the party, and through them Congress influenced both day-to-day matters and broad policies. The Federalist tradition of a permanent civil service, free of party obligations, had been abolished by President Andrew Jackson in the 1820s. The system that replaced it rotated appointments with each shift in party fortunes and placed a premium on political skills and loyalties. The result, argued advocates of civil service reform, was a degradation of standards and a rise in incompetence. In 1868 the National Manufacturers Association passed a resolution that affirmed that "for the integrity and permanence of our government it is indispensable that public affairs be

---

[70] Welch, *Presidencies of Grover Cleveland*, 217.
[71] White, *The Republican Era*, 47.

conducted on business principles, and that the dangerous custom of giving public posts to political paupers and partisan servants, regardless of
their fitness, should be discontinued."[72] Reform threatened the very essence of the patronage system, and opposition was fierce in Congress
and the party machines. As Carl Schurz observed at the time, "A very
large majority of the professional politicians of both parties continue to
hate civil service reform with a sincere and robust hatred, because it
threatens to spoil their business, to throw their arts out of the market,
and to deprive them of their plunder."[73] One such politician, Congressman William Williams of Indiana, charged that the idea of civil service
reform was copied "openly, boldly, and without disguise from monarchical governments. . . . [It is] totally anti-republican and subversive of
elected government."[74]

Given such strong opposition within the traditional loci of power,
progress toward reform was halting. In 1871 President Grant appointed
the first Civil Service Commission, but four years later it was suspended
when Congress refused to provide further funding. Congressional hostility to the commission grew once it became clear that it would not
readily cave in to Congress's whims but was instead an instrument of
presidential authority.[75] Presidents supported civil service reform largely
because it would benefit them in their struggle with Congress. As
Rutherford Hayes explained, "It has seemed to me that as Executive I
could advance the reform of the civil service in no way so effectively
as by rescuing the power of appointing to office from congressional
leaders."[76]

A stalemate continued through the 1870s, but the reformers—mostly
influential lawyers, businessmen, journalists, and politicians—persisted
and in 1881 founded the National Civil Service Reform League.[77] Popular support for reform had been gaining ground and was immeasurably
expanded by the assassination of James Garfield in 1881 by a frustrated
and enraged office-seeker. Upon his death, the league launched a nationwide campaign declaring this tragedy the natural culmination of the
corrupt patronage system. The late president was turned, somewhat dis-
ingenuously, into a martyr for the reform movement; his every word in
favor of reform was emblazoned on league posters. The tactic worked,

[72] Quoted in White, *The Republican Era*, 297.
[73] Carl Schurz, "Civil Service Reform," *North American Review* 134 (1882):451.
[74] Quoted in White, *The Republican Era*, 291–92; also see generally Josephson, *The Politicos*.
[75] Skowronek, *Building a New American State*, 58.
[76] Quoted in White, *The Republican Era*, 34.
[77] Frank M. Stewart, *The National Civil Service Reform League: History, Activities, and Problems* (Austin: University of Texas Press, 1929).

and public anger with the system became evident in every part of the country. After lengthy debate and bargaining, the Civil Service Reform Act of 1883—also known as the Pendleton Act after its sponsor, Senator George Pendleton of Ohio—was passed by Congress and signed by President Chester Arthur, who, ironically, was a prime product of the system he was helping to destroy. It established a new Civil Service Commission with three members appointed by the president and confirmed by the Senate, but the president could dismiss them at his pleasure. The centerpiece of the act was a merit-based system for the civil service, which established open competitive examinations and largely ensured insulation from the political process.[78] The commission was charged chiefly with screening applicants for positions, but it was also asked to recommend rules governing the civil service, conduct investigations of violations of the meritocratic system, and produce an annual report. The president and his department heads were given the power of enforcement of these provisions. Congress had once viewed the federal bureaucracy as its fiefdom, but the Civil Service Reform Act recognized it as an "integral segment of the executive branch."[79]

The existence of a Civil Service Commission did not in and of itself transform the U.S. government or the balance of power between the president and Congress. Repeatedly and in various ways, Congress undermined the commission, and while all presidents were officially supportive of civil service reform, political realities forced them to concede ground to political patronage.[80] In the end, the commission only incrementally eroded patronage. The passage of the Pendleton Act in 1883 was nevertheless a landmark event in the history of the U.S. government. With all its problems, it greatly expanded the role of a professional civil service answerable to the president and placed it at the core of the federal government. In 1883 the act applied to only 14,000 of the approximately 100,000 federal employees. By 1900 it extended to approximately 100,000 people, half of the federal government's full-time staff. More than mere administrative reform, the reforms of the Civil Service "contained the first institutional recognition of the President as the active head of the administrative system." These reforms were only part of an ongoing series of assaults on graft, inefficiency, and pa-

[78] Reformers were disappointed that the act did not create a system based entirely on merit. Amendments allowed for geographic distribution of appointments and preferential treatment for Civil War veterans.

[79] White, *The Republican Era*, 302. The best account is in Skowronek, *Building a New American State*, 47–84; but also see Ari A. Hoogenboom, *Outlawing the Spoils: A History of the Civil Service Reform Movement, 1865–1883* (Urbana: University of Illinois Press, 1968).

[80] This is best dealt with in Skowronek, *Building a New American State*, 68–84.

tronage. Congress's own Dockery-Cockrell Commission (1893–95) called for the implementation of businesslike practices and professionalism in all branches of government. Such moves, which culminated in President William Howard Taft's Commission on Economy and Efficiency, were "visible symbols not only of a transfer of initiative for administrative reform from the legislative to the executive branch, but also of the tipping of the constitutional balance from Congress to the President of the United States. This shift was momentous and was not reversed."[81] Students of the development of the state generally argue that institutional reform is occasioned by crisis conditions.[82] But, as this examination of the civil service reform movement demonstrates, "[n]o major historical event of the late 1860s or the 1870s could be said to cry out that the republic was endangered by the patronage system. . . . an end to the spoils system was not the solution to any specific institution-grinding crisis."[83]

Emergency Powers

Chicago's long, hot summer of 1894 provided the backdrop for one of the most public and violent struggles for constitutional authority in American history. To be sure, the Pullman strike was, like most strikes, chiefly about the relations between business and labor. But it resulted in an important extension of the powers of the president at the expense of state governments.[84] At the trough of the depression of 1893, the railroad manufacturing tycoon George Pullman decided to cut wages drastically to keep profits steady at his Pullman Car Company. The workers struck, and Pullman countered by closing the factory. It was a pivotal moment in American labor history because the American Railway Union (ARU), promising collective action against individual businesses, had been founded by Eugene V. Debs only the year before. By the summer of 1894, the ARU claimed 150,000 members in 465 local unions. The Pullman strike soon turned into a general railroad strike as Debs directed ARU members to refuse to work in any capacity on Pullman

[81] White, *The Republican Era*, 364, 92.

[82] See chapter 2.

[83] Bernard S. Silberman, *Cages of Reason: The Rise of the Rational State in France, Japan, the United States, and Great Britain* (Chicago: University of Chicago Press, 1993), 27.

[84] The best brief account of Cleveland's response to the 1894 strike can be found in Welch, *Presidencies of Grover Cleveland*, 141–56. For a well-written, thorough, but overly sympathetic view, see Allan Nevins, *Grover Cleveland: A Study in Courage* (New York: Dodd, Mead, 1932), 620–30. Also see an interesting monograph by Bennett M. Rich, *The Presidents and Civil Disorder* (Washington, D.C.: Brookings Institution, 1941).

cars. In weeks, rail traffic in and out of Chicago was at 10 percent of its usual volume.

The Pullman strike gained national attention. The railroad owners declared it a threat to law and order. Newspapers agreed; the *Chicago Tribune* called Debs an anarchist. Richard Olney, Cleveland's attorney general, concurred with the railroads. That he came to this conclusion with ease and full conviction was surely aided by his career as a railroad lawyer; in fact, Olney was still on retainer from one railroad company.[85] To prevent what he saw as a breakdown of normal business, Olney obtained "perhaps the most sweeping injunction ever issued by a federal court in a labor-management dispute." The Federal District Court of Chicago outlawed all actions that could result in work stoppages on any train engaged in the delivery of mail or any action that could "interfere with the free and unhindered transportation of interstate commerce."[86] When local officials proved unable to enforce the injunction, Cleveland instructed the secretary of war to send federal troops to Chicago, justifying his action as mandated by his constitutional duties to execute the law and protect life and property. After four days of heightened violence, the troops were finally able to subdue the strikers and restore order to the city.

While the scope of Cleveland's action was large, that was not what made it unprecedented. Rutherford Hayes had used troops to restore order in a railroad strike in 1877. The difference was that Cleveland had acted unilaterally; he had not waited for the governor of Illinois to request assistance. Governor John Peter Altgeld was outraged by Cleveland's actions and wrote to the president to protest this usurpation of state power. He even spoke out publicly against the president, declaring his behavior unconstitutional. And, indeed, the plain meaning of the Constitution appeared to support the governor's interpretation. The relevant passage reads, "The United States shall guarantee to every State in this Union a republican form of government, and shall protect each of them against invasion; and on application of the legislature, or of the Executive (when the Legislature cannot be convened), against domestic violence."[87] Neither Altgeld nor the state legislature had applied for federal protection. Cleveland's dismissive response was that he saw an emergency and acted. He claimed he had a duty to act once he had conclusively determined that "the process of the Federal courts could not be executed through ordinary means, and upon competent proof

---

[85] Allan Nevins sees Olney as the mastermind behind the entire operation, with Cleveland simply acquiescing to his wishes. See his *Grover Cleveland,* 626.

[86] Welch, *Presidencies of Grover Cleveland,* 144.

[87] U.S. Constitution, Article IV, Section 4.

that conspiracies existed against commerce between the States."[88] In other words, the president's perception of an emergency was grounds enough to overrule the local authorities.

Regardless of the legality of this extension of presidential authority, more important for our purposes is the overwhelming evidence that the American people strongly supported Cleveland. One newspaper captured public sentiment in cornball verse:

> The railroad strike played merry hob,
> The land was set aflame;
> Could Grover order out the troops
> To block the strikers' game?
> One Altgeld yelled excitedly,
> "Such tactics I forbid;
> You can't trot out those soldiers," yet
> That's just what Grover did.
>
> In after years when people talk
> Of present stirring times,
> And of the actions needful to
> Sit down on Public crimes,
> They'll all of them acknowledge then
> (The fact cannot be hid)
> That whatever was the best to do
> Is just what Grover did.[89]

Cleveland had run for the White House in 1884 on the usual Democratic platform, trumpeting the rights and sovereignty of state governments. One of his chief themes had been the dangers of the centralization of power in the national government and the presidency. Once president, however, particularly in his second term, he became perhaps the most important enlarger of that office's power since Abraham Lincoln. Cleveland explained the duties of his office to the public in lofty terms. He asserted that as their national leader, as the only official elected by the entire citizenry, he had a special responsibility to them, that he held a position above the partisan bickering of Congress and the myopic interests of the states. With Grover Cleveland, the Democratic conception of the presidency came full circle, returning to the broad interpretation Andrew Jackson had put forth half a century earlier.

---

[88] Quoted in Welch, *Presidencies of Grover Cleveland*, 147.
[89] Ibid.

THE INSTRUMENTS OF FOREIGN RELATIONS

The bureaucracies dealing with foreign and military policy reflected these shifts toward a stronger central administration and a stronger presidency, but the changes in these agencies were less striking. Since the days of George Washington, Americans had viewed foreign affairs as a suspicious enterprise and certainly one that did not require much in the way of government bureaucracy or expenditure. This hostility was not simply a result of the peaceful international environment in which the United States found itself in the late nineteenth century. During its early years, the fledgling nation was in constant danger from great-power neighbors, whose possessions on the continent dwarfed the original thirteen colonies in both physical size and military power. During that era, the United States jockeyed for resources and territory, gaining vast tracts of land in the 1803 Louisiana Purchase through negotiations with the French and Spanish. It fought mighty Britain in 1812, wrested Texas and California from Mexico, and, finally, mobilized itself for the highly industrialized Civil War, during which the North maneuvered to keep Britain and France from openly allying with the Confederacy. Through all this turmoil, Americans continued to believe that their foreign and defense policies were minimal and could be conducted with a small permanent bureaucracy. Even after the Spanish-American War, important organizational changes had to wait for the Progressive movement's zenith and the appointment of a reformer like Elihu Root as secretary of war and then of state. The reason for the long absence of highly developed foreign policy institutions was as much America's antistatist tradition as the lack of foreign and military pressures. Other states with fewer obvious threats, such as Japan and Italy in the late nineteenth century, nevertheless constructed significant foreign and military bureaucracies. Moreover, while the government could not regulate the national economy without an extensive system of bureaucratic controls, a similar apparatus was not seen as crucial to the making of foreign policy. America's weak institutional framework had not stymied presidents and secretaries of state when they sought to forge ahead with a more activist diplomacy or an expansion of American influence abroad.

State power, however, is not assessed by simply counting the number of bureaucrats at work in the foreign service. By the 1890s, the central government and the executive branch had gained broader constitutional authority, greater political power, and increased public legitimacy, making the execution of a unified, and often activist, foreign policy more likely. The absence of these aspects of presidential power and federal authority, not the paucity of clerks in the State Department, was the primary cause of the underexpansion between 1865 and 1889. Nevertheless, bureaucracies are important because, largely through the implementation of orders delivered from above, they daily have an effect on foreign policy. And the foreign policy and military bureaucracies were enlarged and revamped, albeit in the jerky, state-building-as-patchwork style of late-nineteenth-century America.

Foreign Services

The changes in the foreign policy bureaucracies—the diplomatic service, the consular service, and the State Department itself—were part and parcel of the civil service reform movement.[90] In the heyday of untrammeled commerce, nobody understood why the country needed a diplomatic corps in the first place, and enlargement of the foreign service was impossible. Even an ardent civil service reformer like E. L. Godkin suggested that the invention of the telegraph should allow one minister in Paris to replace all American delegations on the continent of Europe.[91] In an antistatist society, suspicious of European great powers and their machinations, the diplomatic profession was viewed with the greatest of unease. It was called variously a "costly luxury," a "relic of medieval monarchical trumpery," and a "nurse of snobs."

But the widespread criticism of the foreign service in the 1870s and 1880s was unrelated to Americans' general hostility. It was just one aspect of the broader civil service reform movement. Leading progressive activists called for the reform of the foreign service as they called for greater honesty, efficiency, and professionalism throughout America's administration. While some discussion referred to America's growing needs and involvements abroad, the reformers' writings on the diplomatic and consular services mainly stressed the ills of corruption, the spoils system, and the "baleful influence of politics." When President Hayes asked Dorman Eaton, the country's leading civil service reformer, to consider how to revamp the foreign service along British lines, Eaton's recommendations were the same as those for the civil service as

---

[90] The two most complete accounts of foreign service reform are Warren Frederick Ilchman, *Professional Diplomacy in the United States, 1779–1939* (Chicago: University of Chicago Press, 1961); and Richard Hume Werking, *The Master Architects: Building the United States Foreign Service, 1890–1913* (Lexington: University Press of Kentucky, 1977).

[91] Milton Plesur, *America's Outward Thrust: Approaches to Foreign Affairs, 1865–1890* (De Kalb: Northern Illinois University Press, 1971), 37.

a whole: security of tenure, promotion by merit, and entrance examinations.[92] In other words, domestic, not foreign, concerns drove this movement.[93]

However, reform of the diplomatic and consular services lagged behind reform of the civil service as a whole. The constituency for a more professional diplomatic corps was dispersed abroad, not concentrated at home, and Congress consequently had little impetus to act. Moreover, once the regular civil service had rid itself to some degree of political appointments, foreign postings became one of the few havens for the spoils system, and Congress was reluctant to eliminate this last bastion of patronage. Finally, some raised genuine concerns that depoliticizing the diplomatic service might rob the country of its most effective diplomats. The United States had a long tradition of distinguished politicians serving as diplomats, from Benjamin Franklin and Thomas Jefferson to Charles Francis Adams and John Hay. Even some advocates of reform urged that political appointments be retained for the highest levels of diplomacy.[94] For all these reasons, the Morgan bill of 1894, which incorporated most of Eaton's recommendations, repeatedly failed to garner sufficient support in Congress for passage, and a diplomatic and consular reform bill was passed only in 1906.

The pace may have been slower, but there was significant reform nonetheless. From the late 1880s onward, Congress annually considered various proposals for streamlining the system. Funding was increased, especially for the consular service, which had a business constituency at home and was regarded as fairly useful by most Americans. Congress did increase the salaries of diplomats, a key request of many reformers who wanted the talented rather than just the wealthy to embrace diplomatic careers. Congress also modestly increased the numbers of embassies and consuls, and secretaries to legations. This last change was important. Since ambassadors were often political hacks, the first and second secretaries were in many ways the most important officers posted abroad. For many years the number of these posts had been stuck at twenty-four; by 1905 it had doubled to forty-eight. Over congressional objections, presidents unilaterally moved to professionalize

[92] Dorman B. Eaton, *Civil Service in Great Britain: A History of Abuses and Reform and Their Bearing on American Politics* (New York: Harper and Brothers, 1880), 311.

[93] Ilchman, *Professional Diplomacy in the United States*, 41–85; and Plesur, *America's Outward Thrust*, 35. The debate about the foreign service was widespread by the 1880s. See, as leading examples, Eugene Schuyler, *American Diplomacy and the Furtherance of Commerce* (New York: Scribners, 1886); "Diplomacy," *International Review* 6 (January 1879); "The Diplomatic and Consular Service," *New York Herald*, April 10, 1880; and *Public Opinion* 6 (February 9, 1889): 367.

[94] Ilchman, *Professional Diplomacy in the United States*, 46.

the services.[95] Turnover, traditionally high at the start of an administration, declined significantly from 1889 onward as presidents chose to keep on and promote long-standing foreign service officers.[96] By the late 1890s, the foreign service was significantly larger, more permanent, and less corrupt than it had been just ten years earlier.

Armed Forces

In 1874 the authorized regular armed forces of the United States of America numbered 25,000 enlisted men and 2,161 officers; the actual force was even smaller. Immediately after the Civil War, an army of any significant size was seen as unnecessary. This view was fueled less by a rational reading of the international balance of threats and opportunities than by simple, old-fashioned antistatism. As Samuel Huntington writes, "Underlying all was the American distrust of government and the belief that the military along with the civil branches of the public service were inherently inefficient and largely unnecessary."[97] In reality, given the tasks that had been assigned to the military, the construction of a standing army should have been a priority. The military had been charged with "taming" the West, and the two decades after the Civil War were marked by a series of intense battles with Indian tribes. Because of its overwhelming technological superiority, the U.S. Army usually triumphed, but it often suffered horrifying losses, in no small part because it was poorly staffed, poorly equipped, and poorly managed.[98]

By the 1880s, a segment of the public began to accept the view that the United States required a larger and better-trained armed forces. Once again, this realization did not stem from international conditions, but from the massive changes wrought by industrialization. The late nineteenth century was a time of peace for America in terms of its relations with the outside world, but it was also a time of internal war. During the last two decades of the century, the United States experienced labor-management violence on a scale unlike anything before or

[95] See Werking, *The Master Architects*, 59.

[96] Ilchman, *Professional Diplomacy in the United States*, 70–82; Werking, *The Master Architects*, 20–44.

[97] Samuel P. Huntington, *The Soldier and the State: The Theory and Politics of Civil-Military Relations* (Cambridge: Harvard University Press, 1957), 228.

[98] James Garfield, "The Army of the United States," *North American Review* 126 (1878): 195–98; also see Russell F. Weigley, *History of the United States Army* (Bloomington: Indiana University Press, 1984).

since in the industrial world. The businessman enjoyed widespread sympathy, particularly among the governing classes, and many believed the army should step in to quell this new industrial violence. In 1877 Secretary of War George McCrary offered an analysis with which most members of the political, business, and intellectual elites would have agreed:

> The Army is to the United States what a well-disciplined and trained police force is to a city, and the one is quite as necessary as the other. As our country increases its population and wealth, and as great cities become numerous it must be clearly seen that there may be great dangers of uprisings of large masses of people for the redress of grievances, real or fancied; and it is a well known fact that such uprisings enlist in greater or lesser degree the sympathies of the communities in which they occur. This fact alone renders the militia unreliable in such an emergency.[99]

The *New York Times* concurred: "We cannot too soon face the unwelcome fact that we have dangerous social elements to contend with, and they are rendered all the more dangerous by the peculiarities of our political system. There should be no delay in the adoption of measures required to impart to the Federal Government sufficient force for the maintenance of domestic order in any conceivable emergency."[100]

Reforming the military to meet these new challenges turned out to be even more difficult than streamlining the foreign services. Both the army and the navy, especially the former, were imbued with the traditions and vested interests of localism, decentralization, and antistatism. The minuscule national army was theoretically supplemented by autonomous militia units in the states that would, in emergencies, join the regular force. The militia system was utterly chaotic, and its soldiers were poorly trained, if they were trained at all. In times of crisis, the results were slow response time, tremendous waste of resources, and needless loss of lives. On the national level, the forces were equally mismanaged. The army and navy were organized into bureaus that were to report to the secretary of war or the secretary of the navy. With no clear lines of command, the bureau system was a recipe for inefficiency. It was also an invitation for congressional influence, which is why it flourished. Pork-barrel projects were funneled through two main outlets, the Army Corps of Engineers and the Navy Yards. The bureau chiefs had close, independent relationships with their respective congressional committees, creating a bilateral decision-making process that bypassed the secretaries of the army and navy, and even the White House. As Skowro-

[99] Department of War, *Annual Report, 1877,* 1:5–6.
[100] Quoted in Skowronek, *Building a New American State,* 100–101.

nek writes, "In peacetime, even the President's authority over the armed forces took a second place to these horizontal relationships."[101]

Congress's interest in the armed forces was limited to patronage and pork. Outside of these two political uses, it allowed the military to run itself. This laissez-faire attitude allowed for a period of introspection within the military that resulted, by the late 1870s, in a burst of reform proposals at the very time that military retrenchment was popular outside the services. The specifics of the military reform programs came from the armed services' "professional needs not from the international situation."[102] The reformers, much like their civilian counterparts, proposed revamping the military's administrative structure and called for "a concentration of power, a centralization of authority, an insulation of army administration from politics, and a penetration of central controls throughout the territory."[103] Borrowing freely from the Prussian model, military theorist Emory Upton wanted to create a strong general staff that would consolidate control over both the bureaus and the troops.

The navy reformers similarly recognized that the key to the military's problems lay in its mode of organization, not its budget. As reform-minded Secretary of the Navy William Whitney pointed out, "Whatever dissatisfaction the country has experienced with the naval arm of government will be found to have its origin, not in the naval service, but in the naval administration."[104] A friendly critic was more blunt: "There must be something radically wrong with our system of naval administration that it cannot, with four times the expenditure, maintain a navy as efficient as that of Austria."[105] The principal reform proposal was the creation of a "General Board." This board would comprise the bureau chiefs (with perhaps some additional members), and the secretary of the

---

[101] Ibid., 96.

[102] Huntington, *The Soldier and the State,* 265.

[103] Skowronek, *Building a New American State,* 91. The quote is Skowronek's characterization of Emory Upton's reform proposals for the army. Upton's long, dull, but influential work is *The Armies of Asia and Europe* (New York: Appleton, 1878). Huntington argues that "in Europe professionalism was normally the outcome of socio-political currents at work in society at large: the Prussian reformers, for instance, were only doing in the army what Stein and his associates were trying to do for the state as a whole. In the United States, however, military professionalism was strictly self-induced. . . . Professionalism was the reaction of an inherently conservative group against a liberal society, rather than the product of a general conservative reform movement within society." Huntington, *The Soldier and the State,* 233. Yet the military reformers consciously borrowed from the progressive reform movement. They railed against corruption and the spoils system and proposed principles of efficiency and sound management. See Skowronek, *Building a New American State,* 89–92, and fn. 11.

[104] Secretary of the Navy, *Annual Report,* 1885, 1:xxvii.

[105] Henry H. Gorringe, "The Navy," *North American Review* 134 (1882): 486.

navy would serve as the group's chairman. The goal was centralization of power within the organization; the plan sought to place the navy's administration and its sailors under the direct authority of cabinet officers and the White House.

Because the solutions both services offered sought to solve, or at least alleviate, the problems of localism and decentralization, their most ambitious reform programs were impossible to implement. State governors, whose control over their precious militias was threatened by an expanding central authority, opposed the plans, and Congress was not pleased by an end to this ready source of patronage and pork. Not until 1898 was a Naval War Board established. In the case of the army, even the Spanish-American War could not spur it on to comprehensive institutional change. Twelve days before the declaration of war with Spain, the House of Representatives, with the active support of the state governors, defeated a bill that would have expanded the regular army from 27,000 to 104,000. Ad hoc and temporary arrangements prevailed until 1900. And even then it took the effective lobbying of Theodore Roosevelt and his secretary of war Elihu Root to gain a general-staff model and the nationalization of the militia. In the next decade, further administrative reforms on all fronts were passed into law.

The lack of sweeping, comprehensive reform in the late nineteenth century, however, should not obscure the important changes that did take place. The most important was that discussed above: the evolution of reformist thought within the armed forces. The radical reformist ideas bandied about within the military—often among the most conservative of a nation's institutions—in the late 1870s and 1880s took decades to implement, but the long germination period within the armed forces ensured that when national leaders found the political strength to overcome state and congressional opposition, the military could adapt quickly. Also among these important developments was a revolution in military education. In 1884 the Naval War College was founded; by that time the army had already established a series of specialized graduate schools, the most famous of which was at Fort Leavenworth, and West Point had finally been thoroughly professionalized. In 1888 the Office of Naval Intelligence was established, as was, a decade later, the Military Intelligence Division. In 1890 the positions of assistant secretary of the navy and assistant secretary of war, abolished after the Civil War, were reestablished. Mandatory retirement and professional examinations for promotions were introduced into the military services. The White House did establish several ad hoc boards for army and navy affairs, moving control of key issues—coastal fortifications, strategic raw material supplies—out of congressional hands and into those of the professional military and the executive branch. The navy in particular flourished in the 1890s. By 1898, thanks to a string of strong, reform-minded secretaries of the navy like William Whitney and Benjamin Tracy, bipartisan support for naval expansion, internal naval reformers like Steven B. Luce, and most famous of all the strategist Alfred Thayer Mahan, the navy had professionalized itself, had gained a vast fleet and a large budget, and was generally regarded with respect around the world.[106] In 1897 Secretary of the Navy John Long reported that the navy would no longer focus on expansion of its capabilities but would turn to consolidation. Over the last few years, he explained, American naval power had doubled, and "class for class, in power, speed, workmanship, and offensive and defensive qualities," the U.S. Navy was the equal of any in the world.[107]

AS THE STATE GOES, SO GOES FOREIGN POLICY

The course of state-building in the United States was long and bumpy. But as this chapter has shown, the surface appearance of a complete absence of state-building during the late nineteenth century is misleading. Along two important axes of state power—the federal government versus the states and the presidency versus Congress—a profound transformation occurred that shifted important constitutional, political, and popular opinions. Even in the areas least affected—the bureaucracies dealing with foreign and military affairs—significant changes were moving them in the same direction: toward Washington, and within Washington, toward the White House. The Progressive Era's more flamboyant reforms were the culmination of long-standing processes with their roots in the 1880s and 1890s. Without the state-building as "patchwork" that occurred in the closing decades of the nineteenth century, the "reconstitution" of the American state at the dawn of the following century would not have been possible.

These shifts in U.S. state structure were not momentous, certainly not by European standards. But the differences in state structure were important when compared with the period immediately after the Civil War. The Civil War had seen a tremendous expansion of the scope and

[106] White, *The Republican Era*, 134–75; Skowronek, *Building a New American State*, 107–20. On the navy in particular, see John A. S. Grenville and George B. Young, *Politics, Strategy, and American Diplomacy: Studies in Foreign Policy, 1873–1917* (New Haven, Conn.: Yale University Press, 1966), 1–39; Robert Seager, "Ten Years before Mahan: The Unofficial Case for the New Navy, 1880–1890," *Mississippi Valley Historical Review* no. 40, 3 (December 1953): 491–512; and Harold and Margaret Sprout, *The Rise of American Naval Power* (Princeton, N.J.: Princeton University Press, 1939), 183–223.

[107] Secretary of the Navy, *Annual Report, 1897*, 3:40–41.

capacity of the American state. The North's ability to extract resources from the population and industry was the key to its success. Lincoln's suspension of habeas corpus, among the most sacred of America's constitutional guarantees, epitomized the change the war wrought. But the end of the Civil War brought severe retrenchment of the power of government and the power of the executive. Beginning with the end of the failed Reconstruction, Democratic and Republican presidents alike, by challenging Congress and the states, paved the way for William McKinley and Theodore Roosevelt. When McKinley took the helm of the American government, he presided over an executive branch that was, to a limited extent, free of congressional influence and that had begun to exercise its young muscles by expanding its scope of activities within the state. The executive reigned supreme, and John Hay could prevail where William Henry Seward had failed. After 1898, England's *Spectator* believed that the Civil War and the Spanish-American War had shown the presidency to be an "elective monarchy."[108]

Despite these important shifts, American diplomacy did not become highly activist by European standards. But the difference was certainly dramatic by American standards. After 1890 the chief executive of the United States could finally pursue a meaningful foreign policy. Congress would not oppose his every move merely because he had taken the initiative.[109] That great struggle had been clearly resolved. Control of the American state and its extraordinary resources had now firmly passed into the hands of central decision-makers who were attentive to the opportunities the international system presented and to the great power at their disposal rather than to the needs of congressional districts. The incipient strength of the new American state made possible the emergence of the United States onto the world stage in the late 1890s.

[108] Quoted in LaFeber, *American Search for Opportunity,* 177.

[109] Among historians of American foreign relations, Walter LaFeber draws attention to the relationship between the increased power of the executive and the heightened American activism in international affairs during 1865–1913. He also identifies the chief motivation for American foreign policy as the search for "more American power and opportunities." See LaFeber, *American Search for Opportunity,* 235–37, 134–36, 144–45. While this aspect of LaFeber's contribution is important, he is less accurate in explaining the origins of greater presidential power. For LaFeber, U.S. foreign and economic policy in this period produced tremendous disorder abroad, and the military force under the president's purview was needed to exploit such disorder when it served U.S. purposes or to crush it when the United States stood to gain from stability. Ibid., 236–37.

CHAPTER FIVE

The New Diplomacy, 1889–1908

THE EMERGENCE OF A GREAT POWER

THE SECRETARY of the navy's *Annual Report* of 1889 marks a turning point in the history of American foreign relations. In it, Benjamin Tracy proposed that the United States construct two battleship fleets—one for the Pacific, one for the Atlantic—with a total of twenty battleships, sixty cruisers, and twenty coastal monitors, turning America into one of the world's great naval powers. The navy secretary's reasoning was clearly set out in the opening paragraphs of the report. He pointed out that many of Europe's leading states had "less than one-tenth of [America's] population, one-thirtieth of its wealth, and one-hundredth of its area," but, despite its superior resources, the United States did "not rank as a naval power." A chart that compared the naval strength of the world's eleven leading powers emphasized this point. To correct the imbalance between America's power and its low ranking, Tracy advocated a major, sustained naval buildup. Financing this buildup was not considered difficult: "We collect in duties in six months at a single port a greater sum than we could spend in building a new navy in six years." Tracy's reasoning comported perfectly with the state-centered realist hypothesis and its focus on increasing state power. Nowhere did the report suggest that new threats or hostile adversaries motivated its proposals. To be sure, the fleet would serve defensive purposes, but defense "absolutely requires a fighting force." Wars, while "defensive in principle," would always have to be conducted offensively.[1] The new navy was, for Tracy, the means by which the United States would assume its rightful place among the world's powers.

Two months later, Tracy released the report of the "policy board," a six-person committee of naval officers he had appointed to conduct an overall strategic review. In justifying a larger navy, the board laid out its theoretical assumptions in terms so explicit as to warm a scholar's heart. "[T]he magnitude of a naval force to be maintained by a government should be adjusted on the one hand to the chances of war . . . and, on the other hand, it should be commensurate with the wealth of

---

[1] *Annual Report of the Secretary of the Navy, 1889,* 51st Cong., 1st sess., House Exec. Doc. 1, pt. 3, pp. 3–5.

the country and the interests at stake." If the threat of war was slight and the nation's interests minor, the navy could be small. If war was likely, a large navy was essential. However, "[w]hatever may be the chances of war, if the interests to be guarded are great then the naval force to be maintained should also be great."[2]

The policy board frankly acknowledged that America's relative geographic isolation had blessed it with immense security that had only increased in recent years. "For the United States it may be confidently asserted that the chances of war with any nation comparable in wealth and power are much less than the chances among the nations of Europe." Indeed, the likelihood of such a war "would seem to be at a minimum." But despite the absence of threats, the board emphasized, a large navy was still vital. "When we consider the wealth of our country . . . and the interests at stake in case of war, we are forced to admit that our navy is insignificant and totally disproportionate to the greatness of the country."[3] The arguments that Tracy and the policy board put forward reflected the logic of classical realism: America's rising wealth and power made necessary the expansion of its influence and hence of its military. This argument was echoed throughout the decade that followed. As a writer in *Forum* simply stated, "We need to be armed as becomes a great Power."[4]

The policy board's recommendations were as extravagant as its rhetoric. It advised the United States to undertake immediately the construction of over two hundred modern warships of all classes. This proposal met strong opposition in Congress, and the Naval Act of 1890 was, of course, a pared-down version of these proposals. But the two reports of 1889 nevertheless marked a shift in the course of American foreign policy. As recounted in chapter 3, the construction of the new navy had begun under the presidency of Chester Arthur, but at that time the central state was still relatively weak, the struggle between the executive and legislative branches had not been resolved, and Congress had allowed only a modest buildup. In his first term, the ideologically antiexpansionist Grover Cleveland joined the Democratic Congress in authorizing the addition of merely some thirty boats to the fleet. But the reports of 1889 vastly enlarged the scope of these plans. Previous construction had been just a prelude; now began the evolution of the modern American navy. When Secretary Tracy and President Benjamin Harrison entered office, the U.S. Navy lay somewhere between twelfth

---

[2] Secretary of the Navy, *Report of the Policy Board, 1890,* 51st Cong., 1st sess., Senate Exec. Doc. 43, 3.

[3] Ibid., 3–4.

[4] Maurice Halstead, "American Annexation and Armament," *Forum* 24 (September 1897): 66.

and seventeenth in the world. Four years later, it ranked seventh and rising.

At home, Tracy's reports changed the terms of debate forever. The House Naval Affairs Committee approved the policy board's blueprint for a new naval command with battleship fleets in the western Atlantic, the eastern Pacific, and the Caribbean. It also endorsed the argument, present in both reports, that a strong offense was the best defense. This logic allowed American statesmen to build and maintain a great battleship fleet that could be used only far from the country's shores, while asserting—when it suited them—that the fleet existed exclusively for the defense of the United States. That final phrase, "the defense of the United States," took on an ever-expanding definition over the years.

Over the next decade, American foreign policy would grow increasingly assertive. Between 1889 and 1908, thirty-two opportunities arose for the United States to expand its interests and influence abroad. Washington seized those opportunities twenty-five times, a dramatically higher rate (78 percent) than in the earlier period of study, 1865–1889 (twenty-two opportunities to expand, six taken, yielding an expansion rate of 27 percent). The country's rising national power—by now widely recognized at home and abroad—was responsible for greater American activism in international affairs. This expansionism was not primarily the result of greater objective or perceived threats to America's security. True, once the desire took hold to expand American influence and interests all over the world, new threats to American interests abounded. In a sense, new threats arose, but only because American interests had expanded.

Perhaps most important, this "large" policy was mainly facilitated by the transformation of the American state in the late nineteenth century. After the Civil War, the United States had been faced with an unprecedented national debt, and a spirit of retrenchment had pervaded the country. Meanwhile, the divided nature of the American state had blocked many of William Henry Seward's expansionist plans in the 1860s and 1870s. In the late 1870s and 1880s, however, the national debt became a regular annual surplus, and the scope and extractive capacity of the American state grew; with the state awash in cash, the financial problems that had militated against an activist foreign policy were no longer an obstacle. Over the same period, the presidency came out on top in a series of struggles with Congress, and the expansion of the government's regulatory powers furthered the reach of the executive branch. With the ascent of the presidency, congressional challenges to presidential foreign policy initiatives became increasingly rare, and a more coherent and activist foreign policy was the result. Increased national power worked in tandem with a stronger state to create what one historian has called a "paradigm shift" in American foreign policy.[5]

AMERICAN POWER AND INTERESTS, 1889–1908

If any questioned America's growing economic might in the 1860s and 1870s, they no longer did by the 1890s. The United States had clearly surpassed Britain as the largest manufacturing nation in the world, with 30 percent of world output by 1900 and 35 percent by 1907.[6] Its steel production, regarded at the time as a crucial indicator of national power, rose to 23.4 million tons by 1907, compared with a mere 6.5 tons for Britain and 11.9 for Germany. Even in the coal industry—in which Britain in 1870 had produced three times as much as its nearest competitor, Germany—the United States had forged ahead by the early 1900s.[7] By virtually every important industrial measure, the United States was clearly the most powerful nation in the world.[8]

The country's prosperity was plain to see. Conspicuous production led to conspicuous consumption. In the great cities—New York, Boston, Philadelphia—grand mansions sprouted, one more lavish than the next. The surrounding countryside in Long Island, Connecticut, and Cape Cod was soon studded with estates and summer homes that vied with the palaces of Europe in extravagance. The newly rich industrialists, financiers, and lawyers made their mark so firmly on this era that it is still today called the Gilded Age.[9] The robber barons may have taken

[5] Robert L. Beisner, *From the Old Diplomacy to the New, 1865–1900*, 2d ed. (Arlington Heights, Ill.: Harlan Davidson, 1986).

[6] League of Nations, *Industrialization and Foreign Trade* (New York, 1945), 13. These figures are slightly different from those for world manufacturing output in P. Bairoch, "International Industrialization Levels from 1750 to 1980," *Journal of European Economic History* 11 (1982), but the rankings are identical.

[7] W. Arthur Lewis, "International Competition in Manufactures," *American Economic Review* 47, no. 2 (1957): 578–87; B. R. Mitchell, *European Historical Statistics, 1750–1975*, 2d ed., rev. (London: Macmillan, 1980); A. J. P. Taylor, *The Struggle for Mastery in Europe, 1848–1918* (Oxford: Oxford University Press, 1954); and D. J. Coppock, "The Causes of the Great Depression, 1873–1896," *The Manchester School of Economic and Social Studies* 29, no. 3 (1961): 205–32.

[8] A good account is Samuel P. Hays, *The Response to Industrialism, 1885–1914* (Chicago: University of Chicago Press, 1957).

[9] The Gilded Age properly refers only to the period spanning the presidencies of Rutherford B. Hayes and William McKinley, but the untrammeled creation of wealth that characterized the times continued well into the early twentieth century. Indeed, the Progressive movement, which lasted from approximately 1902 until 1919, represented the political reaction to this wealth. See the fine collection of essays in H. Wayne Morgan, ed., *The Gilded Age* (Syracuse, N.Y.: Syracuse University Press, 1963).

the lion's share of the riches, but there was wealth enough for everyone. Real wages grew 37 percent between 1890 and 1914. The Gilded Age was in some ways harsh—workers were ruthlessly exploited, and women, children, and the unemployed were treated callously—but still, average American workers saw significant rises in their living standards during the late nineteenth century.[10]

The Columbian world's fair, held in Chicago in 1893, showcased to the world the riches of industrial America.[11] Dozens of gleaming neo-classical facades were interspersed with ornate fountains, lakes, and gardens, all built from scratch for the fair. The exposition focused on America's technological advancement, which was in fact astounding. Agriculture Hall displayed the machines with which America had revolutionized farming and created mass food production. Transportation Hall presented the railroad cars that were, and the great ocean steamers that would in time become, the envy of the world. Machinery and Electricity Halls peered further into the future, portraying "a world that seemed as marvelous in 1893 as it would seem commonplace in 1945"; in these exhibitions, people got their first glimpses of electric trolleys, elevators, long-distance phones, and electric heaters. The fair also displayed the kinetograph, which coordinated recorded sound with recorded images, creating in effect the first talking motion picture.[12]

Twenty million Americans visited this exhibition of their country's material power. It was also visited by writers and diplomats from all parts of the world. Americans were proud, foreigners amazed. A Frenchman observed, "Chicago the enormous town we see expanding, the gigantic plant which grows before our eyes seems now in this wonderful new country to be in advance of the age. But is this not more or less true of all America?"[13] By the late 1890s, this reaction to America's growing power was widespread. In his 1902 best-seller *The Americanization of the World,* the British journalist William T. Stead described the rest of the world, even England, as a commercial colony of the United States. The French, impressed only by empirical proof, collected data on American economic growth, productivity, and management techniques.

---

[10] Stuart W. Bruchey, *The Wealth of the Nation: An Economic History of the United States* (New York: Harper and Row, 1988), 138, and more generally 100–142.

[11] See David F. Burg, *Chicago's White City of 1893* (Lexington: University of Kentucky Press, 1976); Reid Badger, *The Great American Fair: The World's Columbia Exposition and American Culture* (Chicago: Nelson Hall, 1979); and Robert W. Rydell, *All the World's a Fair: Visions of Empire at American International Expositions, 1876–1916* (Chicago: University of Chicago Press, 1984), 38–72.

[12] Emily S. Rosenberg, *Spreading the American Dream: American Economic and Cultural Expansion, 1890–1945* (New York: Hill and Wang, 1982), 6.

[13] Ibid., 3.

British commentators began writing about the superiority of American political institutions and practices, indeed of the people itself. In 1898, on a visit to America, Arthur Conan Doyle regretfully admitted, "The center of gravity of the race is over here, and we have to readjust ourselves."[14]

The American juggernaut began to worry foreign offices in Europe. German diplomats wrote of the impossibility of coexisting with the United States, and kaiser Wilhelm II shared their misgivings about America's growing power. After a meeting between the Kaiser and Czar Nicholas II in 1903, the latter's chief of staff wrote, "England disturbs [the Kaiser] and America even more. The Czar observed that America alarms him too." The phrase "American peril" cropped up in parliamentary debates and press articles across Europe. A former French foreign minister asked, "Are we to be confronted by an American peril . . . before which the Old World is to go down to irretrievable defeat?"[15] These governments were less concerned about America's general cultural and economic influence than about its potential acquisition of a large armed forces, a sizable diplomatic apparatus, and significant imperial baggage. They feared that the United States would adopt the interests of a great power and threaten their own spheres of influence and control. "The United States are forming a navy," wrote the First Lord of the Admiralty in 1904, "the power and size of which will be limited only by the amount of money which the American people choose to spend on it."[16]

Two areas in which rising economic power had already begun to lead—often unintentionally—to the acquisition of interests abroad were trade and finance.[17] The American economy remained largely dependent on its internal market; even after large-scale growth in exports, in 1913 foreign trade stood at just 8 percent of GNP, compared to Britain's 26 percent. But 8 percent of a massive GNP was still a consid-

[14] Ernest May, *Imperial Democracy: The Emergence of America as a Great Power* (New York: Harcourt, Brace and World, 1961), 182, 190–91; Richard H. Heindel, *The American Impact on Great Britain, 1898–1914: A Study of the United States in World History* (Philadelphia: University of Pennsylvania Press, 1940), 53, 130–31; Max M. Laserson, *The American Impact on Russia, Diplomatic and Ideological, 1784–1917* (New York: Collier, 1962), 270.

[15] May, *Imperial Democracy*, 5–6.

[16] Aaron L. Friedberg, *The Weary Titan: Britain and the Experience of Relative Decline, 1895–1905* (Princeton, N.J.: Princeton University Press, 1988), 135.

[17] See Paul M. Kennedy, *The Rise and Fall of the Great Powers: Economic Change and Military Conflict from 1500 to the Present* (New York: Random House, 1987), 244–45; and David M. Pletcher, "Economic Growth and Diplomatic Adjustment," in William H. Becker, Jr., and Samuel F. Wells, Jr., eds., *Economics and World Power: An Assessment of American Diplomacy since 1789* (New York: Columbia University Press, 1984).

erable figure in absolute terms, especially for America's trading partners. Between 1889 and 1913, manufacturing exports rose from $89 million to $805 million, while imports increased from $174 million to only $470 million.[18] Many countries that imported American goods viewed the United States as a colossus that had to be either fought or appeased, and Americans began to develop an interest in maintaining access—the open door—to new markets like Latin America and China. On the financial side, America's large trade surplus with Europe had to be offset by European capital transfers to the United States. These payments combined with European direct investment and Washington's practice of holding one-third of the world's gold in reserve to bring a tremendous capital flow into the United States. The American financial sector lacked the resources and experience to handle this complex international role, and both Wall Street and the U.S. government grew dependent on the City of London as a financial partner. This partnership would become the subject of much populist paranoia over the next twenty years.

As early as the late 1880s, the political implications of the country's new power were being discussed in elite circles. In 1890 Alfred Thayer Mahan published *The Influence of Sea Power upon History*. In the first chapter, which was the most widely read part of the book, Mahan clearly stated his central thesis: as a great productive nation, the United States needed to turn its attention to the acquisition of a large merchant marine, a great navy, and, finally, colonies and spheres of international influence and control. Not only was this necessary, Mahan asserted, it was inevitable, an inexorable step in the march of history.[19] Mahan had expounded on these themes in his lectures at the Naval War College in the late 1880s, and he continued to propagate them through articles, books, and speeches throughout the 1890s.

Mahan may have been the most prominent intellectual figure to advocate expansion, but other leading expansionists, who came to similar conclusions based on entirely different suppositions, also had significant followings. The well-known writer John Fiske had delivered his lecture

---

[18] Mitchell, *European Historical Statistics*, 544–45.

[19] Alfred Thayer Mahan, *The Influence of Sea Power upon History, 1660–1783* (Boston: Little, Brown, 1890). On Mahan, see the thoroughly uncritical Harold and Margaret Sprout, *The Rise of American Naval Power* (Princeton, N.J.: Princeton University Press, 1939), 202–22; and Margaret Tuttle Sprout, "Mahan: Evangelist of Sea Power," in Edward Mead Earle, ed., *Makers of Modern Strategy: Military Thought from Machiavelli to Hitler* (Princeton, N.J.: Princeton University Press, 1943), 415–45. A more balanced assessment is Philip A. Crowl, "Alfred Thayer Mahan: The Naval Historian," in Peter Paret, ed., *Makers of Modern Strategy: From Machiavelli to the Nuclear Age* (Princeton, N.J.: Princeton University Press, 1986), 444–77.

on manifest destiny hundreds of times across the country. His thesis was more ambitious than Mahan's: "It is enough to point to the general conclusion that the work which the English race began when it colonized North America is destined to go on until every land on the earth's surface that is not already the seat of an old civilization shall become English in its language, in its religion, in its political habits and traditions, and to a predominant extent in the blood of its people."[20] The preacher Josiah Strong gave a missionary twist to Fiske's prophecies in the best-selling *Our Country*. The writer Brooks Adams, highly respected for his intelligence as well as his pedigree, presented his vague expansionist ideas in *The Law of Civilization and Decay*.[21]

After Mahan's, however, the most well known theory of expansionism was probably that of Frederick Jackson Turner. At the American Historical Association's 1893 convention, held during the Chicago world's fair, Turner delivered the most famous presidential address in the association's history. "The Significance of the Frontier in American History" argued that free land had been crucial to the development of American democracy. Turner argued that the frontier was closing in the early 1890s.[22] The implication of the frontier thesis was obvious: the republic was in peril, and new lands had to be found to save American freedom.[23] Turner's own views on foreign policy, which he outlined both before and after his 1893 address, regarded expansion abroad as inevitable. The United States was growing economically, he explained, and "once fully afloat on the sea of worldwide economic interests we shall soon develop political interests."[24]

The intellectual atmosphere of the 1890s, full of ideas about national expansion and social Darwinism, deeply affected many statesmen of the day—Theodore Roosevelt, Henry Cabot Lodge, John Hay, Whitelaw Reid, Henry Adams, Albert Beveridge—who had been searching for a

[20] John Fiske, "Manifest Destiny," *Harper's Magazine* 70 (1885): 588.

[21] Josiah Strong, *Our Country* (1885; reprint, Cambridge: Belknap Press of Harvard University Press, 1963); Brooks Adams, *The Law of Civilization and Decay: An Essay on History* (New York: Macmillan, 1895).

[22] Frederick Jackson Turner, "The Significance of the Frontier in American History," *Annual Report, 1893* (Washington, D.C.: American Historical Association, 1894), 199–227.

[23] In point of fact, the frontier had not closed. A larger number of original and final homestead entries were registered after 1900 than in the preceding three hundred years. See Walter LaFeber, *The New Empire: An Interpretation of American Expansion, 1860–1898* (Ithaca, N.Y.: Cornell University Press, 1963), 64. The most significant critiques of Turner are those of Fred A. Shannon and Richard Hofstadter in Ray Allen Billington, ed., *The Frontier Thesis: Valid Interpretation of American History?* (New York: Holt, Rinehart and Winston, 1966).

[24] Quoted in LaFeber, *The New Empire*, 70.

response to the rise in American economic power.[25] Roosevelt gave a long, respectful review to Adams's book and wrote a fan letter to Turner. He sought to remind those for whom the last twenty-five years of external reticence seemed normal that "throughout a large part of our national career our history has been one of expansion. . . . This expansion is not a matter of regret, but of pride."[26] Woodrow Wilson said about Turner, "All I ever wrote on the subject came from him."[27] Two of Mahan's most ardent devotees were Benjamin Tracy and his successor, Hilary Herbert. Until he read Mahan's case for an offensive battleship fleet, Herbert had actually been an advocate of small commerce-destroying cruisers.[28] Many of these statesmen came to believe that the era of Mediterranean dominance had been replaced by the Atlantic era and that the Atlantic era was now being replaced by the Pacific era, in which the United States would shape the global political order.

HARRISON, BLAINE, AND THE "NEW DIPLOMACY," 1889–1893

The administration of Benjamin Harrison is widely accepted among historians as marking a shift in U.S. diplomacy.[29] Observers at the time would have concurred. At the close of the administration's tenure, several newspapers and magazines asked skeptically whether the "series of departures of the gravest nature" from the old diplomacy were to be

[25] Many historians point to the survival-of-the-fittest philosophy of social Darwinism as an explanation for American expansion, but it is important to note that most important social Darwinists of the period—Herbert Spencer, William Graham Sumner, John Fiske— were pacifists. They considered war a stage in the evolution of humankind that advanced, commercial societies had surpassed. See, for example, William Graham Sumner, *War and Other Essays* (New Haven, Conn.: Yale University Press, 1911); and Andrew Carnegie, *Triumphant Democracy* (New York: Scribners, 1888). On the intellectual currents of the 1890s, see David Healy, *U.S. Expansionism: The Imperialist Urge in the 1890s* (Madison: University of Wisconsin Press, 1970); Julius Pratt, *Expansionists of 1898* (Baltimore: Johns Hopkins Press, 1936); and Richard Hofstadter, *Social Darwinism in American Thought* (Philadelphia: University of Pennsylvania Press, 1945).

[26] Quoted in Healy, *U.S. Expansionism*, 34–35.

[27] Quoted in LaFeber, *The New Empire*, 71.

[28] *Annual Report of the Secretary of the Navy, 1893*, 53rd Cong., 2d sess., House Exec. Doc. 1, 3; *Annual Report of the Secretary of the Navy, 1894*, 54th Cong., 2d sess., House Exec. Doc. 3. On Mahan's influence on the navy, see Richard D. Challener, *Admirals, Generals, and Foreign Policy, 1898–1914* (Princeton, N.J.: Princeton University Press, 1973), 12–45.

[29] Beisner, *From the Old Diplomacy to the New*; LaFeber, *The New Empire*; and Charles S. Campbell, Jr., *The Transformation of American Foreign Relations, 1865–1900* (New York: Harper and Row, 1976), among others.

welcomed.[30] For their part, Harrison and his secretary of state, James G. Blaine, were quite candid about their intention to conduct a more active foreign policy. Harrison wrote to Blaine that, regarding the annexations of "naval stations and points of influence, we must look forward to a departure from the too conservative opinions which have been held heretofore." Blaine's most pressing rhetoric was about trade: "I wish to declare the opinion that the United States has reached a point where one of its highest duties is to enlarge the area of its foreign trade. . . . I think we should be unwisely content if we did not seek what the younger Pitt so well termed the annexation of trade."[31] For this speech and similar statements, Blaine is regarded as a moderate expansionist. But such "moderation" included a firm belief that the United States would in the near future need to annex Hawaii, Cuba, and Puerto Rico and that it should annex Canada as well. During his tenure, Blaine also made unsuccessful overtures to foreign governments to acquire those perennial objects of Washington's attention: the Danish West Indies, Samaná Bay, the Môle Saint Nicolas, and Samoa. To these "points of influence" Blaine added Chimbote in Peru.[32]

During the Harrison administration, a little-noticed 1890 Supreme Court case, *In re Neagle,* defined the powers of the presidency, and this expansive definition provided a legal basis for the growing power of the executive branch. In a case not directly related to international affairs, the justices declared that the president was not limited to carrying out Congress's orders. His powers included "enforcing the rights, duties and obligations growing out of the Constitution itself, our international relations, and all the protection implied by the nature of government under the Constitution." This extraordinarily broad view of the presidency—which Theodore Roosevelt would later term "the stewardship theory"—would be used by presidents for decades as a catch-all justification for their actions. The "pressures of international relations" and their duty to "the national interest" allowed presidents to take unilateral actions that would have been difficult to explain within "the literary theory of the Constitution."[33]

[30] See, for example, *Harper's Weekly,* March 18, 1893, 1–4; and A. T. Volwiler, "Harrison, Blaine, and American Foreign Policy, 1889–1893," *Proceedings of the American Philosophical Society* 74, no. 4 (November 15, 1938): 637–38.

[31] *New York Tribune,* August 30, 1890.

[32] For the best general accounts, see LaFeber, *The New Empire,* 102–49; and Alice F. Tyler, *The Foreign Policy of James G. Blaine* (Minneapolis: University of Minnesota Press, 1927). The Harrison administration also undertook many minor efforts to acquire bases abroad, but they have not been included in this study because they do not meet the threshold of seriousness: the attempts were neither persistent nor constant. They would all, however, support the hypothesis of state-centered realism.

[33] Louis Henkin, *Foreign Affairs and the Constitution* (New York: W. W. Norton,

Pan-Americanism

When he came to office, Blaine signaled the change in foreign policy by reviving an idea he had floated during his first stint as secretary of state, during the Garfield administration: Pan-Americanism. Blaine had issued invitations to the leaders of the Central and South American nations to attend a Pan-American conference in 1881, but he had left the State Department after the death of Garfield, and President Arthur and Secretary of State Frelinghuysen had withdrawn the invitations.[34] Seven years later, in July 1888, Grover Cleveland sent out invitations again. For Blaine and others, Pan-Americanism was a means through which the United States would dominate its southern neighbors "in the spirit of the Monroe Doctrine."[35] Blaine structured the conference, held in Washington in November 1889, accordingly: he made sure, for example, that he was elected its chairman. The other members, however, were well aware of the United States' power, and in case they had any doubts, Blaine had arranged for a six-thousand-mile luxury rail tour that visited forty-one industrial centers. The foreign delegations rejected two of Blaine's pet ideas—a customs union and an arbitration treaty—fearing they would result in U.S. economic and political hegemony.[36] The conference did recommend, however, that countries wishing to lower trade barriers should negotiate reciprocity treaties with each other.[37]

Blaine seized on this issue. He had long been concerned with the U.S. trade deficit with Latin America. Not only was it bad for American producers, but it created a serious drain on Washington's gold reserves. Increased exports, in Blaine's view, were the solution, shifting the old imperial trade between Latin America and Europe north to the United States. Congress, however, was less than enthusiastic. Reciprocity appealed to neither the free traders nor the protectionists. Furthermore, reciprocity tended to cede to the president the authority to determine

1975), 309. See also Walter LaFeber, *The American Search for Opportunity, 1865–1913,* vol. 2 of *The Cambridge History of American Foreign Relations,* ed. Warren I. Cohen (Cambridge: Cambridge University Press, 1993), 82.

[34] James G. Blaine, *Political Discussions: Legislative, Diplomatic, and Popular* (Norwich, Conn., 1887), 403–19; *Foreign Relations of the United States, 1882,* (Washington, D.C.: Department of State), 13–15.

[35] Quoted in Arthur P. Whitaker, *The Western Hemisphere Idea: Its Rise and Decline* (Ithaca, N.Y.: Cornell University Press, 1954), 80.

[36] Seven of the delegations did actually agree to an arbitration treaty, but the final treaty had an escape clause that allowed countries to opt out if the dispute concerned "independence." Eventually most, including the United States, did not ratify the treaty.

[37] See *International American Conference, Reports of Committees and Discussions Thereon,* 51st Cong., 1st sess., Senate Exec. Doc. 232, 1:1–30, 130–31, 263–64; 2:1078–83, 1166–68; 3:i–ii (for list of places visited on the railroad tour).

which items stayed on tariff lists and which were removed, an old sticking point with Congress. Senator Justin Morrill still argued that it was an unconstitutional usurpation of power for the president to make reciprocity treaties. In May 1890 a tariff bill was passed without any reciprocity provisions, and chances for an amendment seemed slight. Then Blaine and Harrison went to work, both in Washington and beyond. Harrison lobbied Congress very effectively; Blaine made speeches across the country. The result was a compromise version of the reciprocity amendment, which Harrison signed into law that October. The law gave the president the authority to suspend the importation of sugar, molasses, coffee, tea, and animal hides from another country when he determined that country was engaged in "unequal and unreasonable" trade practices. Harrison and Blaine used this power to force all Latin American countries except Colombia, Haiti, and Venezuela to sign reciprocity treaties. The three that refused were immediately blacklisted.[38]

The reciprocity amendment's passage was aided greatly by the Republican Party's control over both houses. The party struggles of the previous twenty-five years were absent, and so was the instinctive congressional opposition to presidential initiatives. William McKinley of Ohio, in particular, proved to be a crucial ally in the House, persuading his fellow congressmen that reciprocity was a sound policy tool and that the president needed this discretionary power. The other concrete accomplishment of the Inter-American Conference also served to augment the president's power to conduct foreign policy. The conference recommended Blaine's proposal that a Commercial Bureau of the American Republics be established in Washington. This outfit soon became, as Blaine probably intended, "a permanent branch of the State Department and a true intelligence office regarding the Western Hemisphere."[39] The bureau was supported by private funding, and in 1910 it moved— having been renamed the Pan-American Union—to a mansion donated by Andrew Carnegie, who had been chosen by Blaine as a delegate to the Inter-American Conference. This marked the beginning of what later became a routine presidential practice, first employed extensively by Theodore Roosevelt: the use of the power of the White House to raise private funds for foreign policy goals. The Pan-American Union and similar organizations allowed the president to bypass constitutional constraints and limited budgets—the basic weaknesses of the American state.

---

[38] An excellent, brief discussion can be found in LaFeber, *The New Empire*, 112–21.

[39] This is how Blaine's official biographer described it. See Gail Hamilton, *Biography of James G. Blaine* (Norwich, Conn.: Henry Bill, 1895), 680.

Chile

The diplomacy of the Harrison administration was strikingly evident in its response to the *Baltimore* incident in Chile, and even the background to the affair illustrates Washington's new attitude toward intervention. In 1891 a rebellion erupted against the pro-U.S. government of José Manuel Balmaceda in Chile. The U.S. ambassador, Patrick Egan, openly tilted toward the government, supplying it with shipping facilities and information. The American position became even more openly hostile when the rebel ship *Itata* was captured by the American navy. The Balmaceda government was delighted, but the United States could not stop its slide. In August 1891 the rebels took over the government. The United States offered Balmaceda's supporters asylum, delayed recognition of the new regime, and began to draw up contingency plans for a war against Chile.[40]

The *Baltimore* incident, which occurred soon afterward, was much less provocative than the *Virginius* affair in Cuba twenty years earlier, but the American reaction was much more aggressive. On October 16, 1891, sailors from the *Baltimore* got into a fight with some locals at a saloon in Valparaíso. Two Americans were stabbed to death, and seventeen were injured. In his annual message in December, Harrison demanded "full and prompt reparation."[41] Chile defiantly refused to offer any concessions. During the entire episode, Blaine proved to be more conciliatory than the president, who as a former military man took the matter very seriously. "Mr. Secretary," he exclaimed at a cabinet meeting, "that insult was to the uniform of United States sailors."[42] The records of Harrison's private secretary note on January 1, 1892, that "all the members of cabinet are for war." The same could be said of Egan and the naval officers in Chile. That month the British ambassador to the United States, Sir Cecil Spring Rice, wrote back to his government, "We are on the verge of war here."[43] Initially, in part be-

[40] Walter R. Herrick, Jr., *The American Naval Revolution* (Baton Rouge: Louisiana State University Press, 1966), 126–29; Campbell, *Transformation of American Foreign Relations,* 170.
[41] James D. Richardson, *A Compilation of the Messages and Papers of the Presidents* (Washington, D.C.: Bureau of National Literature, 1911), 11:185; also see *Messages of the President Respecting the Relations with Chile,* 53d Cong., 1st sess., House Exec. Doc. 91, 1892.
[42] This point is repeated in both the official U.S. notes to Chile.
[43] Volwiler, "Harrison, Blaine, and American Foreign Policy," 640, 643. Though generally more conciliatory, Blaine waffled somewhat on the question of war with Chile; during much of this period, however, he was seriously ill and may, therefore, have refrained from taking a strong stand against the president and the cabinet.

cause of a change at the Foreign Ministry, it seemed that the Chilean government was coming around, but suddenly it asked that Egan be recalled as ambassador. Harrison decided the matter should now move into the hands of Congress, since it alone had the power to declare war. He also decided to deliver an ultimatum through the State Department to Chile. The terse note threatened the "termination of diplomatic relations" unless Santiago withdrew its offensive statements of December, formally apologized to Washington "with the same publicity that was given to the offensive declarations," and paid reparations for its wrongdoing. The note denied Chile's request for the withdrawal of the American ambassador.[44]

Two days later, Chile capitulated. The government in Santiago issued a public apology for its previous behavior, apologized for the *Baltimore* incident, and suggested that the Supreme Court or an arbitration panel determine the sum of reparations (the figure ultimately agreed upon was $75,000).[45] Chancellories across Europe and Latin America noticed Washington's aggressive stand. In the weeks prior to its retreat, Chile had received messages from Europe that the United States appeared to be in earnest and that the great powers of Europe would not intercede on Chile's behalf in the event of war.[46] Just twenty years before, the United States had allowed a much graver incident ninety miles south of Florida to pass quietly, and now it had almost gone to war because of a barroom brawl in remote Chile. Britain's ambassador drew the connection between America's new power and its new diplomacy: "[T]he moral for us is: what will the U.S. be like when their fleet is more powerful?"[47]

Hawaii

During his brief months as secretary of state in 1881, Blaine had indicated that he viewed Hawaii as vital to "our large and rapidly increasing interests in the Pacific." In a message to the American minister there, he wrote,

> The situation of the Hawaiian islands, giving them the strategic control of the north Pacific, brings their possession within the range of purely American policy, as much so as that of the [Central American] isthmus itself. . . . Hawaii holds in the western sea much the same position as Cuba in the

[44] *FRUS, 1891,* 307–8.
[45] Ibid., 310–12.
[46] Ibid., 309–10; Campbell, *Transformation of American Foreign Relations,* 174.
[47] Quoted in Volwiler, "Harrison, Blaine, and American Foreign Policy," 648.

Atlantic. It is the key to the maritime dominion of the Pacific States. . . . under no circumstances can the United States permit any change in the territorial control of either which would cut it adrift from the American system, whereto they both belong.[48]

Blaine even suggested to the minister that he give Hawaii's foreign minister a copy of Blaine's dispatch so that the islanders realized their importance to U.S. interests. On arriving at the State Department in 1889, Blaine proposed a treaty that would have turned the islands into a de facto colony of the United States. The treaty resembled the Platt Amendment by which Washington would control Cuba after the Spanish-American War; it restricted Hawaii's right to conclude treaties with foreign powers and imparted to the United States the right to maintain troops on the islands.[49] With the help of Canadian businessmen who saw the treaty as a threat to their own interests, the islanders successfully sabotaged this attempt by adding provisions that Washington would obviously not accept.

Two years later, in 1891, Queen Liliuokalani ascended to the throne of Hawaii. The queen did not approve of America's domination of Hawaii, and over the next year the American minister John Stevens and the naval commanders in the Pacific sent back a stream of dispatches outlining the danger to American interests that Hawaii's "instability" represented. The queen holds "extreme notions of sovereign authority," cabled Stevens. American officials offered tacit encouragement to the Annexationist Club, a group of opposition politicians and businessmen who called for an outright American takeover, and in January 1893 the group overthrew Liliuokalani. The USS *Boston* had landed in Hawaii one day before, ostensibly to protect American property, and this image of American strength and support must have helped the annexationists. By January 18, the new government had begun negotiations toward annexation.

For the first few months of 1893, American elites in the government and the media discussed and debated the proposed annexation of Hawaii. Broad support for annexation emerged, with three points generating the greatest consensus. The primary argument was the strategic value of the islands. Benjamin Tracy had explained that Hawaii was crucial to the control of the sea and thus the key to "the future seat of empire." Mahan's arguments about the need for coaling stations and points of influence throughout the Pacific were widely known and ac-

[48] Reprinted in Blaine, *Political Discussions*, 395, and see generally 388–96.

[49] William Adam Russ, *The Hawaiian Revolution* (Selinsgrove, Pa.: Susquehanna University Press, 1959), 12–35; Sylvester Kirby Stevens, *American Expansion in Hawaii* (New York: Russell and Russell, 1945), 187–203; LaFeber, *The New Empire*, 142.

cepted, and Hawaii was an obvious place to apply his theories. Second was the commercial value of the islands. Hawaii was rich in sugar, and some expansionists also recognized its importance as a stepping-stone to the markets of the Far East.[50] But the commercial factor had a complex impact on expansionism. The great plantation owners of Hawaii, for example, opposed annexation. Claus Spreckels, by far the largest planter on the islands, assumed that were Hawaii to be annexed, American immigration laws would prevent him from importing cheap Asian labor. Third was the threat from foreign powers. Over the years, whenever an American official discussed Hawaii, he always mentioned the danger of British and, to a lesser extent, Japanese and German influence growing on the island. Indeed, John Foster, who took over as secretary of state from the ailing Blaine in mid-1892, wrote that unless the United States annexed Hawaii, it would inevitably pass into British or Japanese hands.[51] The impression of many observers was that annexation was inevitable. The American minister in London sent the State Department newspaper clippings showing that the British assumed that Washington would annex Hawaii and that they were resigned to the fact. One member of the House of Representatives said of annexation, "It is the logical outcome and is favored by too many men of prominence in public life to have another outcome."[52]

But despite this apparent elite and governmental consensus in favor of annexation, the effort failed, most immediately because of the American state's divided structure. Harrison was in the last months of his presidency when the treaty was being negotiated and sent to Congress. In 1890 the House had turned Democratic; although the Senate remained Republican, the Democrats controlled more than the one-third of the upper house needed to block ratification of the treaty, and they promised to do so. The president-elect was a Democrat, Grover Cleveland, and he had voiced concerns about the treaty—both because of his well-known opposition to imperialism and because of the means by which the treaty had been obtained. Once in office, Cleveland withdrew the treaty from the Senate and began an investigation into its origins. James H. Blount, former chairman of the House Foreign Affairs Committee, traveled to Hawaii and determined that "the undoubted sentiment of the people is for the Queen, against the Provisional Government and against annexation."[53] By the end of the year, Cleveland

[50] See, for example, Whitelaw Reid's newspaper, *New York Tribune*, February 21, 1893, 1.

[51] John Watson Foster, *Diplomatic Memoirs* (Boston: Houghton Mifflin, 1909) 2:166–68.

[52] Quoted in May, *American Imperialism*, 170.

[53] House Exec. Doc. 47, 53rd Cong., 2d sess., 133.

declared he would abandon the annexation treaty because it had resulted from "unjustifiable interference in Hawaii's internal politics" and "represented a departure from American tradition." Despite this latter concern, Cleveland went on to say that he was not in principle opposed to annexation. Ernest May concludes that "Cleveland did not oppose colonial expansion per se; he only insisted that the U.S. be able afterward to show that she had taken territory with clean hands."[54]

Much of the opposition to annexation, particularly among otherwise activist elites, centered on the difficulty of incorporating "alien" peoples into the dominant American culture. In fact, in the view of some scholars, racism was the chief reason the United States did not annex Hawaii in 1893.[55] While nearly all American elites feared the "contamination" of the white race, this concern—so common in Europe, where it had never prevented expansion—could delay or thwart U.S. expansion only because of the tension between this racism and America's liberal democratic ideology. England and France had worried less about this problem because the new lands would be ruled as colonies. Americans assumed the inhabitants of these new territories would have to be welcomed as future citizens. As *The Atlantic Monthly* opined at the peak of the imperialist fervor of 1898, "The nature of our institutions forbids that we should set up any form of government except one that at the earliest moment shall become self-government."[56] In the end, though, this tension did not greatly affect the course of American expansion. Throughout the 1890s, leaders discussed the option of establishing a protectorate or instituting some informal means of political control over Hawaii, and the United States rarely hesitated to use such means from then on.

Finally, the movement to annex Hawaii also failed because of America's economic troubles. By the time the treaty came before Congress, the panic of 1893—a crisis perhaps even worse than the recession of 1873—had hit the country. Government revenues dropped sharply, and the dominant mood was one of decline and diminished power.[57] In this bleak atmosphere, heady talk of taking over Hawaii, of a "future seat of empire" and of spreading civilization westward, seemed misplaced. Even Walter LaFeber, who generally argues that economic depression caused rising expansionist sentiment in the United States during the late

[54] Richardson, *Papers of the President*, 9, 460–71; May, *American Imperialism*, 170.

[55] Michael Hunt, *Ideology and U.S. Foreign Policy* (New Haven, Conn.: Yale University Press, 1987), 81; Reginald Horsman, *Race and Manifest Destiny: The Origins of American Racial Anglo-Saxonism* (Cambridge: Harvard University Press, 1981).

[56] *The Atlantic Monthly* 81 (June 1898): 432.

[57] Thomas E. Burton, *Financial Crises and Periods of Industrial and Commercial Depression* (New York: D. Appleton, 1907), 292–96.

nineteenth century, admits that in 1893 the opposite occurred: "As economic chaos and social violence again upset the American scene, many people wondered what business the nation had in so assiduously searching for new problems."[58] As the recession deepened, Hawaii slipped further and further back on the nation's agenda.

Under the leadership of Harrison and Blaine, the United States found itself heavily involved in external affairs throughout the Western Hemisphere. Harrison was able to succeed in expanding American interests and commitments where his predecessors had failed in large part because the executive had gained power at the expense of the legislative branch, particularly in the area of foreign policy. During his tenure, the Supreme Court's decision in *In re Neagle* expanded executive authority, and Harrison himself took significant steps to expand the presidency. He had assumed the authority to negotiate reciprocity treaties, and in the Chilean crisis he had brought the country to the brink of war with little congressional input.[59] The balance of power had shifted in Washington and, as a result, in the wider world as well.

CLEVELAND AND THE PERSISTENCE OF EXPANSION, 1893–1897

Although Grover Cleveland's foreign policy record during his first term did not differ greatly from that of his Republican predecessors, Cleveland had managed to preserve an isolationist image, and antiexpansionists were thrilled when he was inaugurated as president in March 1893. He had in some measure embraced isolationism during his earlier term, and that kind of foreign policy had dominated the rhetoric of most high-ranking Democrats during the 1892 campaign. His prompt withdrawal of the Hawaiian treaty seemed to validate this image. It soon became apparent, however, that Cleveland would pursue a foreign policy very similar to that of Benjamin Harrison. The new paradigm crossed party lines and personal beliefs.

The most tangible indication of this continuity in policy was the further expansion of the battleship navy. Hilary Herbert had argued against capital-ship theory, a forward naval strategy, and bigger naval budgets when he had been chairman of the House Naval Affairs Committee. Ten months later, as Cleveland's secretary of the navy, Herbert asked for a budget increase of $3 million to strengthen the battleship fleet. In a letter to Mahan, he stated that under his stewardship, the navy would follow Mahan's policies in full. In fact, Herbert "endorsed

[58] LaFeber, *The New Empire*, 148.
[59] See LaFeber, *American Search for Opportunity*, 81–82.

the capital-ship theory of naval defense in terms even stronger than those used by his Republican counterpart." Despite initial reluctance, brought on by the depression of 1893, Congress went along with the president, in part for reasons of patronage. But by the early 1890s, Americans had also come to accept that as a great power, they had need of a great navy. Cleveland noted that in 1893, American naval craft had been used to promote American interests in Nicaragua, Guatemala, Costa Rica, Honduras, Argentina, Brazil, and Hawaii. That list would only grow longer over the years.[60] At the end of his term, Cleveland could proudly boast that his administration had built three first-class and two second-class battleships, authorized five more battleships, and commissioned two armored cruisers.[61]

The Brazilian Revolution

Under Cleveland, the United States adopted a broad interpretation of the Monroe Doctrine that did not simply forbid new European colonies but declared an American interest in any matter within the hemisphere. Whereas in 1885 Cleveland had argued for an isthmian canal "removed from the chance of domination by any single power," he now wanted one "under distinctly American control."[62] The first sign of such hemispheric American activism came in 1894 when a revolution threatened the pro-American government in Brazil.[63] American economic interests in Brazil were not large but had been growing, particularly after the 1891 reciprocity treaty. The pact had never been popular in Brazil, and denouncing it became one of the rallying cries of the opposition. Helped by the Brazilian navy and indirectly by Great Britain, the rebels laid siege to the harbor of Rio de Janeiro. Adhering to long-standing U.S. practice, the American minister to Brazil at first remained neutral. But he soon received instructions from Washington to adopt an openly pro-government stance. Since Secretary of State Walter Gresham's instructions had not been explicit about military policy, Rear Admiral Oscar Stanton wanted to observe traditional American policy and was soon recalled to the United States. Even Stanton's replacement had to be ex-

[60] Secretary of the Navy, *Annual Report, 1893*; Sprout and Sprout, *Rise of American Naval Power*, 218; Richardson, *Papers of the President*, 9:450–51.
[61] Richardson, *Papers of the President*, 9:731.
[62] Ibid., 11:4912, 5870.
[63] See Lawrence F. Hill, *Diplomatic Relations between the United States and Brazil* (Durham, N.C.: Duke University Press, 1932), 265–81; LaFeber, *The New Empire*, 210–18; and Montgomery Schuyler, "Walter Quintin Gresham," in Samuel Flagg Bemis, ed., *The American Secretaries of State and Their Diplomacy* (New York: Alfred A. Knopf, 1928), 250–57.

plicitly ordered by Gresham not to give belligerent status to the rebels. He also ordered that American goods keep moving through to shore, thus keeping the trade flow constant and bolstering the government.

The policy appeared to be working until December 1894, when the defection of a key Brazilian admiral bolstered the rebel cause. American businesses in Brazil, including the powerful Standard Oil Company, expressed grave concerns to Gresham. Gresham responded by reiterating to his minister in Brazil that American ships must be permitted to continue going about their business; he replaced the rear admiral of the fleet and sent reinforcements, so that by February 1895 the U.S. Navy had five of its six ships from the South Atlantic Squadron in Rio de Janeiro harbor and was by far the most powerful presence in those waters. Challenging the policy of unrestricted commerce, the rebels fired a blank shell at an American merchant ship. The USS *Detroit* then fired a live shell directly into the hull of the rebel craft and warned that if the ship fired again, it would be sunk. It soon became clear that the rebel movement could not succeed in the face of American opposition. Twice more the rebels asked for belligerent status, and twice Gresham refused. By April the rebels were seeking asylum in Portugal.

Nicaragua

Within months of the end of the Brazilian revolution, the United States found itself intervening in a complicated affair in Nicaragua.[64] American strategic planners saw the Mosquito Reservation in Nicaragua as critical because it controlled the eastern access route to the proposed isthmian canal. The native Indians of the reservation were technically independent, but by the 1880s the British had extensively penetrated the area and ruled it in reality. By the early 1890s, however, Americans had come to dominate completely the area's business and trade. In 1893 a revolution brought General José Santos Zelaya to power. Zelaya needed money and began to move on the rich Mosquito Reservation, but British troops overwhelmed the Nicaraguans. When a provisional government was formed in which the Americans did not have much influence, Washington decided to adopt a two-stage strategy: first dislodge the British from their position of influence, and then expand American influence in Nicaragua, particularly in the reservation.

By April 1894, the Nicaraguan government began ignoring—and in some cases even acting counter to—U.S. interests. It discriminated against American property interests, and when an American was mur-

[64] See LaFeber, *The New Empire*, 218–29; also see *FRUS, 1894*, 238–75.

dered on the reservation, the authorities did little to find the killer. Then Nicaragua threatened to terminate the American concession entirely. Gresham moved on two fronts: he first let the British know he regarded these latest moves by the Nicaraguans as part of a British plot, and he pressured Nicaragua through the American minister there, Lewis Baker. Baker protested the government's actions and made clear that the United States would not accept them. And he threatened Nicaragua in a less-than-subtle fashion, pointing to "the presence of two powerful war steamers on your eastern coast" as evidence of the American determination to maintain its concession. Within two months, Nicaragua capitulated. When, in July, Indians on the Mosquito Reservation overthrew the authorities, American, not British, troops arrived to maintain order. Even after the Nicaraguan government regained control of the area, the United States made clear by a show of naval force that it retained veto power over any matter it deemed important. Nicaragua had become a de facto protectorate of the United States.

The Venezuelan Boundary Crisis

Of all the United States' moves in Latin America, its intervention in the Venezuelan crisis of 1895 drew the greatest international attention.[65] Since 1841, Britain and Venezuela had quarreled over the boundary between Venezuela and British Guiana at the mouth of the Orinoco River, a strategically valuable location that was rich in gold. Venezuela had periodically attempted to draw the United States into the border dispute, but the United States had shown little interest. When, in the 1880s, Britain enlarged its claim and Venezuela responded by suspending diplomatic relations, then–Secretary of State Thomas Bayard sent a protest to London. The American minister in London thought it so unimportant as never even to convey the message to Whitehall.

Venezuela's pleas came with increasing urgency during the first months of Cleveland's second term. A Cleveland administration that had during its first term treated these requests casually had since grown accustomed to an activist policy, and it now decided to act more forcefully. Washington protested Britain's enlargement of its boundaries. By December 1894, the matter found its way into Cleveland's annual address to Con-

---

[65] The primary sources on this crisis are full and revealing, particularly *FRUS, 1895*. See also Nelson M. Blake, "Background of Cleveland's Venezuela Policy," *American Historical Review* 47 (January 1942): 261; John A. S. Grenville and George B. Young, *Politics, Strategy, and American Diplomacy: Studies in Foreign Policy, 1873–1917* (New Haven, Conn.: Yale University Press, 1966), 135–50; and Henry James, *Richard Olney and His Public Service* (Boston: Houghton Mifflin, 1923), 96–142.

gress, in which he proposed to work toward a resumption of diplomatic relations between Venezuela and Britain and the arbitration of the border dispute. The State Department forwarded the proposals to London. In February 1895, Congress followed the president's lead and announced its opposition to the British claims. Public support for this hawkish policy toward Britain was great and growing. Venezuela, for its part, was doing all it could to entangle the United States further. It granted a large concession of mineral-rich land to wealthy American investors. It hired William Scruggs to publicize its plight, and his pamphlet, *British Aggressions in Venezuela or the Monroe Doctrine on Trial*, became the most widely read and circulated piece of literature on the issue. Public and congressional interest, Scruggs's persistent lobbying, and a minor incident on the Uruan River all pushed Cleveland and Gresham toward a more activist policy. Then, in May 1895, Gresham died and was replaced by Richard Olney.

Formerly a railroad lawyer and then a labor-busting attorney general in the first Cleveland administration, Olney was not by nature jingoistic. He did not identify with the neo-Hamiltonians, yet his foreign policy was very much in that mold. His memorandum to Great Britain during the Venezuelan crisis defined the new diplomacy of the United States.[66] The first part of Olney's July 20 note outlined the history of the dispute, laying the blame primarily on Britain for the lack of a successful resolution. Occurring within the Western Hemisphere, the controversy necessarily concerned the "honor" and "interests" of the United States, and Washington could not view it "with indifference." Were a European power to deny to any state on the American continent its right to self-government and freedom, the United States would feel compelled to intervene. Asserting an American protectorate over the entire hemisphere, Olney famously went on, "Today the United States is practically sovereign on this continent and its fiat is law upon the subjects to which it confines its interposition." Olney explained that American influence was so strong "because in addition to all other grounds, its infinite resources combined with its isolated position render it master of the situation and practically invulnerable as against any or all other powers." The magnitude of American power and the absence of significant threats made the expansion of American influence in the area inevitable. Olney did not simply act as a classical realist; he thought and spoke as one. Before December 1895, when the British reply to Olney's memorandum arrived, news of the new secretary's actions leaked to the public and was received with great acclaim. Representative Thomas

---

[66] See *FRUS, 1895*, 1:545–62. For an excellent critique, see Dexter Perkins, *The Monroe Doctrine, 1867–1907* (Baltimore: Johns Hopkins Press, 1937), 153–68.

Paschal of Texas wrote to Olney, "Turn this Venezuelan question up or down, North, South, East or West, and it is a winner." Meanwhile, newspapers stoked anti-British sentiment.

In July 1895, as Olney was penning his strong words, a new prime minister entered 10 Downing Street. The Marquess of Salisbury was one of the shrewdest politicians in all Europe, a man of great wealth, position, confidence, and strong will, and possessed of an unyielding belief in Britain's dominant place in the world—particularly vis-à-vis its young offspring, the United States. Dismissive of arbitration in general, he could not have been expected to view Olney's proposal, however delicately framed, with great favor: "Like competitive examinations and sewage irrigation, arbitration is one of the famous nostrums of the age. Like them it will have its day and pass away, and future ages will look with pity at those who could have believed in such an expedient for bridling the ferocity of human passions."[67]

Salisbury's reply was true to form.[68] Britain was in no way interfering with Venezuela's right to self-government or freedom, he argued. It was merely negotiating over territories the British Crown had possessed for decades before the existence of an independent Venezuela. Then Salisbury directly attacked Olney's reassertion of the Monroe Doctrine. While the United States had vital interests in the Western Hemisphere and would naturally act to protect those interests, "no nation, however powerful, [is] competent to insert into the code of international law a novel principle which was never recognized before, and which has not since been accepted by the government of any country." Colonial Secretary Joseph Chamberlain had suggested that Salisbury point out to Washington "that Britain is an American power with a territorial area greater than the United States themselves, and with a title acquired prior to the independence of the United States."[69] With regard to the boundary dispute itself, Salisbury refused arbitration.

Cleveland and Olney were furious. The president's message to Congress that month brought the United States one step closer to war with Britain. Cleveland adamantly defended the basis of the Monroe Doctrine in international law and repeated that the United States regarded British incursions into Venezuela "as a willful aggression upon its rights and interests." He closed with these ominous words: "In making these

---

[67] Quoted in May, *Imperial Democracy*, 52–54.

[68] Salisbury's two-part reply can be found in *FRUS, 1895*, 1:563–76.

[69] In Chamberlain's view, London did not have to worry about provoking a war with Washington because America's unwieldy state structure ensured that action would be slow in coming. "First they would have to get the assent of the Senate—then appoint a commission then make an enquiry—and then?" On the memorandums of Salisbury and Chamberlain, see May, *Imperial Democracy*, 44–48.

recommendations I am fully alive to the responsibility incurred and keenly realize all the consequences that may follow."[70] The administration probably expected public support for its resolute stand, but it was disappointed. Americans reacted to Cleveland's message with great caution. Even Irish Americans showed little zeal in twisting the lion's tail. Many newspapers, traditionally anti-British and proexpansion, were stunned by the possibility of an actual war with Great Britain, and even Joseph Pulitzer's fiery *New York World* called for a peaceful end to the conflict. *The Nation* opined that Cleveland had received "the most unanimous and crushing rebuke that the pulpit of this country ever addressed to a President."[71] The business world, with its extensive financial and trading ties to England, was even more nervous. A few days after the president's message, the stock market crashed and remained highly volatile for the remainder of the crisis. Cleveland was later to write to a friend, "Nothing has ever hurt me so much as to know that these people who praised and flattered me . . . were ready to denounce and abuse me when my obligations to the country at large interfered with their money making schemes."[72]

Despite the rhetorical bravado from some quarters—the Irish National Alliance offered 100,000 men to help conquer Canada—most Americans still regarded Britain as the strongest nation on earth. Although the 1890s in retrospect mark the beginning of Britain's decline, at the time it appeared to be at the pinnacle of its power. Even staunch imperialists like Henry Cabot Lodge were subdued in their reaction to Cleveland's message. Senator Roger Q. Mills of Texas captured the national mood: "It will be no child's play, Mr. President, when we engage in a conflict with Great Britain." The reaction in Britain was less panicked, but the English were certainly not eager for a war with a formidable opponent like the United States. Several hundred members of Parliament called for arbitration. Joseph Chamberlain was sobered into thinking about his true long-term goals of cooperation for the two nations. Arthur Balfour, leader of the House of Commons and Salisbury's nephew, hoped that "some statesman of authority, more fortunate even than President Monroe, will lay down the doctrine that between English-speaking peoples, war is impossible."[73]

With both countries reluctant to escalate tensions still further, the conflict was soon settled. The Anglo-American agreement of November 12, 1896, provided for arbitration of the disputed boundary, exempting

[70] *FRUS, 1895,* 1:578.
[71] *The Nation* 61 (December 26, 1895): 456.
[72] Quoted in May, *Imperial Democracy,* 58.
[73] Campbell, *Transformation of American Foreign Relations,* 212–13.

properties with titles more than fifty years old. The other terms of the accord allowed each side to claim victory. But America's two key objectives had been attained. First, Britain had implicitly acknowledged the United States' right to intervene in any matter relating to any state in the hemisphere. Second, Britain had been forced to accept America's proposals on arbitration and title rights. The United States had involved itself in this conflict mainly to establish its influence in the region. Never, in the one and a half years of the crisis, did it consult Venezuela. In fact, by agreeing to the fifty-year exclusion, it had abandoned one of Venezuela's most cherished principles. And when in 1899 the arbitration panel gave British Guiana most of the disputed territory, the United States was quite unconcerned. Venezuela, on the other hand, regarded America's policy during the crisis as a complete betrayal. Three years later, it offered its strong support to Spain during the Spanish-American War.

The Cuban Revolution

In February 1895, another revolution erupted in Cuba. Cuba's crisis had been exacerbated by the 1894 Wilson-Gorman Tariff, which had denied the island's sugar growers access to the vast American market. As always, Cuban exiles in the United States assisted the rebels, who by September adopted a constitution for an independent Cuba. As the crisis persisted for the last two years of the administration's watch, Cleveland and his team reacted cautiously. Their principal concern was to maintain order and stability on the island, not least because of America's large economic interests there. The high-pitched political rhetoric contributed to the misperception that America's actions in Cuba were largely a result of moral pique, but this was not the driving factor, at least initially. In fact, the first impulse of the Cleveland administration— whose moral impulses have never been questioned—was to support Spain against the rebels, which it hoped would be the easiest way to bring stability back to the island. The administration even tried to pinch off rebel supplies and equipment. However, this approach soon proved inadequate and susceptible to congressional criticism.[74] Olney had determined by September 1895 that "Spain cannot possibly succeed" in quelling the rebellion, and he wondered whether the United States should recognize the independence of Cuba.[75]

The situation in Cuba only grew more dire. The new Spanish general, Valeriano Weyler y Nicolau, was a harsh man who announced that no further reforms would be forthcoming until order was established. In

---

[74] May, *Imperial Democracy*, 87.
[75] LaFeber, *The New Empire*, 289.

October Weyler initiated the *reconcentrado* policy, a systematic establishment of forced-labor camps for prisoners. Spain had observed the Cleveland administration's aggressive stances in Chile and Venezuela, and it was worried enough about American intervention that it requested support—unsuccessfully—from the great powers of Europe. When this news reached Washington, it aggravated the public mood. Congressional opinion moved strongly in favor of intervention, and both houses of Congress passed resolutions demanding that the rebels be recognized and the crisis brought to an end. By December 1896, Cleveland had shifted American policy toward intervention, even as he denied doing so. In his message to Congress, he declared that Spain had definitely lost control of the Cuban situation, and he warned that such chaos endangered American interests "which are by no means of a wholly sentimental or philanthropic nature." Those interests were largely economic and strategic, but Cleveland also noted that Spanish repression went against the American tradition of self-government and freedom. "When the inability of Spain to deal successfully with the insurrection has become manifest and its sovereignty is extinct over Cuba for all practical purposes . . . a situation will be presented in which our obligations to the sovereignty of Cuba will be superseded by our higher obligations, which we can hardly hesitate to recognize and discharge." He promised, at such a time, to bring "the blessings of peace" to Cuba.[76]

Years after the Spanish-American War, Cleveland claimed he would not have intervened in 1898. Whether or not that judgment is true, it is clear that Cleveland and, to a lesser extent, Olney were extremely cautious about intervening.[77] Several factors contributed to their reluctance: the crisis matured in the last year of Cleveland's term, Spanish policy vacillated between concessions and brutal repression, the United States was still mired in a deep recession, the attitude of the European powers was unclear. Above all, Cleveland did not believe that Cuba could be "incorporated into the American system." The tension between racism and liberal democracy that had surfaced in the discussions surrounding the annexation of Hawaii—they could never become "real" Americans, yet they had to be recognized as citizens—returned with greater force

<hr>

[76] Richardson, *Papers of the President*, 9:716–22.

[77] The more accepted view among historians is that "the Spanish-American War turned out to be McKinley's War, not because Cleveland was an old-fashioned isolationist with a stiffer backbone than his successor, but because he left office just in time." Beisner, *From the Old Diplomacy to the New*, 119, and in general 115–19. For the opposite case, see Allan Nevins, *Grover Cleveland: A Study in Courage* (New York: Dodd, Mead, 1932), 713–17; and George Roscoe Dulebohn, "Principles of Foreign Policy under the Cleveland Administrations" (Ph.D. dissertation, University of Pennsylvania, 1941), 51–60.

regarding Cuba.[78] Despite this hesitancy to intervene in Cuba, Cleveland's second term as president essentially continued the more active foreign and military policies begun under Harrison. His personal and his party's isolationist inclinations could not impede the structural pressures that demanded the United States take a more active role in world affairs.

MCKINLEY AND THE BIRTH OF THE AMERICAN EMPIRE, 1897–1901

From the election of William McKinley until 1908, this discussion becomes somewhat simpler. Most historians agree that this period saw a marked expansion of American interests abroad, as the United States pursued formal and informal imperialism. Also widely accepted is the view that the period was characterized by a booming economy, a strong presidency, and a relatively compliant Congress. When McKinley assumed office, institutional power within the government had already shifted toward the executive, but Congress still possessed a constitutional power that could have delayed or altered his plans should Congress have chosen to exercise it. However, with the Republican Party dominant in both the legislative and executive branches after the election of 1896, conflict between Congress and the president was minimized; in this era of Republican presidents, the Senate stayed Republican from 1895 to 1913 and the House from 1895 to 1911. Nor was the American state traumatized any longer by its Civil War debt. By the late 1890s, federal government revenues and expenditures were, by previous standards, consistently large; both hovered around $500 million, double the figure of ten years before.[79] Facing weaker structural constraints than those that had dissuaded his predecessors from pursuing an expansionist foreign policy, McKinley could respond easily to international systemic pressures, further closing the gap between America's power and its interests abroad.

The Road to War

The experience of William McKinley and the Spanish-American War is an excellent example of how structural pressures can overwhelm an in-

[78] Allan Nevins, *Letters of Grover Cleveland, 1850–1908* (Boston: Houghton Mifflin, 1933), 446–49.

[79] Jerald A. Combs, *American Diplomatic History: Two Centuries of Changing Interpretations* (Berkeley: University of California Press, 1983), 73–112; Richard Brandon, ed. *Encyclopedia of American History* (New York: Harper, 1953), 1212; Mitchell, *European Historical Statistics*, 1104.

dividual's personal preferences. Not that McKinley was an isolationist. From the moment he took office, he started work on plans to annex Hawaii, build an American isthmian canal, and continue the navy buildup. But he was not enthusiastic about a war with Spain, in part because he was by nature cautious and in part because he, like Cleveland, did not want to set off a chain of events that would force the United States to annex Cuba. Ruling a subject colony—as was the norm among the European powers—ran against America's values and its tradition; sparsely populated Hawaii could easily be absorbed, he thought, but Cuba, with its Spaniards and blacks, was another matter.[80] The growth of American power juxtaposed with the collapsing Spanish Empire produced a setting in which the persistence of Cuban instability made it virtually inevitable that the United States would intervene, notwithstanding McKinley's, and others', misgivings. What is puzzling about the Spanish-American War of 1898 is not why it happened, but why it was so long in coming.

When McKinley entered the White House, the depression that had begun three years before was still relentlessly raging. His first priority was to get the American economy back on its feet, and ambitious plans to "free" Cuba were hardly uppermost in his mind. McKinley's key constituency, the northern business elite, was for the most part opposed to hostilities with Spain. War, it feared, would bring uncertainty, spark volatility in the stock market, and potentially usher in looser monetary policies and inflation in the form of free silver. Of course, the segment of the American business community that traded with Cuba wanted an end to the hostilities that were ruining their commercial ventures, but the vast majority of their business colleagues were wary of war. As Senator Eugene Hale reported in 1896, "I have had hundreds of letters from businessmen all over the country . . . protesting against this whole crusade." Two years later, one week before the war started, Senator Benjamin Tillman explained to the Senate that his expansionist views were popular with most Americans save one important class, "the few thousand who live within the purview or within the influence of boards of trade and chambers of commerce and banking houses."[81]

Like Cleveland, McKinley held a conception of American interests

[80] See Healy, *U.S. Expansionism,* 52–53.
[81] Quoted in Campbell, *Transformation of American Foreign Relations,* 248. In the debate on this issue, LaFeber, *The New Empire,* makes the most sophisticated case that the commercial classes drove the war. A strong case for the opposite view is presented in Julius W. Pratt, *Expansionists of 1898: The Acquisition of Hawaii and the Spanish Islands* (Chicago: Quadrangle Books, 1964). Also see Charles S. Campbell, Jr., and David Pletcher, "Rhetoric and Results: A Pragmatic View of American Economic Expansion, 1865–1898," *Diplomatic History* 5, no. 2 (Spring 1981): 93–106.

that was less business-oriented than strategic, and like Cleveland, he in the end found himself advocating a more activist position than he had at first.[82] McKinley's original secretary of state, John Sherman, made clear in his initial instructions to the U.S. minister to Spain, General Stewart Woodford, that the United States had vital interests in Cuba and its environs and would not sit idly by if Spain did not bring peace to the island. Woodford, in conveying this message to the Spanish government, added a timetable. If Spain could not give satisfactory assurances to the United States of "an early and certain peace" by November 1, 1897, the United States would feel free to do "whatever she should deem necessary to procure this result."[83]

Despite Madrid's promises to Washington that it would ensure stability on the island and undertake significant political reform, in the period between the issuance of the ultimatum and the declaration of war, the situation on Cuba worsened considerably. In January 1898, in brutally quelling a riot in Havana, local officials made clear that, regardless of Madrid's orders, they would not implement any far-reaching reforms. As Spanish efforts to crush the rebellion failed, the cruelty of those attempts generated waves of sympathy in the United States. The highly respected Senator Redfield Proctor of Vermont, who opposed war with Spain, returned from Cuba devastated by the conditions there: "I went to Cuba with a strong conviction that the picture had been overdrawn. . . . I could not believe that out of a population of 1.6 million, 200,000 had died within these Spanish forts [the concentration camps]. . . . the case has not been overstated."[84]

That same month came the infamous sinking of the American battleship *Maine,* an episode identified in popular legend as the immediate cause of the war. The "yellow press" of Joseph Pulitzer and William Randolph Hearst played up the incident in gory detail, and those who wanted a war anyway, like Theodore Roosevelt, used it to stir up the public's wrath. But E. L. Godkin felt that most people were not taking these war cries seriously.[85] Several incidents actually triggered the conflict; it was a war waiting to happen. A crisis of equally grave proportions, certainly one that angered McKinley more, was the de Lôme letter. Dupuy de Lôme, the Spanish minister in Washington, wrote a

---

[82] Most historians note the continuity between the policies of Cleveland and those of McKinley. See Beisner, *From the Old Diplomacy to the New;* Healy, *U.S. Expansionism;* May, *Imperial Democracy;* LaFeber, *The New Empire;* and John M. Dobson, *America's Ascent: The United States Becomes a Great Power, 1880–1914* (De Kalb: Northern Illinois University Press, 1978).

[83] *FRUS, 1898,* 559, 567.

[84] *Congressional Record,* 55th Cong., 2d sess., 2916–19.

[85] *The Nation* 66 (February 24, 1898): 139–40.

private letter to a friend in which he called McKinley "weak," "a bidder for the admiration of the crowd," and "a would-be politician." To these insults, he added that Spain's diplomatic concessions were only "for effect."[86] When this indication of Spanish duplicity was leaked to the press, it created an uproar. De Lôme resigned in disgrace. Soon after, the Naval Board issued its report on the *Maine,* concluding that the battleship had been destroyed by a submarine mine. Even those inclined to believe the Spanish government, which fervently denied a role in the sinking, concluded that it had lost control over its own sailors, who might at any point harm Americans and their property. By late February 1898, the atmosphere was so tense that Secretary of the Navy John Long wrote in his diary that "the slightest spark is liable to result in War."[87]

McKinley had begun to contemplate seriously the possibility of war. He in effect asked Joe Cannon, chairman of the House Appropriations Committee, that national power be converted into state power, which he could then turn into military might: "I must have money to get ready for war. I am doing everything possible to prevent war but it must come, and we are not prepared for war." His request came at an opportune moment. The depression was over, and the economy—and treasury revenues—were expanding. Both the Senate and the House were Republican by solid majorities, and the mood in Congress was considerably more belligerent toward Cuba and more acquiescent toward the president than it had been in a long time. Congress passed $50 million in emergency military funds. The Spaniards were, in Minister Woodford's phrase, "stunned." "To appropriate fifty millions out of money in the treasury, without borrowing a cent, demonstrates wealth and power. Even Spain can see this," he reported.[88] Through the 1890s, American national power had grown, with state power following in its path. The time was ripe for a massive expansion of American influence abroad.

At the end of March 1898, the administration made a final attempt to negotiate with Spain. Woodford was asked to probe to see whether Madrid would agree to an armistice, an end to the concentration camps, and the acceptance of the president as an arbiter between Spain and the insurgents. The message was framed somewhat ambiguously; it did not explicitly state what specific actions would constitute compliance, what U.S. action was threatened, and what the third condition really meant. Spain responded quite moderately, agreeing to end the

[86] Quoted in LaFeber, *The New Empire,* 347.
[87] *The Journal of John D. Long,* ed. Margaret Long (Rindge: Richard Smith, 1956), 216.
[88] Quoted in LaFeber, *The New Empire,* 349–50.

concentration camps, making some vague noises regarding an armistice, and ignoring the third point altogether. Woodford interpreted Spain's reply as meaning a "continuation of this cruel, destructive and now needless war."[89] Despite Madrid's concessions, the mood in Washington demanded no less than full compliance with its terms.

On April 11, McKinley sent his message to Congress. Congress had been anxious to recognize the independent government of Cuba. McKinley strongly opposed this move; he wanted to keep America's options open. By now the crucial issue was no longer whether the United States would go to war but, as Paul Holbo writes, "who was to direct American policy."[90] Twenty years before, the president would not have stood a chance in such a struggle; now, within weeks, Congress backed down. On April 20, McKinley signed the congressional joint resolution directing the president to use force to ensure that Spain evacuate Cuba. The resolution also specified that Cuba was not to become an American colony. Thus humiliated, Spain broke diplomatic relations with the United States. On April 25, Congress declared war on Spain.[91]

McKinley has been unfairly portrayed as a weak, vacillating figure pushed into war by a jingoistic press and a war-hungry Congress. A shrewd man, cautious and conservative by nature, McKinley steadily sought the expansion of American influence in Cuba. He hoped he could achieve this end peacefully, by forcing Spanish concessions. Congress and the "yellow press" had consistently been calling for war since 1895. McKinley could have dealt with their posturing as Cleveland had. But as it became increasingly clear that Spain did not want to cede its authority in Cuba and was too weak to transfer control to the United States, his analysis of the costs and benefits of war changed. McKinley's concerns about the effects of war on commerce were allayed by shifting views within the business sector; it began to prefer a quick resolution to the crisis rather than a longer, drawn-out civil war. The calculation of cost in terms of U.S. lives also shifted in favor of war: with the new appropriations, most estimated that the United States was by far the stronger power. Churchill's famous phrase could be applied to McKinley's policy in Cuba: McKinley wanted not war, but the fruits of war— the expansion of American power and influence. He found, however, that he had to fight a war to pluck the fruits.

---

[89] Ibid., 352.

[90] Paul S. Holbo, "Presidential Leadership in Foreign Affairs: William McKinley and the Turpie-Foraker Amendment," *American Historical Review* 72 (July 1967): 1322–34.

[91] Actually, it declared that a state of war had existed between the two countries as of April 21.

The Scramble for Colonies

If not "splendid," the Spanish-American War was certainly "little."[92] With under four hundred battle deaths, it was, at the time, the least costly war in American history. The war, however, is memorable for its aftereffects, for it conferred upon the United States the mantle of a great power. "Between wars," Ernest May writes, "judgments [about power] are entirely subjective; war is the only objective test."[93] America had triumphed in this test, and both the United States and the rest of the world knew it. Although the American army in Cuba was badly prepared and badly outfitted—Theodore Roosevelt's legendary Rough Riders almost killed themselves in a senseless charge into enemy fire— the United States routed Spain on land and sea, culminating in the destruction of the Spanish fleet off Santiago in July. Within a week of the declaration of the war, the most dramatic event took place thousands of miles away from Cuba. Following instructions from Assistant Secretary of the Navy Roosevelt that had been approved by Secretary Long, Commodore George Dewey attacked the Spanish fleet in the Philippines. More than anything that occurred on Cuba, this was the shot heard round the world. Humiliated, but almost relieved that the trauma was brief, Spain capitulated, and on August 12, 1898, an armistice was announced.

The mood in the United States was utterly triumphant. McKinley asked Americans to thank the Lord for this magnificent victory. Newspapers were filled with editorials, articles, and speeches extolling the power, virtue, and glory of the United States. The reaction abroad, though not quite as strong, was impressive. The London *Times* declared in a long editorial, "In the future America will play a part in the general affairs of the world such as she has never played before." John Hay, the U.S. ambassador to London, wrote to the president of the European reaction: "We have never in all our history had the standing in the world we have now." This dramatic domestic recognition of American power brought with it, as state-centered realism would predict, the desire for the expansion of American influence. As a contemporary historian wrote, "The brilliancy of their [Americans'] achievements in the war had quickened their imagination and greatly broadened their aspirations and ambitions." The *Chicago Times-Herald*, expressing a common sentiment, found that things had suddenly changed: "We now find that we want the Philippines. . . . We also want Puerto Rico. . . . We

---

[92] The phrase "splendid little war" is usually attributed to John Hay.
[93] May, *Imperial Democracy*, 6.

want Hawaii now . . . We may want the Carolines, the Ladrones, the Pelew, and the Marianna groups." This anti-imperialist newspaper had difficulty accepting these new ambitions, but it admitted that "the people now believe that the United States owes it to the world to accept the responsibilities imposed upon it by the fortunes of war." *The Literary Digest* asked editors nationwide whether the United States should keep the Philippines, and the results reflected this change in the national mood: 84 favored outright annexation, 17 sought a protectorate, 66 wanted only a naval station, 3 suggested selling the islands, and not one suggested returning the islands to Spain or granting them independence.[94]

In this heady atmosphere, within one year the United States expanded into Hawaii, Cuba, Puerto Rico, Guam, the Wake Islands, the Philippines, and Samoa. Hawaiian annexation had been a goal of McKinley's from the start of his administration, and reports of recent Japanese interest strengthened his conviction. In June 1897, the president had sent a treaty of annexation to the Senate, but with the recession still lingering and many Democrats reluctant to approve a project that their president, Cleveland, had once shelved, McKinley failed to muster the sixty votes needed for approval. Two days after news reached Washington of Dewey's triumph in Manila, McKinley sent the treaty back to the Senate. "We need Hawaii just as much and a good deal more than we did California," he argued. "It is manifest destiny."[95] Although the military victories had strengthened McKinley's hand, he did not want to take a risk again in the Senate, so he proposed a joint congressional resolution, which required just a simple majority of both houses. This device had been used by President James Polk to acquire Texas, but in the 1860s and 1870s it had been widely denounced and considered unconstitutional. In 1898 it passed easily—in fact, in the Senate it passed with a two-thirds majority—and on August 12 of that year Hawaii became a U.S. territory.

With regard to Samoa, after fresh trouble there in 1898 the United States decided to settle the matter with Great Britain and Germany. Britain withdrew in favor of the other two countries, and Berlin and Washington carved up the islands. The native chiefs of Tutuila, America's prize, ceded the island to the United States in 1900. The president accepted on behalf of the country and did not even bother presenting an annexation treaty to Congress.

Cuba, Puerto Rico, Guam, and the Wake Islands were seized from the

---

[94] Walter Millis, *The Martial Spirit* (Chicago: Ivan R. Dee, 1959), 316–18; May, *Imperial Democracy*, 220–21; Campbell, *Transformation of American Foreign Relations*, 299; Healy, *U.S. Expansionism*, 64.

[95] Russ, *The Hawaiian Revolution*, 240.

THE NEW DIPLOMACY 161

Spanish, in all cases without the support of the populace. The Cubans wanted independence and were wary of becoming an American colony. The Puerto Ricans, who enjoyed great autonomy under Spanish rule, were angered by America's military takeover of their island. These were not haphazard acquisitions; McKinley used America's enhanced power position at the end of the war to achieve objectives he had outlined earlier. In June 1898, he had maintained that Cuba, Puerto Rico, a Philippines naval base, and perhaps some other island bases should end up with the United States. In the Treaty of Paris, signed on December 10, 1898, Spain ceded "all claims of sovereignty over and title to" Cuba, Puerto Rico, the Philippines, Guam, and any other islands in the Spanish West Indies. For the first time in a treaty acquiring territory, the United States made no promise of citizenship. Since the formal status of Hawaii and Cuba was already clear, and Puerto Rico, Guam, and the Wake Islands were too small to raise concerns, debate in the Senate focused on the Philippines. While the public favored imperialism, the elite anti-imperialist tradition was still strong, and fears of associating with a distant land of nonwhite savages were great.[96] In February 1899, the Senate passed the treaty by a margin of 57 to 27, one vote more than the required two-thirds. The American mood in general, however, was ebullient. The dour Henry Adams complained, "I find America so cheerful, and so full of swagger and self-satisfaction, that I hardly know it." Adams attributed this changed America to "McKinley's prosperity" and the war of 1898.[97]

China and the Open Door

China had always held an important place in the American imagination. The twin goals of bringing goods and God to the Chinese people had lured scores of businessmen and missionaries to the country for almost two centuries. The fabled "China market" actually constituted just over 1 percent of American exports in the 1890s, but the potential was thought to be limitless. For missionaries as well, the attraction of China lay in its immense population. The thought of Christianizing hundreds of millions of Chinese made other missionary work seem trivial. The 1890s saw these impulses grow in strength. The U.S. government was interested in expanding its influence in China, and after the Spanish-American War it was determined to do so. The acquisition of the Philip-

[96] The Anti-imperialist League included among its members Grover Cleveland, Benjamin Harrison, William James, Andrew Carnegie, and Mark Twain.

[97] Quoted in Bradford Perkins, *The Great Rapprochement: England and the United States, 1895–1914* (New York: Atheneum, 1968), 89.

pines, Guam, and Samoa moved American attention from the Caribbean and the Americas to the Pacific. The Republican expansionists had always believed that the country's future lay in the Pacific and not the Atlantic. Secretary of State John Hay regarded China as "the key to world politics for the next five centuries."[98]

Around 1898, the great-power rivalry in China began to heat up. At the end of the Sino-Japanese War in early 1898, the great powers of Europe had carved out "spheres of influence"—essentially trading ports with some adjoining territory. Britain had asked the United States if it would join in a condemnation of this approach and a defense of the Open Door to China. The United States, distracted by the situation in Cuba, refused. One year later, its confidence boosted after the Spanish-American War, the United States harbored greater ambitions in the Far East. In mid-1899 Russia and Germany threatened to close their ports to the other powers. Hay regarded this possibility with great concern. The other industrial powers could always enter China through their designated ports, but for the United States, the only great industrial state without a specific sphere of influence in China, the Russian and German moves portended the closing of the Chinese market. Hay's famous Open Door note of September 1899 was the U.S. response to this threat to its economic interests. It asked the great powers to observe and enforce the commercial treaty rights of all nations within their spheres of influence. Less out of any concern for the Chinese, who were not consulted, than to prevent the diminution of American access, Hay further declared U.S. support for the maintenance of China's territorial integrity and the equitable application of Chinese tariffs. Through some clever diplomacy, Hay succeeded in gaining the assent of all the major powers involved—Great Britain, France, Germany, Japan, and Russia.

The Chinese, offended by the dominance of outsiders in determining their country's fate, launched the Boxer Rebellion in early 1900, which erupted in a series of attacks on foreigners and their property. As the Manchu dynasty's dowager empress watched and even encouraged them, the Chinese rebels laid siege to consulates and murdered the German minister in Peking. The central government feebly attempted to quell the revolt. The reaction of the American minister was similar to that of the representatives of the other major powers. He requested that the fleet be sent to the Chinese coast "to frighten the Chinese into compliance. . . . The Chinese Government really cares little about anything

---

[98] Quoted in William Neumann, "Determinism, Destiny, and Myth in the American Image of China," in George Anderson, ed., *Issues and Conflicts: Studies in Twentieth Century American Diplomacy* (Lawrence: University of Kansas Press, 1959), 1. The best book on this general subject is Michael H. Hunt, *The Making of a Special Relationship: The United States and China to 1914* (New York: Columbia University Press, 1983).

but power and an earnest exhibition of it always promptly moves them."[99] McKinley responded by sending five thousand troops to China—without any congressional approval—to protect American property and restore order. But a larger problem emerged from the aftermath of the rebellion: the great powers were planning to use it as an excuse to seal off their spheres. Hay retaliated by sending the second Open Door note, in which the United States again asked that all the powers preserve China's territorial and administrative integrity. The nervous great powers fell into line.

George Kennan has criticized Hay's policy as dangerous because the United States was unwilling (and unable) to back up its insistence on these lofty principles with force.[100] But Hay was always acutely aware of the limits of America's power in the Far East, and therefore his policy took the form of trying to convince the other major states to accept "neutral" principles that also happened to protect and enhance America's position. As Hay explained to McKinley, "The inherent weakness of our position is this: we do not want to rob China ourselves, and our public opinion will not permit us to interfere, with an army, to prevent others from robbing her. Besides, we have no army. The talk in the papers about 'our preeminent moral position giving us the authority to dictate to the world' is mere flap-doodle."[101] The United States would extend its influence as far as it possibly could at little cost, but when, one year later, Japan strongly objected to the American request of the Chinese for a naval base at Samsah Bay, Hay backed down immediately. In the Western Hemisphere, U.S. power was dominant, and the European states lacked the means to project enough power to challenge the American position; expansion of American influence in the Caribbean and Central and South America was a relatively simple task. American expansion in Asia would have to be of a different order.

Under William McKinley's leadership, America undertook the most dramatic extension of its interests abroad since the annexation of Texas. McKinley also so brazenly expanded presidential power that some have called him the first modern president. He cleverly formed a cabinet that had relatively few members with independent political bases; his appointees were men well versed in the ways of corporate America and with extensive administrative skills, but their political power depended entirely on their allegiance to him. The Senate, a powerful voice in domestic affairs, normally deferred to the president on matters of foreign

[99] Hunt, *United States and China to 1914*, 154.
[100] George F. Kennan, *American Diplomacy, 1900–1950*, (Chicago: University of Chicago Press, 1951) 21–38.
[101] Quoted in Walter LaFeber, *The American Age: United States Foreign Policy at Home and Abroad Since 1750* (New York: W. W. Norton, 1989), 209.

policy. McKinley took advantage of his executive power to enlarge the presidency still further: he dispatched troops to China to help put down the Boxers without consulting Congress. Never before had a president used force against a recognized government without obtaining a declaration of war. "In a centripetal-centrifugal effect, as U.S. foreign policy spread globally, authority over that policy centralized in the chief executive's office."[102]

Yet the policies he pursued were not terribly different from those of his two predecessors. Had another figure been president, the expansion of American influence abroad would likely have occurred anyway, just as it continued after McKinley left office. McKinley's tenure certainly does represent an exception to the American rule in that his policies led to formal colonialism, which Americans would soon regret and to which they would not again aspire. But through a variety of means, presidents after McKinley ensured that the United States had access to and a large measure of control over sea lanes, port facilities, strategic locations, and even the domestic order of foreign countries in the Caribbean and Latin America. While imperialism may have come and gone with McKinley, American expansionism and foreign policy activism remained vigorous under his successors.[103]

THEODORE ROOSEVELT AND THE SEVENTH GREAT POWER, 1901–1908

Theodore Roosevelt represented the second coming of William Henry Seward. Like Seward, he was an unabashed expansionist who believed America had come of age as a mighty nation. Like Seward, he sought expansion across the full range of its expression—a larger army and navy, an expanded diplomatic corps, an activist diplomacy, and American political control over foreign territories. America's economic power was ample; indeed, the country was so wealthy as to be in danger of decadence. It needed strategic goals and a vigorous foreign policy that would help it "take the position to which it is entitled among the nations of the world." For Roosevelt, expansionism was not just necessary, but morally praiseworthy as well. "Our people are neither craven nor weaklings," he proclaimed, "and we face the future high of heart and confident of soul eager to do the great work of a great world

---

[102] LaFeber, *American Search for Opportunity*, 135–36, 177.

[103] Theodore Roosevelt repeatedly drew this same distinction between expansionism and imperialism. See Howard K. Beale, *Theodore Roosevelt and the Rise of America to World Power* (Baltimore: Johns Hopkins Press, 1956), 68–69.

THE NEW DIPLOMACY 165

power." He saw himself in the line of American statesmen who, like Seward, had historically matched American power with new interests.[104]

The difference between the two men, however, lay in their ability to realize their expansionist dreams. Roosevelt came to power after thirty years of sustained economic growth, at a time when the national government and the executive had grown in stature and power, and immediately after an international war that had crystallized the image of American strength in the minds of diplomats around the world. As a result, Roosevelt presided over the fulfillment of most of Seward's pet projects. Hawaii, Samoa, and Puerto Rico were already American, as was, in effect, Cuba. The navy was large, continuously expanding, and steadily acquiring new bases abroad. Roosevelt continued the enlargement of the armed forces and also began American expansion into the Danish West Indies and Santo Domingo, built the Panama Canal, and effectively established, through the Roosevelt Corollary, the American hemispheric empire of which Seward had but dreamed. He even took up Seward's interest in broader great-power diplomacy, taking part in the Algeciras Conference on the future of Morocco and brokering peace in the Russo-Japanese War. During Roosevelt's presidency, the world came to see America as a full-fledged great power. At the close of Theodore Roosevelt's administration, William Henry Seward could have rested in peace.[105]

Britain Falling: Panama and Canada

Roosevelt immediately set out to fulfill certain long-standing American goals, the most important of which was the construction of an isthmian canal. The project had never received sustained U.S. government support in part because a canal controlled exclusively by the United States would have violated the 1850 Clayton-Bulwer agreement with Britain, which had promised that Britain would be a full partner with the Americans in any canal. Congress had always been dismissive of this problem, and anti-British sentiment was high even as late as Roosevelt's presidency. But the executive branch had always been more responsible in its concern about observing treaty provisions and also more impressed

---

[104] Healy, *U.S. Expansionism*, 35; Beale, *Theodore Roosevelt*, 38–39.

[105] Other than Beale, *Theodore Roosevelt*, good studies of Roosevelt are John Morton Blum, *The Republican Roosevelt* (Cambridge: Harvard University Press, 1954); William Henry Harbaugh, *Power and Responsibility: The Life and Times of Theodore Roosevelt* (New York: Farrar, Straus and Cudahy, 1961); and Frederick W. Marks III, *Velvet on Iron: The Diplomacy of Theodore Roosevelt* (Lincoln: University of Nebraska Press, 1979).

by British power. And, as the Venezuelan boundary crisis showed, if a situation ever threatened to make anti-British rhetoric more concrete, the congressional hawks turned into doves.

Yet by the late 1890s, Britain had adopted a rather different attitude toward the United States. It had recognized that America was the most significant rising power in the world and that British interests in the Western Hemisphere were exposed. Britain had two choices: it could either contest this nascent power or accommodate it. A declining Britain opted for the latter approach.[106] While British officials were rethinking the two countries' relationship, two events settled the issue in their minds: the Spanish-American War and the Boer War. The first vividly displayed American power, and the second showed the limits of Britain's force-projection capabilities. In 1900 the naval attaché to Washington wrote to London, "It cannot be questioned that [America] in general is in favor of a fleet commensurate with the wealth of the nation and strong enough for all purposes." The political implications of the naval buildup were clear. Whitehall's internal documents of the period are full of references to the "necessity for preserving amicable relations with the United States" and "the painful decision to rely on American goodwill" to protect British interests in the Western Hemisphere.[107] Beginning in the mid-1890s, Britain withdrew substantial military forces from the Americas and limited its political interests there. (Paul Kennedy has pointed out that appeasement of America was largely responsible for the longevity of the British Empire.)[108] The Republican expansionists drew the very same lessons from the Spanish-American and Boer Wars. The Boer War in particular stunned them. "It certainly does seem to me that Britain is on the down-grade," then—Vice President Roosevelt wrote privately to a friend. Even John Hay, who was an Anglophile, confessed to Henry Adams, "The serious thing is the discovery, now past doubt, that the British have lost all skill in fighting, and the whole world knows it, and is regulating itself accordingly."[109]

To open the path for a U.S. isthmian canal, Hay had negotiated a new treaty in early 1900, the Hay-Pauncefote Treaty, which absolved the United States of the need to share control of a canal with Britain or even to get Britain's permission to build it. But the treaty had been

[106] Many books have been written on this subject. The best are Friedberg, *The Weary Titan;* Kenneth Bourne, *Britain and the Balance of Power in North America, 1815–1908* (Berkeley: University of California Press, 1967); and Perkins, *The Great Rapprochement.*

[107] Friedberg, *The Weary Titan,* 164, 177–78, 187–88.

[108] Paul M. Kennedy, *Strategy and Diplomacy, 1870–1945* (London: Allen and Unwin, 1983).

[109] Beale, *Theodore Roosevelt,* 95–102; also see John H. Ferguson, *American Diplomacy and the Boer War* (Philadelphia: University of Pennsylvania Press, 1939).

perceived at home as being too pro-British; even Henry Cabot Lodge and Roosevelt had opposed it, and it had been quite easily defeated in the Senate. Hay began renegotiating with the British, who offered further concessions, and on November 18, 1901, the second Hay-Pauncefote Treaty was signed. It overturned all the provisions of the Clayton-Bulwer Treaty and allowed the United States to construct, fortify, and operate an isthmian canal entirely on its own terms. As one historian notes, "This treaty granted to the United States everything James G. Blaine had unsuccessfully sought from Great Britain in 1881. Britain's friendly acquiescence in 1901 illustrates how much the United States' international stature had changed in two decades."[110]

Now that the United States had cleared the legal hurdles to building the canal, it had to settle on a location. Nicaragua was the obvious choice. Official commissions had twice recommended it as the cheapest place to build a canal. The second possible route was across Panama, a rebellious province of Colombia. Congress left the decision to the president. Roosevelt leaned toward the Panama option, and he gained supporters when a volcano erupted in Nicaragua. The secretary of state negotiated the Hay-Herran Treaty, which allowed the United States to build and fortify the canal across Panama and to control a zone of land running three miles on either side. The Senate swiftly approved the treaty, but Colombia stalled, hoping for a better offer. This was not how Roosevelt envisioned dealing with a small Central American country. He publicly called the Colombian leaders "banditti" and quietly encouraged the Panamanians to revolt. In November 1903 they followed his advice, and the U.S. Navy provided cover for them, preventing Colombian troops from landing to snuff out the rebellion. Two days after the rebellion began, Roosevelt recognized the Republic of Panama and began negotiating a new treaty for the canal. The terms of the revised treaty were even more favorable to the United States: it widened the canal zone from six to ten miles and named the United States the guarantor of Panama's independence. Over the next ten years, political instability in Panama ensured that the United States was a constant political and military presence in the country. By 1913 Panama had accepted de facto protectorate status, with an arrangement much like Cuba's.[111]

---

[110] Dobson, *America's Ascent*, 154; on this point also see Norman Penlington, *The Alaska Boundary: A Critical Reappraisal* (Toronto: University of Toronto Press, 1972).

[111] For the details of these events, see Richard H. Collin, *Theodore Roosevelt's Caribbean: The Panama Canal, the Monroe Doctrine, and the Latin American Context* (Baton Rouge: Louisiana State University Press, 1990); Howard C. Hill, *Roosevelt and the Caribbean* (Chicago: University of Chicago Press, 1927); and for a briefer account, Dana G. Munro, *Intervention and Dollar Diplomacy in the Caribbean, 1900–1921* (Princeton, N.J.: Princeton University Press, 1964).

Roosevelt did not bother to consult with Congress while he negotiated with the Nicaraguans and then the Colombians, incited Panama to
revolt, recognized the new country, and finally drew up a new treaty. In
a famous speech years later, in 1911, he justified his behavior: "If I had
followed the general consultative method I should have submitted an
admirable state paper, occupying a couple of hundred pages detailing
the facts to Congress and asking Congress consideration of it; in which
there would have been a number of excellent speeches on the subject
. . . and the debate would be proceeding at the moment with great
spirit, and the beginning of the canal would be 50 years in the future."
Roosevelt then added the well-known quip, "I took the Canal Zone and
let Congress debate, and while the debate goes on the Canal does too."
Though many congressmen were outraged by the arrogance of presidential power—they even formed a committee to investigate the matter—it
did not have any repercussions. Roosevelt was unyielding in his defense,
outlining a broad interpretation of presidential powers in foreign affairs: "When the interests of the American people demanded that a certain act should be done, and I had the power to do it, I did it unless it
was specifically prohibited by law."[112]

Settlement of the U.S. rights to an isthmian canal had always been
linked to a boundary dispute between the United States and Canada.
The area in dispute, a long stretch of the Alaskan coastline about thirty
miles wide, was of interest in large part because gold had been discovered in it. The United States had the stronger case; the area was clearly
part of the land purchased by Seward in 1867. Yet the Canadian government, extremely eager to obtain the land, had asked Britain to negotiate on its behalf. Grover Cleveland had futilely tried to settle the issue
by asking for a bilateral deal between America and Canada. Roosevelt,
on the other hand, did not want any solution that might divide the
territory. He knew that Britain would give in on an issue it did not care
much about. "I am going to be ugly," he told a British friend. An arbitration panel was created with three Americans, two Canadians, and
one Englishman. Roosevelt appointed three blatantly partisan Americans, so the decision rested on the shoulders of the British member,
Lord Alverstone, the Lord Chief Justice of Great Britain. In the course
of the negotiations, Hay had made noises about a possible war if Britain
did not settle matters to America's satisfaction. Alverstone ruled with
the Americans, giving most of the land to the United States. Once again
Britain had backed down to accommodate America's increasingly expansive interpretation of its interests.[113]

[112] See Collin, *Theodore Roosevelt's Caribbean*, 322–26.
[113] Lawrence Martin, *The Presidents and the Prime Ministers: Washington and Ottawa*

Central and Latin America

After Spain gave Cuba its independence, American troops, led by General Leonard Wood, ruled the island. Both McKinley and Roosevelt intended to prepare Cuba for self-government, but they also wished to maintain a strong measure of American influence over the island. In 1900 Wood convened a constitutional convention in Cuba and asked that the representatives include provisions that prevented Cuba from entering into treaties with foreign governments and that gave the United States the responsibility and right to intervene in Cuba as it saw fit "for the preservation of Cuban independence, the maintenance of a government adequate for the protection of life, property and individual liberty."[114] The Cubans refused to incorporate these articles, and the American troops refused to leave until they did. The Cubans finally capitulated, and on May 20, 1902, the troops left. The new constitution contained the articles better known by the name of the relevant bill passed by Congress—the Platt Amendment. The provisions made Cuba virtually a protectorate of the United States. The United States took advantage of this clearly stated theoretical right to intervene just a few years later. In 1905 a series of events, mainly rigged elections, led to the collapse of the liberal, pro-American government of Cuba. Chaos ensued, and in the summer of 1906 Washington, which by then saw itself as the guarantor of order in the entire region, dispatched troops to Cuba. The occupation lasted three years.

Further south, Roosevelt revived the plan to purchase the Danish West Indies. Hay negotiated a treaty of annexation with Denmark, and the Senate easily approved it. The Danish Senate, however, rejected it, postponing yet again Seward's pet project. In 1917 Woodrow Wilson would finally consummate the deal and create the U.S. Virgin Islands.

Roosevelt adopted a highly aggressive foreign policy to prevent European penetration of the hemisphere. The German government, having tried and failed to collect outstanding debts from Venezuela by other means, had decided to turn to a show of force.[115] Conscious of American power and interests in the region, Germany informed the United States that it intended to stage a naval demonstration off the coast of Venezuela and that it had no territorial ambitions whatsoever. England decided to join in the display and similarly informed Washington. The

---

Face to Face: The Myth of Bilateral Bliss, 1867–1982 (Garden City, N.Y.: Doubleday, 1982), 58–61; also see Beale, *Theodore Roosevelt,* 110–31.

[114] Munro, *Intervention and Dollar Diplomacy,* 56.

[115] Ibid., 65–78. See also Nancy Mitchell, "The Height of the German Challenge: The Venezuela Blockade, 1902–3," *Diplomatic History* 20 no. 2, (Spring 1996): 185–209.

United States seemed unconcerned; in fact, Roosevelt was pleased that the two great powers recognized America's sphere of influence. It was the first time European powers had asked America's permission before dealing with a Latin American country.[116] But the attempt at intimidation did not work, and the foreign ships sank some Venezuelan gunboats. Caracas turned to America for help. Roosevelt decided that the Europeans had gone too far and intervened, demanding that they accept American arbitration. The British agreed; the Germans initially did not. Roosevelt leveled a not-so-veiled threat at the German ambassador in Washington and asked Admiral George Dewey, hero of the Philippines, to conduct full fleet operations in Culebra.[117] The kaiser swiftly agreed to arbitration.[118] Once again, Latin Americans complained that Washington and Europe were determining their fate. Roosevelt was actually moving to cut Europe out of the equation altogether.

The trigger event for a full-scale reevaluation of U.S. Latin American policy was turmoil in Santo Domingo. The republic, whose annexation had been Seward's very first project, was in debt to several European and American companies. Roosevelt decided to revive a plan that James Blaine had attempted to implement in 1881: the United States took over the Santo Domingo customhouse and collected its duties. In December 1904, in a message to Congress after the fact, Roosevelt explained that while the United States had no further territorial claims or ambitions in the hemisphere, it reserved "an international police power" when a country's "inability or unwillingness to do justice at home or abroad had violated the rights of the United States or had invited foreign aggression to the detriment of the entire body of American nations."[119] This Roosevelt Corollary to the Monroe Doctrine, as it became known, made the United States the sole arbiter for both the Europeans and the countries of the region. The United States was asserting the right of intervention to maintain order in its vast backyard. Two years later, when the Guatemalan civil war spread into Honduras and El Salvador, the United States and Mexico intervened and brokered a peace settlement. The United States even established a Central American Court of Justice, like the court in The Hague, to arbitrate disputes among Central American republics.

The Roosevelt Corollary and its application to the case of Santo

[116] Perkins, *The Monroe Doctrine*, 394.

[117] There is some controversy as to whether Roosevelt did, in fact, make such a threat. He claimed to have done so, and much scholarship bears him out. See Seward Livermore, "Theodore Roosevelt, the American Navy and the Venezuelan Crisis of 1902–1903," *American Historical Review* 51 (April 1946): 452–71.

[118] The International Court ruled that the Europeans had acted within their powers.

[119] Hill, *Roosevelt and the Caribbean*, 113.

Domingo was presented by both admirers and detractors as an alternative to annexation.[120] Roosevelt sent the Santo Domingo treaty to the Senate for approval, but the Senate saw it as too great an expansion of American interests in the Caribbean and decided to reject it. But the president of the United States would not be thwarted. Roosevelt signed an executive agreement with the government of Santo Domingo, which did not require any Senate action. Roosevelt's agents took control of the island, and the agents of the major New York banks assisted in its daily administration. Debts to all parties, European and American, were repaid. This episode completed the process by which the United States turned the Monroe Doctrine on its head. Formulated when the United States was a weak nation, still surrounded in North America by great European powers, the doctrine originally espoused nonintervention and support for revolutionary movements. With the growth of the United States into the dominant regional power and a world power, the doctrine had been reinterpreted to sanction American intervention against Latin American revolutions.[121] Santo Domingo was also a clear example of a previously rare practice that Theodore Roosevelt made into a normal presidential tool: the executive agreement. Roosevelt used this device often to bypass Congress in the making of foreign policy. Unlike a treaty, this understanding between two governments is honored only for the life of the administration; in essence, it is a personal promise from the president. "But Roosevelt judged (correctly) that future presidents would uphold his agreements—in part because they would want their successors to uphold their deals."[122] The practice, of course, continues to this day.

Going West to Asia

For all of Roosevelt's braggadocio in the Western Hemisphere, he approached Asia much more cautiously. Not that he did not want to expand American interests there; on the contrary, he was among those who believed that America's future lay in the Pacific. But Roosevelt knew what Secretary of State John Hay had explained to his predecessor: the United States' power position in the Far East was relatively weak, and there were limits as to how much American interests could be expanded there. Roosevelt's careful expansionist behavior in Asia clearly demonstrates that classical realists do not expand recklessly; as Roosevelt did, they perform a cost-benefit analysis, and whereas the

[120] Ibid., 162.
[121] See Perkins, *The Monroe Doctrine.*
[122] LaFeber, *The American Age,* 224.

United States could penetrate the Caribbean at its whim, that was not the case in Asia. The Pacific rim encompassed several great powers, some old like Russia and China, and one important new one, Japan. Roosevelt's respect for Japan was enormous. He wrote in 1905 to Henry Cabot Lodge, "As for Japan, she has risen with simply marvelous rapidity, and she is as formidable from the industrial as the military standpoint. She is a great civilized nation. . . . [I]n a dozen years I think she will be the leading industrial nation of the Pacific."[123]

After the Boxer Rebellion, Russia alone had refused to withdraw from northern China. It was attempting, not very secretly, to intimidate the Chinese government into granting it certain exclusive rights in the area, particularly that of building and operating mines, railroads, and factories. Hay feared the other powers would respond similarly and China would once again be in danger of being carved into exclusive spheres of influence with the United States completely excluded. Having had some success with his previous methods, Hay sent a memorandum to the great powers in February 1902, objecting to any actions that undermined the spirit of the Open Door. Britain joined in, and so did its new ally, Japan. With so much pressure, the Russians gave in, and the Sino-Russian Treaty of October 1903 redressed the situation.[124]

Tension between Japan and Russia had been rising, however, over Russian ambitions in Manchuria and Korea. In February 1904 it erupted into war, instigated by the Japanese. Initially, Roosevelt leaned toward Japan, in part because he saw Russia as the greatest new U.S. enemy— an autocratic, aggressive regime with designs on China. The entry of Japan into the equation could check Russia's power and redress the balance in northern Asia. In part, however, Roosevelt simply admired the Japanese thrust to great powerdom. They seemed to be living fully the strenuous life. "Wasn't the Japanese attack bully!" he exclaimed in 1904. Roosevelt's anti-Russian feelings were widely held. "Everyone is interested, and excited, and all are anti-Russian, almost to dangerous extent," complained Henry Adams.[125]

Russia's performance in the war was humiliating, and after the revolution against the czar in 1905, the Russians sued for peace. They asked Roosevelt, as a seemingly neutral party, to arbitrate the dispute. Roosevelt was delighted. This was exactly how he wished the great powers to view the United States—as a judicious peer. His position at the Portsmouth Peace Conference, though, was somewhat pro-Japanese. Though

---

[123] Quoted in Tyler Dennett, *Roosevelt and the Russo-Japanese War: A Critical Study of American Policy in Eastern Asia in 1902–5* (Garden City, N.Y.: Doubleday, 1925) 165.

[124] Ibid., 118–44.

[125] Quoted in LaFeber, *The American Age*, 237.

he persuaded Tokyo to drop its demand of a large indemnity payment, Japan emerged from the peace with a controlling interest in Korea, important Chinese ports that had been Russian before the war, the southern Manchurian railroad, and the southern half of Sakhalin Island. One month after Portsmouth, the Japanese turned Korea into a protectorate, a status that it maintained until 1945. Far from objecting to this development or viewing it as a threat, the United States moved to accommodate Japan and simultaneously shore up vulnerable U.S. possessions in the area. The Taft-Katsuhara agreement of July 1905 recognized Japanese suzerainty over Korea in return for an understanding that America's colonies in the Pacific were safe. In 1908 the Root-Takahira agreement further accepted a greater Japanese sphere of influence. While Japan agreed to uphold the Open Door and the territorial independence of China, the accord did not speak, as had previous agreements, of the territorial integrity of China, and it implicitly recognized southern Manchuria as Japanese. Two years earlier, at the Algeciras Conference on Morocco, it had become clear that the Open Door was for Roosevelt not an abstract principle but a means to achieve influence by limiting the influence of other great powers and by ensuring access for American goods. The United States voted against Germany, which wanted to maintain the Open Door in Morocco, and with France, which preferred spheres of influence.[126]

Roosevelt took several other opportunities to expand American influence in Asia. The United States used its monetary power in 1907 to release China from its Boxer Rebellion debts in exchange for reductions in Chinese emigration to the United States. Japanese policies proved harder to change. The number of Japanese immigrants coming into California had grown to twenty-four thousand in 1900, over ten times the figure from a decade ago, and anti-Japanese riots erupted in San Francisco. In 1907 Japan unofficially agreed to halt emigration if the United States ensured better treatment of the Japanese immigrants in California. Roosevelt decided that the Japanese would be impressed only by force, and he arranged to have the entire American fleet of twenty-two battleships sail around the world, paying a special visit to Japan. Congress was angered at this decision, which had been made without its knowledge. Roosevelt replied that he had enough money in the treasury to send the ships halfway across the world; if Congress wanted them back, it could appropriate the other half. Congress authorized the funds for the full trip.

At the close of the Roosevelt administration, the United States was

[126] Beale, *Theodore Roosevelt*, 279; Dennett, *Roosevelt and the Russo-Japanese War*, 161.

clearly regarded by the world—and clearly regarded itself—as one of the most powerful nations in the world. It had effectively established hegemony over the Western Hemisphere, penetrated East Asia, and even been involved in that great taboo, European diplomacy. The new presidential powers that Harrison, Cleveland, and McKinley had used haltingly, Roosevelt had employed consistently and with great flourish. Throughout his term as president Roosevelt bypassed America's small but growing diplomatic apparatus; he relied instead on private sources of information and often used friends to conduct negotiations.[127] The expectations of congressional and presidential behavior had changed so much that Roosevelt's relationship with Congress, like McKinley's, was generally cordial and productive.[128] The American president now presided unchallenged over not just the American nation, but the American state.

THREATS AND RESPONSES, 1889–1908

Undeniably, fears of foreign intervention played some part in America's expansionist moves. Many of the countries in Central and Latin America that the United States eyed had long colonial histories with Europe's great powers. Others were rich in resources, making them attractive to the Europeans as they scrambled for colonies in the 1880s and 1890s. But, as table 5.1 shows, the vast majority of cases studied here show that American expansion and activism were not caused by either the perception or the reality of threats. The areas of expansion, the timing of expansion, and, finally, the decision-making process that explains the causes of expansion clearly demonstrate that defensive realism's hypothesis does poorly in predicting events. By and large, the United States intervened in areas and against nations that were weak and posed no threat to it. It acquired Caribbean and Pacific islands that were sparsely populated and expanded its influence in Latin American countries with weak governments. It intervened against Europe's weakest power, Spain, and did so only after Spain had shown itself to be exhausted and almost ready to surrender anyway. Theodore Roosevelt mournfully remarked in 1897, "It is indecent to fight Spain anyhow."[129] The United States did perceive Europe's great powers as threats, and it prepared plans for

[127] Robert Wiebe, *The Search for Order, 1877–1920* (New York: Hill and Wang, 1967), 254.

[128] Wilfred E. Binkley, *President and Congress* (New York: Vintage Books, 1962), 228–46.

[129] Quoted in Joseph B. Bishop, *Theodore Roosevelt and His Time Shown in His Own Letters* (New York: Scribners, 1920), 1:84.

TABLE 5.1
America's Opportunities to Expand, 1889–1908

Period	Case	Outcome	Hypothesis Validated
1889–1893	1) Naval buildup	E	SCR
	2) Pan-American conference	E	SCR
	3) Chile	E	SCR
	4) Hawaii	NE	Other
1893–1897	5) Brazilian revolution	E	SCR
	6) Nicaragua	E	DR
	7) Venezuelan boundary crisis	E	SCR
	8) Cuban revolution	NE	Other
1897–1901	9) Cuba	E	Other
	10) Hawaii	E	Other
	11) Philippines	E	SCR
	12) Puerto Rico	E	SCR
	13) Guam	E	SCR
	14) Wake Islands	E	SCR
	15) Samoa	E	SCR
	16) Intervention in China	E	DR
	17) Samsah Bay	NE	SCR
	18) Hay-Pauncefote Treaty	NE	SCR
1901–1908	19) Panama Canal	E	SCR
	20) Alaskan boundary	E	SCR
	21) Cuba—Platt Amendment	E	SCR
	22) Danish West Indies	NE	SCR
	23) Venezuelan/German affair	E	DR
	24) Santo Domingo	E	SCR
	25) British Open Door	NE	DR
	26) Open Door notes	E	DR
	27) Boxer Rebellion	E	DR
	28) Portsmouth Peace Conference	E	SCR
	29) Algeciras Conference	E	SCR
	30) Cuban coup	E	SCR
	31) Guatemalan civil war	E	SCR
	32) Appeasement of Japan	NE	SCR

Note: E = expansion; NE = nonexpansion; SCR = state-centered realism; DR = defensive realism; Other = cause too varied to code as either state-centered realism or defensive realism

wars against them. But—indeed, because of these threats, because of the power the European states possessed—it rarely ventured into the European theater.

When confronted by Britain, an established great power, the United States was wary, expanding very cautiously, around the edges and on issues that were not central to British security. The United States was twice confronted by a tangible British threat; both times it backed down. The first occasion, a minor event, took place when the United States was in the process of replacing Britain as the dominant power in Nicaragua. In 1894 the Zelaya regime deported the British proconsul in Nicaragua. London was furious; it sent warships steaming to Central America, broke diplomatic relations with Nicaragua, and presented it with an ultimatum. Nicaragua turned to the United States for help. Were U.S. expansion motivated by threats, this would have been the perfect moment for Washington to expand its control of Nicaragua. Instead, it refused to invoke the Monroe Doctrine even rhetorically and told the Nicaraguans they should meet London's demands. The Zelaya government stalled, still hoping for an American intervention. Britain escalated, occupying Corinto. The United States did nothing. Two weeks later, Nicaragua came to an agreement with Britain.[130] The second episode, described above, was the Venezuelan boundary crisis of 1895, when Britain refused to back down and war appeared to be a distinct possibility. Not only did the United States adapt its policy, but popular opinion, usually reliably anti-British, turned on a dime and advocated accommodation. When the British reduced their military forces in the region and reoriented their diplomacy, American activism and expansion followed. As with Spain, the United States pushed when it saw threats diminishing, not the reverse. Similarly, London's perception of America's rise and the threat that this posed to its interests in the Western Hemisphere led it to seek accommodation with Washington.

One of the reasons McKinley vacillated over Cuba in the first year of his presidency was that he had received reports that France, Russia, and Germany might back Spain in a war with America.[131] After the war, the United States was probably more secure than at any point in its history until then. Spain had withdrawn from the Americas; Britain had made patently clear its decision to reduce its naval presence in the region and to appease Washington diplomatically; and the German threat was still distant on the horizon. In that heady atmosphere of victory and security, the United States, far from relaxing its efforts, moved to expand its influence and control in the hemisphere, annexing islands and naval

---

[130] LaFeber, *The New Empire*, 226–27.
[131] May, *Imperial Democracy*, 119.

stations, forging protectorates, and even setting up formal imperial rule in the distant Philippines.

Even Theodore Roosevelt, for all his swagger, was cautious when dealing with the rising sun in the east. Japan's actions in China and the Pacific were clearly a threat both to the Open Door and, more tangibly, to American colonies in the region. As Tyler Dennett writes regarding Japan's proximity to the Philippines, Roosevelt "was never really sure that all would be well."[132] His response, which conforms to the prediction of state-centered realism, was to appease Tokyo. The Taft-Katsuhara and Root—Takahira agreements were remarkable events in American diplomacy—formal agreements recognizing Japan's sphere of influence in the Pacific and southern Manchuria. Roosevelt's decision to accommodate Japan and, by implication, thwart Russia stemmed directly from his view that Russia was a decaying monarchy and Japan a new rising power that could pose a real threat to U.S. interests.[133]

Some argue that the reason for America's increased activism and expansion during the 1890s and 1900s was the rise of the German threat.[134] According to this view, the United States had been sheltered by the Royal Navy for decades, never confronting any threats in its immediate vicinity, and had therefore been isolationist. The rise of the German threat, which in these accounts dates to the mid-1890s, forced the United States to become active on the world stage. This account of American expansion is highly problematic. First, the Royal Navy was not, nor was it viewed as, America's protector. For most of the period of this study, Britain was seen as the country with which the United States had the largest and most numerous political conflicts and with which it was most likely to go to war. The myth was born during World War I, and Theodore Roosevelt—that great Anglophile—attempted to snuff it out in the crib. In a remarkable letter to Rudyard Kipling in 1918, he pointed out that "for the first ninety years the British Navy, when, as was ordinarily the case, the British Government was more or less hostile to us, was our greatest danger."[135] The war plans of the period confirm this assessment. As Geoffrey Barraclough writes, before 1914 "for Americans the tangible threat of British sea-power was more real than the hypothetical threat of German land-power."[136]

[132] Dennett, *Roosevelt and the Russo-Japanese War,* 159.

[133] Ibid., 150–70.

[134] Stephen R. Rock, *Why Peace Breaks Out: Great Power Rapprochement in Historical Perspective* (Chapel Hill: University of North Carolina Press, 1989).

[135] *The Letters of Theodore Roosevelt,* ed. Elting E. Morison (Cambridge: Harvard University Press, 1951–54) 1407.

[136] Geoffrey Barraclough, *An Introduction to Contemporary History* (New York: Basic Books, 1964), 111–12.

The myth was perpetuated in the 1920s by writers like Walter Lippmann and Nicholas Spykman, who were determined that the United
States should abandon its isolationism and join the world—a worthy
goal.[137] To convince people, however, they misinterpreted American history. They argued that isolationism was understandable in the late nineteenth century, when America was secure under the Royal Navy's protection. The rise of Germany made such a stance impossible; the ocean
that served as a moat was now a causeway for the German fleet. America had no choice but to enter world politics, for its very security was
imperiled. As Barraclough writes, "this is reading history backwards."[138]
Ironically, this redefinition of the concept of the ocean—from moat to
highway—had in fact taken place, but during the 1890s and for a very
different purpose. In justifying American expansion, Mahan had reversed the traditional idea of the ocean as protection against European
intrigue and compared it to a "great highway; or better, perhaps . . . a
wide common, over which men pass in all directions."[139] The point, of
course, was not that the Germans could use this highway to attack
America, but that America could use it to gain colonies.

The Germans, for their part, assumed in the 1880s and 1890s that
were a war involving the United States to break out, the configuration
would be as follows: "an American-French alliance would certainly be
opposed by a German-English one."[140] Bismarck had advised Salisbury
in the 1880s that England had to confront America's rising naval power
in the Atlantic, which meant allying with Germany. Such an alliance
between a great naval power and a great land power made geopolitical
sense, but England instead chose to accommodate the United States and
challenge Germany. The reasons for this are clear. Britain had exposed
interests in the Western Hemisphere, especially Canada, and it had a
healthy respect for American power. A second, important reason was
the cultural, political, and ideological affinity between the two peoples,
particularly at the elite level. Leaders of both countries consciously attempted to turn these "natural affinities" into a political and strategic
bond. Both these factors predate the rise of the German threat, which
certainly gave a strong impetus to an already burgeoning entente.

The rhetoric surrounding expansion does, of course, contain some
references to threats, though the paucity of even that kind of evidence

[137] Walter Lippmann, *U.S. Foreign Policy: Shield of the Republic* (Boston: Little, Brown,
1943); Nicholas J. Spykman, *America's Strategy in World Politics: The United States and
the Balance of Power* (New York: Harcourt, Brace, 1942).
[138] Barraclough, *Introduction to Contemporary History*, 111–12.
[139] Quoted in LaFeber, *The New Empire*, 25.
[140] Alfred Vagts, "Hopes and Fears of an American-German War, 1870–1915," *Political
Science Quarterly* 54, no. 4 (December 1939): 519.

for defensive realism is remarkable. When such language was used, it was often obviously designed to persuade Congress and the public that the action was one of necessity, not ambition. James Blaine revealingly wrote to President Harrison in 1893 that the annexation of Hawaii could be "represented as being necessary to prevent English conquest." By the time McKinley inherited the situation, the use of the British threat was becoming incredible, so the Japanese threat was mentioned in vague terms. Even this did not catch on. As Ernest May writes, "by the time the [annexation] treaty was drawn up even Roosevelt had been forced to admit that Japan posed no immediate menace."[141] It is worth quoting the distinguished historian Albert Weinberg at some length on Hawaii and the general problem of the rhetoric statesmen use to justify expansion.

> One sees now for the first time a fact which will be met again and again in the history of this doctrine of inevitability. It is that the doctrine tends to be invoked in just the circumstances which upon analysis seem to give it least justification. Though it was now alleged that Hawaii was in danger of falling under foreign control, there was adduced no substantial evidence of acquisitive designs by Great Britain or any other power. The danger was now probably less than ever in the past, for whereas previously Hawaii had been under what Harrison called the "effete" monarchy, open to foreign influence, it was now under the rule of former Americans who were vigorously disposed to cultivate intimate relations with their native country. It is further true that the excluded alternative of a protectorate was no longer subject to the chief objection which Stevens had urged against it—that of assuming responsibility for a bungling regime. The fact that the doctrine of political necessity was applied precisely when the situation in Hawaii took a turn favorable to American interests may mean merely that not the best logic was used. But it is difficult to avoid the inference that the expansionists were fundamentally not interested in the logic of political necessity.[142]

Doris Graber concurs. "The preventive interventions which occurred in Hawaii, Samoa, and Cuba were largely inspired by a desire to annex these regions, rather than by a need to prevent non-American intervention."[143]

As state-centered realism predicts, while rising power did beget rising interests, American expansion cannot be characterized as a mad lust for power. It took place in a rational—which is not to say wise—manner,

[141] May, *Imperial Democracy*, 17, 122–23.

[142] Albert K. Weinberg, *Manifest Destiny: A Study of Nationalist Expansion in American History* (Baltimore: Johns Hopkins Press, 1935), 258.

[143] Doris A. Graber, *Crisis Diplomacy: A History of U.S. Intervention Policies and Practices* (Washington, D.C.: Public Affairs Press, 1959), 107.

weighing costs and benefits, pushing into areas where the costs and risks were low and the perceived benefits high. The closer the instability, the less Washington tolerated it and the more it preferred its own control to letting things take their course. Hence the obsession with revolutions in Latin America but the lack of concern over threats from Europe. Therefore, Canada, long the great prize for American expansionists, dropped off the American strategic radar. It was clear that Canada would be a stable and predictable part of the Western Hemisphere even though it remained an arm of the British Empire. The risks of leaving it alone were low, and the costs of acquiring it high.

The rise to great powerdom is said to involve the transformation of a country from a revolutionary power to a status quo one. To become a status quo power, however, a nation has first to expand its influence to the point where it has created a status quo with which it is satisfied and which it wants, at the very least, to preserve. To use Robert Gilpin's terms, a state stops expanding only when it has reached the point of diminishing utility. In 1908 America had not yet reached that point, and William Howard Taft would pick up where Theodore Roosevelt had left off. The United States—under the leadership of presidents of both parties—continued to pursue an activist foreign policy through its intervention in World War I. The crucial American role in the Great War and Woodrow Wilson's idealistic Fourteen Points and participation in the negotiations at Versailles marked the height of American involvement in great-power politics. No country's expansionist path is linear, however, and the 1920s—and more so the 1930s—saw a retreat, albeit partial and haphazard, from the involvements of the previous thirty years. However, the United States would soon resume its expansionist ways, reaching unprecedented levels in the first decade of the Cold War. After World War II, the United States possessed virtually unchallenged control over its international environment, and it used its overwhelming power to construct an international order favorable to American interests. The transformation to great power was finally complete.

CHAPTER SIX

Conclusion

STRONG NATION, WEAK STATE

REALISM HAS been discussed self-consciously and explicitly in the United States only since the 1950s. During those years, Hans Morgenthau, George Kennan, and Walter Lippmann articulated an outlook on diplomacy that was to dominate the postwar debate. Rejecting proponents of isolation and overextension alike, they advocated a restrained but forceful foreign policy that would protect America's vital interests but avoid idealistic goals. It would eschew lofty rhetoric and grand promises that could not be fulfilled except at great cost. Containment was realistic, rollback impossible. Involvement in Europe was essential, the Third World was irrelevant. Kennan was good, Dulles bad.

To justify their worldview, these thinkers firmly grounded their limited internationalism in the American tradition by tracing it back to the Founding Fathers.[1] Alexander Hamilton was the realist father figure, but even his ideological antithesis Thomas Jefferson was portrayed as pursuing a diplomacy that was shrewd and sensitive to the balance of power, reflected in his restrained rhetoric. Nineteenth-century foreign policy, with the acquisition of Oregon, Texas, and California as the highlights, continued a pattern of limited goals backed by sufficient force to execute them. American policymaking was easier, to be sure, because Britain's Royal Navy helped create what Lippmann called "unearned security," but it was also restrained.[2] This tradition of restraint evaporated with the presidency of William McKinley, whose declaration

---

[1] See Hans J. Morgenthau, *In Defense of the National Interest: A Critical Examination of American Foreign Policy* (New York: Alfred A. Knopf, 1951); George F. Kennan, *American Diplomacy, 1900–1950* (Chicago: University of Chicago Press, 1951); and Walter Lippmann, *U.S. Foreign Policy: Shield of the Republic* (Boston: Little, Brown, 1943). See also Robert Osgood, *Ideals and Self-Interest in American Foreign Policy: The Great Transformation of the Twentieth Century* (Chicago: University of Chicago Press, 1953). The diplomatic historian most closely associated with the realist school is Norman A. Graebner; see in particular his *Empire on the Pacific: A Study in American Continental Expansion* (New York: Ronald Press, 1955); *An Uncertain Tradition: American Secretaries of State in the Twentieth Century* (New York: McGraw-Hill, 1961); and *Ideas and Diplomacy: Readings in the Intellectual Tradition of American Foreign Policy* (New York: Oxford University Press, 1964).

[2] Lippmann, *U.S. Foreign Policy*, 49.

of war on Spain and annexation of the Philippines and other overseas territories launched the United States on a different path. Since McKinley, Washington had alternated between idealistic pledges it could not fulfill (and had no intention of fulfilling)—like the Open Door notes, the 1928 Kellogg-Briand Pact, which outlawed war as an instrument of national policy, and the Stimson Doctrine, which refused to recognize the Japanese subjugation of Manchuria in 1932—and well-meant but misguided crusades to change the world, as at Versailles. Lippmann stated it bluntly: in the nineteenth century, the United States had responded to genuine threats, but now it was seeking broader goals that were "mirages," like peace and collective security.[3]

In fact, it was Walter Lippmann and his like-minded colleagues who had invented mirages. Driven by normative concerns, the realist interpretation of history depicted American expansion in the nineteenth century as a response to threats from European powers when these moves actually reflected the desire of a growing power for greater influence. Then as later, American foreign policy was driven by an awareness of American strength and by the search for greater influence over the international environment. American statesmen had led the spread of the country across the continent—the Louisiana Purchase, Texas, California, Oregon Territory, Alaska. Throughout the nineteenth century, they had their eye on Cuba and Mexico to the south and Canada to the north. The process by which thirteen colonies nestled east of the Allegheny Mountains became one of the world's largest and greatest powers was one motivated more by power than by threats. Theodore Roosevelt's interpretation of American foreign policy—"our history has been one of expansion. . . . This expansion is not a matter of regret, but of pride"—is accurate and frank.[4]

What changed at the turn of the century—and what realists like Lippmann and Kennan have always been uncomfortable with—was the sheer magnitude of American power. The United States had grown so strong and had so many resources at its disposal that its behavior came to resemble that of other great powers. It enlarged its military and diplomatic apparatus; it annexed territories; it sought basing rights; it participated in great-power conferences. It sought influence beyond limited security aims because it was strong enough to do so. Great powers have the luxury of defining their interests in ways that far exceed minimal security requirements; the United States proved no exception to this rule.

[3] Ibid., 3–5, 30–31, 47–49.
[4] Quoted in David Healy, *U.S. Expansionism: The Imperialist Urge in the 1890s* (Madison: University of Wisconsin Press, 1970), 34–35.

Like the defensive realists, who are the modern heirs of this error, the Lippmann-Kennan school wanted the United States to expand for limited strategic interests alone, and from this hope developed the theory that all states expand only to ensure limited security objectives in the face of clear threats. Countries that violate this rule and expand in the absence of such threats must then be abnormal, and the roots of their behavior must lie in domestic pathologies. America's disease, Kennan wrote, was its "legalistic-moralistic" tradition that ran "like a red skein" through American history and produced terrible consequences in the twentieth century.[5]

But a theory must predict, not implore. A theory of foreign policy explains and forecasts how countries will behave and under what conditions they will expand. Yet most realist theories of foreign policy entreat states to act in certain ways; hence their focus on threats as the factor motivating a country's behavior abroad. Since defensive realists wish that states responded only to clear, objective threats, they have argued that this is indeed how the world works, and they have interpreted history from this perspective. In fact, even a cursory examination of diplomatic history confirms that this proposition accounts for little great-power behavior.

This study's test of the validity of two first-cut theories of foreign policy, state-centered realism and defensive realism, confirms the power-based interpretation of American expansion. Between 1865 and 1889, America's policymakers perceived twenty-two serious opportunities to expand and acted less than one-third of the time. This period was generally characterized by an absence of threats from the European powers, and at first glance defensive realism would seem a good guide: few threats, little expansion. However, defensive realism has a hard time explaining the few cases of expansion during this period, such as the acquisition of Alaska and of basing rights in Samoa. More important, even in those cases in which the United States did not expand its political interests abroad, the impulse driving the advocates of expansion was more often related to relative increases (or decreases) in power than in threats. Defensive realism also could not account for the United State's tendency to *retract* its interests when it encountered serious threats, such as France's role in Mexico in the mid-1860s and Britain's presence in Canada. Thus, of the twenty-two opportunities to expand between 1865 and 1889, state-centered realism proved the better explanation in fifteen cases and defensive realism in just two; the causes of five cases were too vague to confirm either hypothesis.

The more expansionist period, from 1889 to 1908, further confirmed

[5] Kennan, *American Diplomacy,* 95.

the predictions of state-centered realism. Of thirty-two distinct opportunities that arose, twenty-five were seized. As in the previous quarter century, the United States faced few threats during this era. But now it expanded vigorously, and that expansion was specifically linked, in time and place, to its growing power. The United States did not expand against strong states that posed a great threat to its security but largely against areas that were weak and in which expansion would entail a small cost. Of the thirty-two opportunities, state-centered realism explained twenty-two cases and defensive realism only six; the causes of four cases were too varied to code as confirming the predictions of either theory. The success rate of the two theories is quite similar in both the period of expansion and the period of nonexpansion—a further sign of the robustness of the results. State-centered realism explained 68 percent of the cases in the earlier period and 69 percent in the later one. Defensive realism explained just 9 percent of the cases in the first period and 19 percent in the second.

Were defensive realism an adequate starting point, it should help explain the dramatic shift in American foreign policy from nonexpansion to expansion. However, after 1865, and throughout the period under study, the United States was free of serious threats; the European powers had come to recognize that they could not easily project their power into the Western Hemisphere. State-centered realism, on the other hand, does provide the explanation: state power. The American economy grew rapidly during the 1870s and 1880s, and by the early 1880s it had overtaken even Britain by most important measures. But this national power was obscured by a state that was too weak to consistently extract resources to fulfill its objectives and that was too divided to act in a coherent fashion. Expansion was often proposed but rarely consummated. When state power was lowest, almost no expansion occurred. In the 1870s and 1880s, as industrialization proceeded and the need arose for an extensive regulatory state, the scope and strength of the central government increased. Power shifted from the states to the federal government and from the legislative branch to the executive branch. By the 1890s, the expansionist pipe dreams of the 1860s and 1870s could become reality.

Clearly, statesmen do at times expand out of legitimate concern for the country's security and in response to threats. This behavior is most apparent when threats are black and unmistakable; the balancing behavior that greeted the expansion of Hitler's Germany is a good example. Much of international life, however, consists of grays: periods of ambiguous threats and opportunities. Uncertainty is the dominant feature of international life. States have a greater range of choices than we might think, and they choose to highlight certain threats and downplay others based on their conception of their interests. Thus the interesting question is how states come to define their security—what threatens them and when. This is not to suggest that statesmen cynically put forward national security rationales every time they intend to embark on a flight of imperial ambition, though that certainly happens. Most policy is explained as protecting—and often genuinely formulated to protect—the nation's security; but the definition of security, of the interests that require protection, usually expands in tandem with a nation's material resources. The definition of these interests is shaped by individual statesmen, by domestic politics, by the general values and culture of the society, but in the first instance by a state's power. This dynamic aspect of a great power's foreign policy eludes defensive realism. Karl Deutsch put it exactly right twenty-five years ago:

> [There is] a kind of Parkinson's law of national security: a nation's feeling of insecurity expands directly with its power. The larger and more powerful a nation is, the more its leaders, elites, and often its population increase their level of aspirations in international affairs. The more, that is to say, do they see themselves as destined or obliged to put the world's affairs in order or at least keep them in some sort of order that seems sound to them. . . . Only the largest and strongest nations can develop an at-least-plausible image of a world in which they, by their own national efforts, might mold, change, or pressure wholly or in large part according to their own desires; and their fears, worries, efforts, and expenditures go up accordingly.[6]

As American power grew, areas that were not earlier seen as crucial became vital interests, and crises that the United States had blissfully ignored in the past were perceived as threatening. The objective threats had not increased, but America's desire to control its environment had. A scholar looking at great-power behavior over time—even in a secure, relatively benign nation like the United States—must conclude that states seek more than mere security: they seek influence over the international environment. And the more powerful they become, the more influence they seek.

A theory of foreign policy should eschew the concepts of threat and security: these terms are highly malleable and have been manipulated in the past by both statesmen and scholars. When statesmen expand their nation's interests abroad, they often claim to be motivated by the search for "security"—which is hardly surprising, since the alternative is to admit to imperial or hegemonic motives. However, it makes the concept difficult to define and the theory difficult to falsify. Realism has always

---

[6] Karl W. Deutsch, *The Analysis of International Relations* (Englewood Cliffs, N.J.: Prentice-Hall, 1968), 88.

been weakened by the difficulty in operationalizing its predictions. Almost all state behavior can, in retrospect, be accounted for by realism in the same sense in which—by ingenious post hoc definitions of "costs" and "benefits"—rational-choice theory can also account for any choices an actor makes.[7] A version of realism that adds to its problems in this area cannot be considered a step forward.

State-centered realism and defensive realism are theoretical competitors, but both are essential for explaining reality. A more complex theory of state action would specify the conditions under which each theory makes its greatest contribution. State-centered realism clearly does a better job of explaining the rise of a great power in the long run and its changing goals over time. It better accounts for the behavior of states during periods of relative peace and stability, when great powers have the "luxury" of choosing their interests and goals.[8] When power is high and threats low, a state has greater freedom to determine its interests and pursue them, and under such circumstances state-centered realism is a good guide to its behavior. Though deficient as a general theory, defensive realism might be useful in explaining "snapshots" of international life—short-term responses to the surrounding environment—particularly in periods of international turmoil. When a state must act to ensure its survival and territorial integrity, the concept of threat is remarkably unambiguous. Such a crisis curtails the consideration of broader interests.

Thus while defensive realism, pointing to the Soviet threat, might explain why the United States built up its armed forces and allied with Western Europe in the late 1940s, state-centered realism can explain more broadly how the United States had expanded the definition of its interests in the first half of the twentieth century and thus expanded the list of countries it viewed as vital and behaviors it viewed as threats.[9] The possibility that a single power would dominate Europe had arisen four times in America's history. The threat from Napoleon Washington was disturbed by but did nothing about; that from Wilhelmine Germany it ignored until the third year of World War I and then mobilized against in a limited manner; that from Hitler's Germany it countered

---

[7] See, for example, David A. Lake, "The State and the Production of International Security: A Microeconomic Theory of Grand Strategy," paper delivered at the American Political Science Association annual meeting, August–September 1990.

[8] Stephen D. Krasner, *Defending the National Interest: Raw Materials Investments and U.S. Foreign Policy* (Princeton, N.J.: Princeton University Press, 1978), 138.

[9] This perspective is well presented in what some call the definitive history of the origins of the Cold War; see Melvyn P. Leffler, *A Preponderance of Power: National Security, the Truman Administration, and the Cold War* (Stanford, Calif.: Stanford University Press, 1992).

more speedily and with considerable force; and that from the Soviet Union it opposed very early—indeed, preemptively—and with a comprehensive political, economic, and military strategy. As American power grew, its statesmen regarded the security of Europe as increasingly vital to the nation's interests. In 1950 the Soviet threat was real and great, but in large part because America had become, and accepted its role as, a world power.

Obviously, state-centered realism, like any theory, cannot explain every period in American history. American diplomacy during the 1920s and 1930s is most fully explained by a number of other factors, though a few points are worth making. America was both powerful and active in the 1920s. While politically disengaged in the central balance-of-power discussions in Europe, Washington was the key player in the economic rehabilitation of the continent. The 1930s were a period of more genuine isolationism, but caused in part by the collapse of the American economy and the sense of powerlessness that pervaded the country. Finally, people and plans matter. Woodrow Wilson presented Americans with an all-or-nothing choice regarding internationalism and they chose against his vision, but the fallout from the battle over entry into the League of Nations turned into a political disgust with world activism that echoes to this day.

STATE STRUCTURE AND FOREIGN POLICY

State-centered realism extends beyond the classical realist tradition linking national power and national intentions to draw on a tradition that treats the state as an autonomous actor with great impact on national policy. Nations do not formulate and implement foreign policy and extract resources to those ends; governments do. The state-centered scholarly tradition dates back to Alexis de Tocqueville's *The Old Regime and the French Revolution* and was particularly popular on the European continent during the nineteenth century, with Otto Hintze and Max Weber its most well known exponents. Even some Anglo-American scholars—a group usually less enamored of such an approach, perhaps because they lived in countries with relatively weak states—devoted themselves to constitutional and political analysis that focused on the structure of the state, notably Walter Bagehot, Leonard White, and A. Lawrence Lowell. In post—World War II America, this approach has seemed less in favor, though certain scholars, like Samuel Huntington, remained resolutely state-centered. The last two decades, however, have seen a renaissance of such scholarship, its practitioners often infelicitously referred to as the "bringing the state back in" school. While most of this new work has concerned domestic policy, some important studies have combined the study of state structure with traditional international relations theory. This work hopes to add to that body of scholarship. The statism of state-centered realism, however, is limited. It does not discard an international systemic explanation for a domestic one, but rather uses both levels of analysis. State-centered realism's central concept, state power, builds on classical realism's key variable, national power. It simply applies a discount on national power based on state structure; the weaker the state, the bigger the discount. While state-centered realism is as parsimonious as unadulterated classical realism, it is more general and abstract because it incorporates a broader range of phenomena. "A general theory is not less parsimonious, as long as the principal ideas that organize its relevant variables are as few in number as the principal ideas in the less general theory."[10]

Is this emphasis on state power and its absence unique to the American case? Does studying the exception tell us much about the rule? Based on this study, it is impossible to state definitively such a general conclusion, yet a cursory glance seems to confirm its relevance to other countries. The most obvious example of state power's greater importance than national power comes from early European imperialism. Michael Doyle has pointed out that at the time of Britain's eighteenth-century confrontation with India, the two countries probably had similar levels of GNP Britain's state apparatus, however, had harnessed that national power far more efficiently than could the diffuse Mogul empire. The confrontation in the Indian subcontinent was not between a strong nation and a weak one, but between a strong state and a weak one. Doyle comes to a more general conclusion: "[T]he weakness of periphery, which allows it to be conquered and indeed encourages aggression from the metropole, is a product primarily of its social organization."[11] It is hardly a coincidence that Britain experienced a small burst of state-building in the early nineteenth century, which was followed by foreign policy activism; next came a period of retrenchment of state power, followed by the mid-nineteenth-century Victorian policy of "splendid isolationism." In 1870 the "collectivist trend" began again in a qualitatively more significant manner, and within thirty years Britain had added five million square miles to its empire, mainly through its encounter with weak states in Africa.[12]

[10] Stephen M. Walt, *The Origins of Alliances* (Ithaca, N.Y.: Cornell University Press, 1987), 263–64.

[11] Michael W. Doyle, *Empires* (Ithaca, N.Y.: Cornell University Press, 1986), 131.

[12] F. H. Hinsley, "Introduction," in Hinsley, ed., *The New Cambridge Modern History,* vol. 11, Material Progress and World-Wide Problems, 1870–1898 (Cambridge: Cambridge University Press, 1970), 18.

The European great powers were no longer pure monarchies by the late nineteenth century, but they continued to jockey ceaselessly for advantage as their national power grew. Why were the new legislative structures not creating friction between relative national power and national policies? Did the distinction between state power and national power not exist? Although the executive in these states had constitutionally been weakened, the de facto state structure left that branch supreme:

> [N]one of these parliaments, with the exception of those of Britain, Belgium and the U.S., had more than nominal powers against the executive. In the next 30 years [after 1870] no new parliament was introduced except in Japan; and in no country except France did the legislature make significant strides towards a system of parliamentary control over the executive comparable to that which Britain, Belgium and the U.S. had developed. Elsewhere the executive government, whether it was monarchical or republican, easily retained its power and position or enlarged them. Even in Britain, Belgium and the U.S., while parliamentary control remained established, the legislature entered upon the beginning of a decline in relation to the executive.[13]

The rise of Germany is instructive. After the unification of 1866, the new German constitution was "a compromise between unification and federation and between the monarchist principle and the sovereignty of the people."[14] Chancellor Otto von Bismarck's much-praised restraint in foreign policy surely reflected his wisdom, but he was also limited by the structure of the new German state. Like many American presidents, he tried to overcome it, an easier task given the inherent powers of his office; by the late 1870s he had created a large imperial administration through which he, as chancellor, would determine and implement national policy. In 1879 German state structure reached a breaking point: as Werner Conze writes, "This year must be viewed as the decisive turning point in the economic and domestic policy of the empire, one which basically determined the whole age of William II."[15] The unification constitution did not allow the monarch to impose taxes on the states. Bismarck tried to wrest control of this crucial means of extracting resources from society, but he largely failed. This tension in Germany's state structure persisted and increasingly resulted in an imperial disregard for the legislative branch, particularly in the areas of foreign and defense policy, in which the executive wielded much broader powers.

[13] Ibid., 26, 36.
[14] Werner Conze, "The German Empire," in Hinsley, *New Cambridge Modern History*, 11:276–77.
[15] Ibid., 289–90.

While Wilhelm I was on the throne, he chose to reign, not rule, and Bismarck exercised these imperial powers wisely. With the accession of Wilhelm II, Bismarck was dismissed, and the bizarre emperor and his sycophants inherited the state Bismarck had carefully assembled.

The strengthening of the state went hand in hand with a manufacturing boom that moved Germany swiftly up the world-power ranks; it displaced Britain for second place, after the United States, in share of world manufacturing output by 1910.[16] Between 1872 and 1913, the proportion of industrial finished goods in total exports rose from one-third to two-thirds. Agriculture also fared well, doubling its yield between 1871 and 1914 and making Germany self-sufficient in food. Until the 1880s, Berlin had been an importer of capital, but exports had risen so much that by 1913 it had thirty million marks invested abroad. Conze describes the mismatch between German power and German interests:

> Germany's foreign trade was already second in Europe after that of Great Britain, but her navy was still far behind Britain's and those of France, Russia, and Italy as well. Now Germany, belatedly enough, was to join the general trend of "new navalism." It seemed impossible also to stand aloof from "world politics." In view of the growing foreign trade and the colonial footholds newly won, in China and the South Pacific, Germany's maritime interests claimed attention. The interrelation of foreign trade, seapower and international politics guided the Emperor's whole statecraft, and his dearest wish came to be to have a powerful German navy.[17]

Wilhelm II was a uniquely strange and aggressive man. And he came to power at a time that gave his eccentricities free range, as tremendous economic growth combined with rising state strength. With an extraordinary personality like Wilhelm II, as Paul Kennedy argues, one can easily forget that structural pressures, both international and domestic, contributed to German expansion even if this expansion would not have been as grandiose or ill considered had Wilhelm not been emperor.[18]

THE RISE AND FALL OF STATE POWER

The world today is in the midst of what Oswald Spengler so ominously termed "a historical change of phase." Transformations of the international system have in the past been fraught with danger, as new powers

---

[16] League of Nations, *Industrialization and Foreign Trade* (New York, 1945), 13.

[17] Conze, "The German Empire," 295.

[18] Paul M. Kennedy, "The Kaiser and German Weltpolitik: Reflections on Wilhelm II's Place in the Making of German Foreign Policy," in John C. G. Rohl and Nicolaus Sombart, eds., *Kaiser Wilhelm II: New Interpretations* (Cambridge: Cambridge University Press, 1982).

rise and old ones fall. Some scholars have argued that conflict in these situations is almost inevitable.[19] While this study does suggest that the newly rich nations of the world will demand seats at the great-power table, it finds a silver lining in this cloudy prophecy.

Power, not threats, drives states toward an expansive interpretation of their interests abroad, and thus the particular configuration of states in any one area—the geography of threats, the geometry of unipolar, bipolar, and multipolar systems—matters less than scholars often claim and pundits often declare. Europe's multipolarity does not present a uniquely dangerous environment that will cause all the powers of yore to rise in competition. Nor does Japan's island position provide a safe atmosphere that will keep the rising sun in "splendid isolation," uninterested in worldwide or regional influence. Whether state power rises quickly and without obstruction will determine the shape, nature, and timing of the rise of new great powers more than divining the degree of minimal security each of these states needs and has.

Herein lies the good cheer. States today are simply not as autonomous or as powerful as they were 150 years ago. We have grown used to one kind of state, thinking of it solely in its post—French Revolution form. The nineteenth century saw the rise of the "integral state" that completely dominated its nation's economy, society, and military in a way that government before had not. In 1968 Samuel Huntington suggested that the structures of Europe's modern states could soon change. "[A]s other societies become fully modern, as the need to disestablish old, traditional, feudal and local elements declines, the need to maintain a political system capable of modernization may also disappear." He foresaw the possibility of "evolution toward an American-type system. . . . The end of ideology in western Europe, the mitigation of class conflict, the tendencies toward an 'organic society' all suggest that European countries could now tolerate more dispersed and relaxed political institutions. Some elements of the American system seem to be creeping back into Europe from which they were exported three centuries ago."[20] The Tudor polity of the medieval world may be the state structure of the future.

The European integral state has been in decline for the last thirty years, ceding its power to regional and international organizations like the European Commission, to subnational units like local and state governments, and to powerful nongovernmental actors like global financiers, speculators, foundations, and the international media. The end of

---

[19] Robert Gilpin's *War and Change in World Politics* (Cambridge: Cambridge University Press, 1981) could be read in this way, though the author is not quite so pessimistic.

[20] Samuel P. Huntington, *Political Order in Changing Societies* (New Haven, Conn.: Yale University Press, 1968), 138–39.

the Cold War has only exacerbated this trend. Consider Germany today, with its federal structure, weak central government, and fiercely independent central bank; many of the government's powers have been delegated to Brussels, others have slipped out of its hands as Bonn has loosened its grip on the economy and the welfare state. Japan is trapped on the one hand by its postwar constitution, which restrains its military might, and on the other by its entanglement in a world of international institutions. Even China, the most thoroughly traditional—and therefore frightening—of the new great powers, finds that its central state is challenged by local authorities and constrained by international ones. The long absence of great-power war and the growth of the global economy have weakened the state and intertwined it in structures that will make the once-straightforward rise and fall of great powers a complex, friction-filled process.[21] These complications may create greater uncertainty for scholars, but they could help blunt the otherwise aggressive temperament of great powers and tame the fierce nature of international life.

[21] Michael Lind, "The Catalytic State," *The National Interest* 27 (Spring 1992): 3–13. See also Michael C. Desch, "War and Strong States, Peace and Weak States?" *International Organization* 50, no. 2 (Spring 1996): 237–68.

Index

India, state structure of, 188
industrialization: and immigration, 99; and military reform, 122–23; and state-building, 95, 96–97. *See also* economics; wealth
influence: American, 5, 11–12, 44, 57; costs and benefits of, 163; distinguished from power, 33–34; and expansionism, 3, 10, 21–22, 30; maximization of, 19n, 30, 33–34; as result of wealth, 88, 129, 185
interests. *See* national interests
Interstate Commerce Act, 105
Interstate Commerce Commission, 101, 103, 105
isolationism, American, 5, 8, 43, 49, 178, 187. *See also* non-expansion
isthmian canal: American plans for, 59, 62–63, 74–75, 147, 155, 165–68; French plans for, 79–80

Jackson, Andrew, 97; and patronage, 113; and presidential powers, 118
Japan: expansion of, 4, 12, 26, 172; U.S. relations with, 163
Jefferson, Thomas, 70, 97, 181
Jensen, Lloyd, 14n
Jensen, Ronald J., 64n
Jervis, Robert, 11, 15n, 21n, 24, 26–27
Johnson, Andrew, 11, 61, 62, 63, 66, 67, 68, 111
Jones, Edward E., 33–34n
Juárez, Benito, 84

Kahn, Alfred E., 30n
Keller, Morton, 98n
Kellogg-Briand Pact, 182
Kennan, George F., 50, 163, 181, 182, 183
Kennedy, Andrew, 46
Kennedy, Paul M., 3–4, 9, 17n, 20, 46n, 166, 190
Keohane, Robert, 17, 19n, 28
Khong, Yuen F., 31n
Kipling, Rudyard, 177
Kuhn, Thomas, 23n

Labor, Bureau of, 101
labor, centralization of, 100
LaFeber, Walter, 50, 51, 94n, 127n, 135n, 144–45, 155n

Lakatos, Imre, 23n, 28
Lake, David A., 36n, 37n
Leffler, Melvyn P., 53
Lenin, Vladimir I., 15 and n
Levy, Jack S., 23n
Liliuokalani, Queen, 142
Lincoln, Abraham, 44, 98, 118; and state-building, 127
Lippmann, Walter, 178, 181, 182, 183
Livermore, Seward, 170n
Lodge, Henry Cabot, 90, 151, 167, 172
Long, John, 126, 157
Louis, William Roger, 18n
Lowell, A. Lawrence, 187
Luce, Steven B., 126

Madison, James, 56, 95
Mahan, Alfred Thayer, 81, 94, 126, 134, 135, 136, 142, 145, 178
Maine incident, 156–57
Mandelbaum, Michael, 3
manifest destiny, 8, 55, 57, 160
Marshall, John, 97
Mastanduno, Michael, 36n, 37n
Maximilian, Archduke of Austria, 84
May, Ernest R., 31n, 49, 50, 74, 144, 159, 179
McCormick, Richard L., 92n
McCormick, Thomas J., 51n
McKeown, Timothy, 24n
McKinley, William, 8, 12, 91, 93, 127, 131n, 139, 169, 179, 181–82; and expansionism, 154–64
Meinecke, Friedrich, 32n
Mexico: Austrian and French intervention in, 84; as target for U.S. expansion, 58
Midway Islands, annexation of, 47, 59, 63–64, 85
Milgram, Stanley, 33n
military reform, and U.S. state formation, 53, 122–26. *See also* Navy, U.S.
Mills, Roger Q., 151
Modelski, George, 14n
Monroe Doctrine, 84, 146, 150, 151, 170–71, 176; and Pan-Americanism, 138; Roosevelt Corollary to, 170–71
Monroe Doctrine Committee, 57–58
Monroe, James, 56, 70
Morgan, H. Wayne, 131n
Morgenthau, Hans J., 9, 18, 32, 36, 181
Morrill, Justin, 139